BADGES, BEARS, AND EAGLES

BADGES, BEARS, AND EAGLES

The True-Life Adventures of a California
Fish and Game Warden

Steven T. Callan

coffeetownpress

Seattle, WA

coffeetownpress

Coffeetown Press
PO Box 70515
Seattle, WA 98127

For more information go to: www.coffeetownpress.com
callan.coffeetownpress.com

The following is a work of nonfiction. Names and identifying details have been changed, except when used by permission.

Cover design by Sabrina Sun

Badges, Bears, and Eagles
Copyright © 2013 by Steven T. Callan—All rights reserved.

ISBN: 978-1-60381-158-3 (Trade Paper)
ISBN: 978-1-60381-159-0 (eBook)

10 9 8 7 6 5 4 3 2

Library of Congress Control Number: 2012955784

Printed in the United States of America

FSC
www.fsc.org
MIX
Paper from
responsible sources
FSC® C011935

To my father, Wallace J. Callan,

The first game warden I ever knew

And one of the best.

Acknowledgments

First and foremost, I would like to thank Catherine Treadgold and Jennifer McCord, at Coffeetown Press, for giving me the opportunity to tell my stories. I have never met two nicer ladies. Throughout the process of producing Badges, Bears and Eagles, Catherine and Jennifer have provided guidance, expert advice and constant encouragement.

Kathy Callan, my wonderful wife, could not have been more supportive during the long two years it took me to write this book—hours and hours of sitting at the computer. "Kathy, would you look this over for me—Kathy, what do you think of this—Kathy, how do you spell ..."

What can I say about Dave Szody? We have been close friends for thirty-eight years. All that time, Dave has never failed to come through when I needed him. Thanks for the nice "Foreword," Dave, and for providing many of the details contained in this book.

I am indebted to Fish and Game Patrol Captain Rick Banko, retired Fish and Game Patrol Captain Nick Albert, retired Fish and Game Patrol Lieutenant Don Jacobs, and retired Fish and Game Patrol Lieutenant Bob Taylor for providing invaluable information used in the writing of this book.

For their kind words, I cannot begin to thank former California Department of Fish and Game Director Boyd Gibbons, former California Department of Fish and Game Director Don Koch, former Shasta County District Attorney McGregor Scott, Sierra County District Attorney Larry Allen and Major League Baseball Sports Agent Randy Hendricks.

Finally, I would like to thank my dad, Wally Callan, for inspiring me to make wildlife protection my life's work. What great times I had, as a boy, riding on patrol with you.

Contents

Foreword

I remember it like it was yesterday. It was a hot July afternoon in 1975. I had graduated from the Riverside Sheriff's Academy the previous month and was finally a full-fledged Fish and Game warden for the State of California. My Captain, Jim Reynolds, had instructed me to drive up to Lake Havasu to meet one of my new squad mates, Warden Steve Callan. Jim said, "Callan is a real go-getter. You two will get along."

The plan was to work Lake Havasu that night—nothing special, just routine sport fisheries enforcement. We went out and worked from late afternoon until after midnight. As I recall, we wrote about two dozen citations. Steve and I got along well and made plans to work together again. Little did I know that we would work together again and again over the next thirty years.

Steve was eventually promoted to lieutenant and moved to Riverside. I was transferred to Fortuna, on the North Coast. He was transferred to Shasta County in 1981 and I followed in 1983, when a warden's position opened up in his lieutenant's district.

Working for Lieutenant Steve Callan was easy. He made the same work-related demands as Captain Reynolds, but there was one big difference: Steve Callan was the most focused, tenacious investigator I had ever worked with.

The bald eagle investigation, described in Chapter 1, is an excellent example. Two local poachers killed a bald eagle and had the temerity to threaten the life of one of Steve's wardens by dumping the dead eagle, with a note attached, at the front gate of the Fish and Game office. At the time, Steve was supervising a diverse squad of Fish and Game wardens and had a heavy workload. It was a balancing act that I would witness again and again. The ensuing months were classic Steve Callan. He would phone at all hours of the day or night to bounce questions and theories off me. Days spun into weeks. Sometimes I wouldn't hear from him for three or four days; it wasn't unusual for Steve to sequester himself in his office so he could write and think without distractions. These absences would be followed by frantic activity in the field, search warrants, interviews, interrogations, arrests and then more report writing.

After the bald eagle case, all manner of people asked me for details. There was little evidence to begin with and, as is typical of most wildlife investigations, there were no witnesses. Everyone—prosecutors, other law enforcement officers, wardens and pathologists—was amazed that this case was made and successfully prosecuted.

This was the first of many cases that Steve made with little or no evidence and a scarcity of witnesses. Fellow officers sometimes walked away from investigations, believing they were a "waste of time" and couldn't be solved. Steve loved the challenge of these cases and literally picked them out of waste paper baskets at the regional office.

Enjoy this book—it's a fun ride and a glimpse into wildlife enforcement at its best!

Dave Szody
California Department of Fish and Game Lieutenant (retired)
Shingletown, California
Summer 2012

Introduction

One September morning in 1975, California Fish and Game Warden Dave Szody and I were working dove hunters down along the Colorado River. A few miles south of Blythe, I spotted two men sitting in the shade of an old cottonwood tree. "Pull over there," I suggested, pointing to a wide spot on the opposite side of the road. "Let's see what those guys are up to." As Szody turned his patrol car to the left, two citation books and a stack of mail slid to the right and across his dash. "When are you gonna stop using your dashboard for a book shelf?" I said. Without responding, Szody picked up a filthy, tobacco-stained coffee cup and deposited a wad of freshly-chewed spittle.

"How does your wife like that disgusting habit?" I said, as I directed my binoculars toward our suspected dove hunters.

"She hates it," answered Szody, laughing. "What do you see?"

"Looks like a couple old-timers. They must be finished hunting for the day; their shotguns are leaning up against the tree."

"Let's go see how they did," said Szody, opening the driver's-side door and preparing for a 200-yard hike across the field.

"You might want to wipe that stuff off your chin first," I said.

At a distance, the elderly dove hunters might have mistaken Dave Szody and me for brothers. We were only a year apart in age and recently out of the academy. Both of us stood six-feet-tall, or a little more, and weighed about 180 pounds. Unlike most game wardens, who preferred the traditional "cop-like" appearance, my working partner and I went a little longer between haircuts.

As Szody and I approached, one of the hunters stood up from his lawn chair and greeted us. Tall and slim, this elderly gentleman wore a wide-brimmed hat, a tucked in long-sleeved shirt and neatly pressed Khaki pants.

What I noticed most was the curious grin on his face that told me he knew something I didn't.

I asked to see the man's hunting license, while my partner contacted his companion. The name scrawled across the top of the license looked familiar, but at the moment I was more interested in how many doves these guys had killed. "Looks like you had some luck," I said, staring down at a heavily laden game bag that was hanging from the back of his chair. The man smiled and, without my asking, handed me the bag. I counted exactly ten doves—the legal limit. About the time I had pulled the last bird out of his bag, it dawned on me who this man was.

"You're George Werden," I blurted, a look of surprise on my face. "Why didn't you say something?"

Werden laughed. "I was just letting you do your job."

In his eighties, Werden had retired many years earlier as a patrol captain. He will always be remembered as Warden Werden, one of the pioneers of California wildlife law enforcement. Szody and I enjoyed a brief conversation with this Fish and Game icon and were about to leave when Werden called us back. "Do you boys mind if I give you some advice?" We had only been on the job about a year, so questions raced through our minds: *What did we do wrong? Did we miss something?* Werden seemed to enjoy making us squirm a little. With great anticipation, we waited for his words of wisdom. The old gentleman looked us both in the eyes and said, "You boys are just starting out on the best job in the world. Don't take yourselves too seriously and above all, always think of it as a game."

We never saw George Werden again, but his simple advice remained with us for the rest of our careers. Anyone lucky enough to become a wildlife protection officer should think of his occupation not as a job, but as a career-long adventure. We were getting paid to roam the fields, forests, and waters of California, searching for anyone breaking the law or harming our precious natural resources.

This book describes what it was like to be a California Fish and Game warden during the last quarter of the Twentieth Century—working routine details from one end of the state to the other and conducting some of the most successful wildlife-related investigations in California history.

It's important to point out that the overwhelming majority of North America's hunters and fishermen are conscientious, law-abiding sportsmen who contribute hundreds of millions of dollars, every year, toward the purchase of wildlands and the improvement of fish and wildlife habitat. They do it through the excise taxes they pay on firearms, ammunition, and fishing equipment. State and federal fish and wildlife programs are dependent upon funds from the purchase of hunting and fishing licenses, tags, and stamps.

Some people oppose hunting because they dislike the idea of individual animals being killed. I don't want to go into exhaustive detail, but here is the theory of wildlife management in a nutshell: literally billions of animals exist today because of habitat saved, improved, or created with funds provided by legal sport hunters and fishermen. These funds help not just game species, but nongame birds, mammals, fish, reptiles, amphibians, and beneficial insects—butterflies, pollinating bees, and hundreds of others.

Along with the good guys, there will always be a small percentage of individuals who choose to break the law—the outlaws, the game hogs, the poachers and worst of all, those who would exploit our fish and wildlife resources for personal profit. These people have little or no regard for the law or the rights of others. They often justify their actions with narrow-minded, self-serving rationalizations. Here is one example: Fish and Game Warden Rick Banko arrested a Del Norte County poacher for killing an elk inside Redwood National Park. When Banko asked this outlaw what he thought should happen to someone who kills an elk in the National Park, the man responded, "These animals were put here for us to use." California's elk population wouldn't last a week if everyone shared that attitude.

"Habitat is where it's at," as they say, but the only way to maintain healthy populations of fish and wildlife in a state with thirty-eight million people is by establishing laws and providing dedicated, well-trained officers to enforce those laws.

Badges, Bears, and Eagles is based on events that actually happened. The dialogue has been reconstructed from my memory, but also from interviews, officers' records, transcripts, and court documents. Some scenes involving the perpetrators have been dramatically enhanced in a way that fits the available facts.

I wrote this book because I want people to know that there are wildlife officers out there who are passionate about wildlife, proactive, and capable of putting together complex investigations. More than just ticket writers and fishing license checkers, many of today's state and federal wildlife officers are highly sophisticated professionals, putting their lives on the line for the protection of our rapidly diminishing natural resources.

The Eagle Case

I

"Hey, we caught a fox!" shouted Jake Stillwell, looking down over the steep embankment at his slower and much larger partner. It was early December, 1984, and recent rains had turned the exposed red clay hillsides of Cottonwood Wilds Subdivision into slop. With each stride, Mitch Davis added another pound of sticky mud to the soles of his size-thirteen boots. His pant legs were soaked through from repeated falls. Both forearms were caked with mud in an effort to keep the muzzle of his .22 caliber rifle from auguring into the wet ground. "Hurry up with that rifle," ordered Stillwell, the thirty-four-year-old self-appointed leader of this duo of destruction.

Stillwell was a devious little creep with shifty eyes, a pear-shaped body and an uncanny ability to make people believe things that weren't true. Davis, a stout, twenty-seven-year-old "tow head," had an annoying habit of clearing his throat every ten seconds. He might have had a good side to him, but it didn't have much of a chance when he was with Stillwell; he followed the man around and did his bidding like a well-trained puppy.

Davis looked up at Stillwell just in time to see him disappear over the rise. Stillwell walked back toward the third trap in their line of seventeen. As he approached, a small salt-and-pepper-colored animal watched him through the branches of a manzanita bush. Weakened and panting heavily, the little gray fox had been unable to free its right front paw from the trap's metal jaws. The bone was broken, just above the paw, and the fur around it had been chewed away. Given another hour, the desperate little canine might have chewed its leg off and escaped. Now it was staring into the eyes of its captor.

As Stillwell came closer, the fox began thrashing from side to side, but only succeeded in wrapping its body in the anchor chain. Stillwell looked over his shoulder and told Davis, "Bring that rifle over here before this thing gets away."

Davis handed the rifle to his impatient partner and cautioned him to make sure there was no mud in the barrel. Stillwell raised the rifle to his shoulder and sighted the scope on a spot near the fox's left ear. A curious look came over his face as he squeezed off the trigger. Snap! The sharp trill of a .22 caliber high-velocity bullet echoed through the canyon. The fox's head dropped to the ground and its body fell limp. One of its back legs continued to quiver for a few seconds and a small stream of blood flowed from behind its left ear.

Mitch Davis walked over and stepped on the trap's release mechanism. He pulled the fox free and threw it aside. Davis then reset the trap and covered it with debris. Taking a small chunk of jackrabbit flesh out of his backpack, he hooked it to a wire that hung over the trap. This practice is illegal, but effective for attracting curious foxes and bobcats.

By noon, Stillwell and Davis had checked all seventeen of their traps and walked back to Stillwell's Jeep. Finding a low spot in the barbed wire fence, they each straddled the top wire and carefully stepped over. A few feet away was a white, ten-by-twelve-inch sign, reading:

> NO HUNTING OR TRESPASSING
> VIOLATORS WILL BE PROSECUTED.

Neither man gave the sign a second look.

Cottonwood Wilds Subdivision was a section of private land near the isolated foothill community of Platina. The absentee land owner had graded a lengthy road over the hills and across several canyons in hopes of eventually selling off forty acre parcels. At the time it remained undeveloped fenced-and-posted property, which Stillwell and Davis saw as their own private trapping grounds.

On December 28, 1984, California Fish and Game Warden Merton Hatcher received an anonymous tip regarding illegal trapping activity in the Cottonwood Wilds Subdivision. Hatcher, a middle-aged throwback to the fifties, proudly displayed his greased-down, graying hair in a "ducktail"—combed back on the sides and flat on top. Tall and thin, he had feet that were so large, he had to order his boots out of a catalog.

The informant had seen the trespassers driving two different vehicles, depending on the day—a red Ford pickup and a blue Jeep.

Although trapping has become unpopular and pretty much unprofitable over the last twenty-five years, it was still common and borderline profitable back in the 1980s. Those who did trap in California were required to have a license and follow a strict set of regulations. One of those regulations prohibited the use of "sight bait"—exposed fur or meat within thirty feet of a trap. The purpose of sight bait was to entice an unsuspecting bobcat, fox, or other furbearing mammal. Unfortunately, the exposed animal flesh also attracted raptors—hawks, owls, and eagles. It was not uncommon to find these state and federally protected birds caught in steel-jawed leg-hold traps with their legs broken or severely injured.

Having taken time off for the holidays, Warden Hatcher had not responded to the first report. He received a second tip on January 7, 1985, from a different informant, providing license plate information for the two suspect vehicles. Hatcher ran the plates through Shasta County Sheriff's dispatch and learned that the blue Jeep belonged to a well-known violator named Jake William Stillwell. The Ford pickup was registered to an unfamiliar name—Mitchell Wayne Davis. Hatcher had once pinched Stillwell for a minor fishing violation but the longtime outlaw always seemed to be just out of reach when it came to the more serious crimes. Now that he suspected Stillwell was involved, the veteran warden set out to investigate the following day.

Heavy rains had fallen the night before, making the steep dirt roads inside Cottonwood Wilds Subdivision muddy and too slippery to drive on. Warden Hatcher parked his patrol vehicle near the entrance and hiked two miles into the area where the violations were occurring. He was an experienced trapping investigator so it didn't take him long to find the illegal trap line. There were seventeen traps, all illegally baited with exposed rabbit parts.

By the time Hatcher located the last trap, it was almost dark, so he decided to return early the following morning. Although California trapping regulations required that traps be checked once a day, Stillwell or Davis would probably not return any time soon. After all, they were already committing at least three violations—trespass, sight bait, and unnumbered traps. That night, Warden Hatcher lost sleep thinking about the illegal trap line. *Could this be my chance*, Hatcher wondered, *to finally bust Stillwell for something more serious than taking a couple extra trout?*

Up the next morning before daylight, the sleepy warden reached Platina sometime around 6:00 a.m. He hid his patrol vehicle and again hiked to the violation site. Accustomed to stakeouts, Hatcher found a dry log to sit on and waited for the trappers to return. For the first two hours he occupied his time by watching a hungry scrub jay. This intelligent, close relative of the common crow had discovered a chunk of rabbit meat hanging above one of the illegal traps. Gliding in from a nearby perch, the large, bluish-gray bird would land on the ground, hop in the air and attempt to rip bits of flesh from the dangling piece of tissue. With every attempt, it landed closer to the deadly trigger plate and ultimate doom. Hatcher tried to discourage the determined corvid by tossing debris in its direction. Undeterred, the bird would fly back to its perch, turn around and immediately return.

By noon, Warden Hatcher's own hunger began to affect his decision-making process. He wanted to wait another hour or two, but his stomach convinced him that the two outlaws were probably not going to show up.

One by one, Hatcher collected the seventeen illegally-set traps. Each time he removed a trap he replaced it with one of his business cards, writing the same message on the back: *Contact me if you want your traps back*. Knowing what a cagey adversary Jake Stillwell was, Warden Hatcher did not expect to hear from the illegal trappers.

On February 12, 1985, Jake Stillwell and Mitch Davis pulled into a private trout hatchery on Lanes Valley Road, near the foothill community of Manton. Stillwell was at the wheel of his blue Jeep. He had worked at the hatchery a few years earlier and befriended the manager, Al Hollis. Stillwell and Davis were apparently out plinking that particular day and dropped by to talk with Hollis. Al Hollis was adjusting the boards on one of his fish ponds when Stillwell and Davis walked up beside him.

"What are you guys up to?" asked Hollis, as he came to an upright position.

"That game warden, Merton Hatcher, took seventeen of our traps," Stillwell groused.

"How did that happen?"

"We were trapping up by the Ditch Grade. He must have heard that we were in there because he walked all the way in, took our traps and left his business cards. His cards said if we wanted our traps back, we had to contact him. Can he do that?"

Having once worked trappers as a Fish and Game warden, Hollis could think of several possible violations. "Were your traps numbered?"

Stillwell and Davis looked at each other for a second. Most of the traps belonged to Davis's dad. Davis answered, "No, not really."

Appearing embarrassed by Hollis's response to their question, Stillwell changed the subject. "What if we kill a mountain lion?"

Knowing that mountain lions were protected in California, Hollis was taken aback by the question. "Why, did you get one?"

"Yeah, we killed one off Ponderosa Way. It's all skinned out if ya know anybody who wants to buy it. Ya know, everyone is pissed off at Hatcher. Whaddaya think would happen if we put a bullet through his windshield?"

Hollis was not eager to continue this discussion, which involved the killing of a protected mountain lion and a threat of violence against a peace officer. He pretended to lose interest and walked toward the next pond.

"What's the big deal about sight bait?" shouted Davis.

"Sight bait could attract a soaring bird, like a hawk or an eagle." said Hollis.

Stillwell and Davis thought that was hilarious. "Maybe we ought to kill a couple eagles!" said Stillwell, with his typical bravado. Stillwell and Davis looked at each other, snickering. They mentioned doing something with an eagle, but by then Hollis had reached the next pond and couldn't quite hear what was said.

Before the men left, Hollis clearly overheard Stillwell say, "We should kill a deer for every one of the traps Hatcher took and dump them at the Fish and Game office."

On February 15, 1985, at 7:55 a.m., Inspector Dave Nelson, enforcement chief for the California Department of Fish and Game's Redding Regional Office, was arriving for work. Nelson was a lean, six-foot-three-inch, former World War II army officer, rapidly approaching retirement. A nice enough guy, he always seemed distant and impersonal when dealing with subordinates. I figured that had something to do with his military background. Although Inspector Nelson never let on that he knew me any better than the fifty other people he supervised, he had actually been my father's boss back in the sixties. Young and spry then, Nelson sometimes played catch with my brother and me when he came by the house to see my dad. Now his hair was almost gone and his hands were so shaky he couldn't write anything without using the old Underwood typewriter that sat on his desk, but the veteran inspector still showed up every morning, bright and early.

As he pulled into the office parking lot, Nelson noticed a black garbage bag lying at the base of the locked west entrance gate. Thinking that someone had thoughtlessly discarded his garbage, Inspector Nelson walked over and picked up the bag. His first inclination was to drop it into a dumpster at the back of the office, but something told him to look inside. The bag contained a magnificent raptor, which the veteran wildlife protection officer immediately identified as a bald eagle.

Fresh blood dripped from the bird's nostrils and breast area, indicating that it had recently been shot. "I'll be damned!" mumbled Nelson. "Somebody shot an eagle." As he was about to close the bag, Inspector Nelson noticed something attached to the eagle's leg. It was a message. "What the hell?" exclaimed the surprised inspector.

Like most fifty-eight-year-olds, Dave Nelson couldn't read much of anything without his glasses. He fetched them from his car and quickly returned. The note—hand-printed on a piece of white, six-by-eight-inch paper—was littered with expletives, a mixture of upper and lower case letters and a lot of misspelled words. More importantly, it threatened the life of Fish and Game Warden Merton Hatcher.

Inspector Nelson brought the bag inside the regional office. A few minutes later, Jack Weaver, the Redding area patrol captain, arrived for work. Weaver, a two-hundred-sixty-pound chain-smoker, always wore a zipped-up uniform jacket to hide his enormous belly. Seldom was the captain seen without a cigarette in one hand and a thirty-two ounce fountain drink in the other.

Captain Jack, as he was often called, supervised the warden force in four Northern California counties—including Shasta, where the office was located. His relatively small army of wildlife protection officers consisted of three field lieutenants and sixteen wardens. Inspector Nelson intended to turn the matter over to Weaver and his crew as soon as possible.

With long, slow strides, the soon-to-be retired inspector carried the bag up the hallway toward Captain Weaver's office. Nelson supervised Weaver, but I always had the impression that he preferred to deal with him as little as possible. Weaver had pretty much run the enforcement branch of the office for several years before Nelson arrived and there seemed to be an underlying tension between them. Their antipathy had reached a boiling point during the previous summer, when all the enforcement personnel attended an annual training campout in the nearby mountains and Nelson and Weaver got into a heated argument over how to cook corn. That was the first time I had ever seen Dave Nelson drop his guard and become one of the guys. We all found it hilarious, but since that time, the two strong-willed supervisors seemed to keep their distance from each other whenever possible.

"Jack, you'll want to look into this," said Nelson, as he entered Weaver's office. "It involves Warden Hatcher." As was his custom before the state smoking ban went into effect, Weaver was sitting behind his desk, leaning back in his chair, smoking an unfiltered Camel cigarette. The captain regularly polluted the north wing of the building and pretty much dared anyone to complain about it.

"What has Hatcher gotten into now?" grumbled Weaver, as he took a long drag on his cigarette.

"See for yourself," replied Nelson. "I found this lying in front of the gate this morning."

Nelson placed the bag on Weaver's desk and stepped away. Weaver opened the bag and looked inside. After reading the note attached to the eagle's leg, the perplexed captain said, "I'll take care of it," and Nelson walked back down the hallway toward his own office.

That's where I came in. I had just gone 10-8 (on duty and subject to radio call) when I received a radio report that Captain Weaver wanted to see me.

I worked out of my residence and tried to avoid the regional office as much as possible. I was a former athlete and admitted health nut, so the thought of being trapped in the captain's office with the door closed made me want to head for the hills; I could count on the usual nicotine headache and the overwhelming urge to go back home and change my uniform. As I entered the front door of the building, the receptionist advised me that Jack was waiting to see me in the office adjacent to hers.

"Come in and close the door," instructed Weaver. "I need to talk to you about Warden Hatcher and something that's happened." Captain Weaver snuffed out his cigarette in an ash tray already brimming with cigarette butts and lit up a fresh one. After we had stayed in the captain's office long enough for me to get a splitting headache, he led me down the hallway to the evidence freezer. Inside the freezer was the black garbage bag Inspector Nelson had found, along with the dead bald eagle and the threatening note. "I don't know what you're going to be able to do with this," said Weaver, "but do what you can."

I opened the garbage bag and examined the eagle. It was obvious that the bird had been shot through the chest, probably with a .22 rifle. Captain Weaver watched as I read the note for the first time. I was careful not to touch the paper and avoided placing my fingers on the bag. The first thing I noticed was the unusual spelling of Hatcher's name—"Hather." The curious mixture of upper and lower case letters appeared to have been written with a black felt-tip pen. Although the captain seemed fairly pessimistic about making a case, I enjoyed a good investigation and was confident about eventually finding the culprit.

This time I wasn't just confident, but I was also determined to find the miserable bastards who had killed that eagle. For me this would be not just another investigation, but a mission. I loved all wildlife, but eagles—golden eagles as well as bald eagles—were at the top of the list. Having been fortunate enough to handle and even rehabilitate these majestic birds while working in Southern California, I couldn't imagine anyone stooping so low as to kill one. It was downright sacrilegious!

II

Merton Hatcher was one of the strangest Fish and Game wardens who ever pinned on a badge. For a number of years, during the 1970s, he was just about the only Fish and Game representative that Redding area hunters, fishermen, and trappers ever encountered. From the time Warden Hatcher got up in the morning until the time he went to bed at night, he wore his uniform and packed a sidearm. Whether he was out patrolling for deer poachers or shopping at Sears with his wife, Hatcher would be in uniform and packing a .357 Magnum revolver on his gun belt.

Merton fancied himself an amateur preacher and self-proclaimed ambassador from whatever church he happened to be attending at the time. Much to the chagrin of his supervisors, he was not shy about expressing his strong religious opinions, on duty or off. At the same time, Hatcher had the reputation of being a "hard-assed" game warden who would not hesitate to arrest his own mother if he caught her doing something wrong.

Warden Hatcher believed that a person couldn't possibly be a real game warden without also being an experienced hunter and fisherman. He often bragged about the time he killed his first bear. According to Merton, he killed the bear way down in the bottom of a canyon and was unable to carry it out before dark. As the temperature dropped, his only source of warmth was the gutted bear carcass, which he climbed inside to spend the night. If anyone else had told me that story, I would have accused him of pulling my leg. Well aware of Hatcher and his eccentricities, I figured it had to be true. He probably pretended to be *Grizzly Adams* so he would have that story to tell.

I began the investigation by discussing the eagle and the note with Warden Hatcher, asking if he knew of anyone who might want to threaten or discredit him. Hatcher thought for a few minutes and mentioned the trapping investigation from a month earlier. When Warden Hatcher had confiscated the seventeen traps, he had failed to tell any of his supervisors. Time passed, no one claimed the traps and he had gone on to other business. Therefore Hatcher's supervisors were unaware of anyone out there with an ax to grind.

"The trappers never came back, so I picked up all their traps and left my business cards in their place," explained Hatcher.

"How many traps did you take?" I asked.

"Seventeen."

"Anything else you can tell me?"

"I have their names and vehicle information if you want it."

Warden Hatcher provided me with the vehicle information he had been given and the names Mitch Davis and Jake Stillwell. With very little to go on, I contacted Paul Wertz, the regional public information officer, and asked him to write a press release about the eagle incident. Wertz was an effective, professional writer, who could create a compelling story for the local newspaper. Soon everyone in town was wondering who had shot the bald eagle and left the threatening note. The actual content of the note and the name of the officer involved were not published, for obvious reasons.

I transported the infamous contents of the plastic garbage bag to the Shasta County Sheriff's Evidence Laboratory. The evidence officer, Sergeant

Art Wooden, used all the most sophisticated techniques available at the time to pull up some kind of usable fingerprint. Much to our disappointment, nothing was found. Stillwell and Davis were prime suspects, but for the time being I had no tangible evidence to use against them.

No sooner had the newspaper article appeared in Redding's *Record Searchlight* than it began to pay off. On February 19th, I received a telephone call from a man who said he wanted to keep his identity confidential. At the time of the initial call, I did not know the caller or recognize his voice.

"Yeah, I read the story in the paper about the eagle being killed and the threat to one of your wardens. I might have some information about that," said the caller.

"We appreciate any information we can get," I replied.

"Last Tuesday these two guys came into the hatchery where I work. One of them used to work here. Their names are Jake Stillwell—that's the one that used to work here—and Mitch Davis. They were driving a dark blue Jeep. That belongs to Stillwell. Anyway, we started talking and Stillwell said that Merton Hatcher had picked up seventeen of their traps."

"Are you sure he said *seventeen* traps?" I asked.

"I'm positive," said the caller. "I read the article in the paper and figured it had to be them."

During the remainder of our conversation, the caller provided a detailed account of the February 12th conversation with Stillwell and Davis at the private fish hatchery. He described how the two outlaws had talked about putting a bullet through Warden Hatcher's windshield and killing a mountain lion. He went on to say that Stillwell and Davis had joked about killing a couple eagles and dumping deer carcasses at the Fish and Game office. As excited as I was about receiving this invaluable information, the caller's next statement was troubling: "I can't testify in court," he said in an apologetic tone. "The two guys I work for would be mad if they knew I was even talking to you."

My new informant's reluctance to testify would make things more complicated, but he had given me the information I needed to prepare two detailed search warrants. For the time being, it would be necessary to convince the judge to seal the affidavits. Having dealt with similar dilemmas, I knew some tough decisions might have to be made if and when we went to trial.

I carefully documented what my informant had said, along with facts provided by Warden Hatcher and physical evidence found at the Fish and Game office. The remainder of my work day was spent preparing search warrants and affidavits for the district attorney's approval. Once approved by the district attorney and signed by the judge, the search warrants would cover the persons, residences, and vehicles of Jake William Stillwell and Mitchell

Wayne Davis. More specifically, Fish and Game officers would be authorized to search:

> … any and all freezers, refrigerators, kitchen drawers, cabinets, drawers, closets, gun and ammunition storage areas, tool storage areas, garages, outbuildings, surrounding property, sumps, pits, garbage containers, barrels, and boxes.

Also included were:

> … the persons and vehicles of Jake Stillwell and Mitch Davis.

The warrant continued:

> Items to search for include indices of ownership or occupancy; tablets or pieces of plain white paper of the size 6 and 1/8 by eight inches; black felt-tip pen; handwriting examples; small caliber firearms, live rounds or cartridges; steel traps, stakes, steel drags, wire attached to traps; wire in bulk; wire cutters or wire cutting pliers; Warden Hatcher's business cards, containing notes left at the trap site; raw furs or carcasses; knives; fur stretching frames; mountain lion hides; eagle feathers or blood; mud and snow tires; black plastic bags; dead rabbits or parts thereof; and clothing or footwear that may contain fragments of blood, hair, or feathers.

As required by law, I concluded the search warrant with legal justification for the search:

> Your affiant, Lieutenant Steven Callan, had reasonable cause to believe that the subjects were in possession of property constituting a means of committing a felony (evidence of threatening a public officer) and property or things with the intent of using them to commit a public offense (misdemeanor take and/or possession of an endangered species [bald eagle] and/or take and possession of a protected mountain lion).

A coordinated, simultaneous search was conducted at both residences on February 20, 1985. Warden Dave Szody, Warden Don Jacobs and I went to Mitch Davis's residence. Davis lived out in the country on a small piece of fenced acreage owned by his parents. Two mobile homes were on the property: One belonged to Davis and his wife; the other belonged to Davis's parents. I expected that most of the illegal items would be found on Davis's property, since Stillwell lived in town, with limited space.

Mitch Davis, his wife, and both parents were home when we arrived. I handed copies of the search warrant to Mitch Davis and his father. If a picture is worth a thousand words, Mitch looked like his fun-and-games world of shooting anything that moved had just come crashing down around him. His face turned red, partially out of fear, but mostly from embarrassment. Davis's wife and parents obviously had no idea what their fair-haired boy had been up to.

The first place Szody and I searched was the freezer in Mitch Davis's kitchen.

"I'm guessing this is the kitty they killed on Ponderosa Way," I said, as I opened a large plastic bag containing a complete mountain lion hide.

"What's in that little bag?" asked Szody, holding a clipboard and recording the items I seized into evidence.

"I'll be darned. I believe we have a ring-tailed cat!"

"You know, I've never seen one in the wild."

"Don't feel like the Lone Ranger," I said. "Very few people have. These little guys only come out at night and even then you never see 'em."

"Have you ever seen one?" asked Szody

"Only once. I was working Shasta Lake one night, about three years ago, when I saw one running through the rocks on the shoreline."

California law classifies the ring-tailed cat as a "fully protected mammal" and the mountain lion as a "specially protected species." The take or possession of either one of these animals was considered to be a serious offense. I carefully bagged both items and sealed the bags with evidence tags.

While Szody and I continued our search of Davis's mobile home, Warden Jacobs was looking around outside. It didn't take him long to find three plastic garbage bags in a field next to the residences. One of them contained the decomposing carcass of a fisher. Fishers are rare furbearing mammals, seldom seen in California. As was the case with the mountain lion and the ring-tailed cat, fishers are protected by California law.

"What do we have here?" muttered Jacobs, as he opened the second bag and peered inside. "Wow! This one's ripe." Jacobs had discovered what was left of a bobcat that had been thrown into the field to rot. Examining the contents of the last bag, he said, "A little gray fox," and held the bag at arm's length. "Looks like he might have been trying to chew his paw off to escape."

"None o' them carcasses is mine," announced Mitch Davis's father, who was standing nearby and watching Jacobs. "I ain't trapped in years. Mitch is responsible for anything you find out there."

Szody and I concluded our search of Mitch Davis's trailer with the discovery of a blood-spattered knife. The blood was later identified as rabbit.

Before leaving, I handed Mitch Davis a receipt for the items that were being seized into evidence. I also pulled a card out of my wallet and read Davis his Miranda rights. He had cooperated up until that point, but claimed to know nothing about a dead bald eagle or a threatening note. There was no question in my mind that Davis was not being truthful, but I also knew that we would have to prove it.

Meanwhile, Wardens Hatcher and Martens were busy searching the residence of Davis's partner, Jake Stillwell. Stillwell lived in a small house in town. Sitting on the north side of Stillwell's residence were two plastic milk carton boxes—the kind with the printed notice on the side telling people it's against the law to take them. Both boxes were filled with steel-jawed leg-hold traps and trapping tools.

"There's another trap, a bloody towel and fur of some kind here in the Jeep," said Martens, as Hatcher recorded the seized items.

"Yeah," said Hatcher. "That's probably rabbit fur. I found four jackrabbits in his kitchen freezer."

Warden Martens, who had been on the job a year or two longer than Hatcher, pulled a card out of his pocket and read Stillwell his Miranda rights. Believing that he could outsmart what he viewed as a couple country-bumpkin game wardens, Stillwell waived his rights and agreed to answer questions.

"Who do all these traps belong to?" asked Martens.

"They all belong to Mitch," said Stillwell. "The other day we pulled a trap line up by Whitmore. That's where all these came from."

"Have you guys been trapping near Platina?"

"Yeah, we were trapping somewhere up there, but I'm not sure of the exact location."

"May I see your trapping license?"

"I don't have one, but I think Mitch does."

Martens and Hatcher didn't believe anything that Stillwell had told them. They ran a records check through Sacramento headquarters and learned that neither Davis nor Stillwell had a California Trapping License.

While searching Jake Stillwell's residence, Hatcher and Martens documented Stillwell's possession of several rifles, including a .22-.250 Winchester, with scope; a .22 Winchester, with scope; and a Ruger .220. Empty casings from the .22-.250, along with live ammunition for the same rifle, were found in Stillwell's Jeep. One of the most interesting items found inside Stillwell's residence was a black felt-tip pen, with virtually the same-sized tip as the one used to write the note threatening Warden Hatcher. A few samples of Stillwell's handwriting were also taken into evidence; the best were found in a book of recorded firearm sales.

"I would like to ask you one more question before we leave," said Martens.

Stillwell stopped what he was doing and waited for the veteran warden's question.

"What can you tell us about a dead bald eagle that was dumped at the Fish and Game office?"

"I don't know anything about any eagle."

The next day I began working my way through the pile of evidence that Martens and Hatcher had seized from Stillwell's residence. All those traps were the first items that caught my eye. One by one, I examined each trap, looking for blood, feathers, or anything else that might provide a clue as to what Stillwell and Davis had been up to. The jaws of one trap were closed around a group of large, tan-colored, down-type feathers. *Could these feathers have come from a bald eagle?* I wondered. It was clear that they had come from a large bird, but an expert would have to confirm the species. Some white feathers and a few partial feathers were scattered in one of the boxes, along with the traps.

I personally carried the feathers from the trap, along with the scattered feathers, and the dead bald eagle, to the California Department of Fish and Game Forensics Laboratory in Sacramento. Unable to make a definitive identification, Pathologist Jim Banks sent the feathers on to the Smithsonian Institute in Washington, D.C. While at the Smithsonian, the feathers were examined by Roxy Laybourne, one of the foremost ornithologists and feather experts in the world; Ms. Laybourne specialized in the microscopic structure of bird feathers. With the aid of an electron microscope, she identified the feathers as having come from the lower leg (tarsus) of an eagle—not a bald eagle, however, but a golden eagle. Unlike bald eagles, golden eagles' legs are feathered to the feet.

I was a little disappointed that the feathers had not come from a bald eagle. Such a finding might have tied Stillwell and Davis to the dead bald eagle at the Fish and Game office and the threatening note. On the other hand, golden eagles were also fully protected: taking one or possessing any parts thereof would constitute a serious crime. Although irrelevant to the case, Ms. Laybourne identified the white feathers as having come from the underwing of a mallard duck. The scattered partial feathers belonged to a ring-necked pheasant.

Charges were piling up against Stillwell and Davis, but I was determined to convict one or both of them for killing the bald eagle and leaving the threatening note. Without the testimony of the original informant or additional evidence, that might not be possible.

Returning to square one, I began examining the limited handwriting samples from Stillwell's firearms sales record book. I was disturbed by the thought that someone as unstable as Stillwell could be authorized to sell firearms; after all, this habitual wildlife poacher had recently threatened to put a bullet through a state peace officer's windshield.

I was no handwriting expert, but it was fairly obvious to me that Stillwell had authored the threatening note. Before submitting anything to state or federal handwriting experts, I aimed to find additional examples of Stillwell's writings. With that in mind, I contacted Fred Hoffman, one of Stillwell's former employers. Hoffman owned a business in the Redding area. I introduced myself and asked Hoffman if he had once employed a man named Jake Stillwell.

Hoffman's face lit up immediately. "I figured what you were here for when I saw you walk in the door," exclaimed Hoffman. "Yeah, I fired Jake about three years ago."

"I was hoping you might have a few samples of Stillwell's handwriting lying around here somewhere," I said.

"I read the article in the newspaper," said Hoffman. "It sounds just like something Jake Stillwell would do."

"Why do you say that?" I asked.

"He was always bragging about poaching," said Hoffman.

"If you can find any samples of his handwriting, it would be a big help."

"Give me a little time. I'll see what I can come up with." My instincts told me that this man knew a lot more than he was telling me, but I decided not to press him too hard until he came up with the handwriting samples I needed.

That evening, about 8:00 p.m., I received a phone call from Fred Hoffman. Just as I figured, Hoffman was much better informed about Jake Stillwell than he originally let on.

"You know," he began, "Stillwell did seem to have it in for one particular game warden."

"Was it Merton Hatcher, by any chance?" I asked.

"That's it!" replied Hoffman. "Me and Jake used to go squirrel hunting in Tehama County. Several times I had to stop him from shooting deer. He never paid attention to whether or not deer season was open. The further away he could shoot something, the better he liked it." Hoffman went on to say that Stillwell was a very good shot and had scopes on all of his rifles.

"What kind of rifles does he use?" I asked. Hoffman said Stillwell's favorite rifle was a .22-.250. I remembered that Hatcher and Martens had documented a .22-.250 rifle during the search of Stillwell's residence and found scattered .22-250 casings inside his Jeep. It seemed unlikely that Stillwell was picking up spent casings off the ground. More likely, he was shooting from the window of his Jeep.

Hoffman began rambling about his experiences with Stillwell. "I was with him once, when he shot a hawk at two or three hundred yards. Hatcher once stopped Jake near Black Butte Lake. Jake had a bunch of illegal ducks, but Hatcher never found them. Jake was always bragging about killing deer. Several times, he would say this would be a good place for Hatcher to catch us. One time Jake got a citation for taking some illegal trout. He said that makes up for the twenty-five other times that he didn't get caught. He can't hunt legitimately. Jake used to talk about Merton Hatcher like he was on a personal basis with him."

I thanked Hoffman for the information and carefully documented everything he had said. We agreed that I would come by his business the next day.

The next morning I dropped by Fred Hoffman's business to pick up a couple of Jake Stillwell's handwriting samples and ask a few more questions. Hoffman's statement about Stillwell shooting hawks bothered me. If Stillwell would shoot a hawk, I reasoned that he would have no qualms about shooting an eagle. I questioned Hoffman about this.

"I saw Jake shoot hawks at least ten times," replied Hoffman.

"Are you sure that you're not exaggerating a little?"

"At least ten times," Hoffman insisted.

I left Hoffman's business and drove to the Fish and Game office. More than ever, I was convinced that Jake Stillwell was our man. I also knew that without more evidence or the testimony of our original informant, we would not be able to pin the crime—threatening a public officer (a felony) and take or possession of an endangered species (a misdemeanor)—on either Stillwell or Davis. The trapping and protected species violations would hold up, but these guys, particularly Stillwell, were as bad as poachers get. They deserved to be prosecuted to the full extent of the law.

With no other viable options, I decided to give our original informant another try. He managed a private trout hatchery out in the Manton area, so I telephoned him and asked if Warden Szody and I could drop by to talk. Dressed in civilian clothing and driving an unmarked car, we arrived early the next morning.

I spotted a man walking across the hatchery grounds wearing rubber hip boots and a yellow rain parka. "Be right with ya," he shouted.

"I recognize that bow-legged walk from somewhere," I said, as the man approached.

"I'm Al Hollis, the one who called you."

"Thanks for meeting with us, Al. I'm Steve Callan and this is Dave Szody."

"Just a minute while I take this stuff off. I was moving some fish around."

We waited while Hollis removed his parka and changed his boots. There was nothing remarkable about his appearance—average height and weight—short graying hair, but something about him rang a bell.

"I don't remember if I told you this over the phone, but I used to be a warden, said Hollis, coming to his feet. "I had a drinking problem and they let me go."

"I must have met you at one of the training conferences," I said. "You look familiar."

"The Department wouldn't give me a break," Hollis went on, his voice gruff and cracking. "I was pretty bitter about it for a couple years."

I suspected there was another side to that story, but we needed Hollis's help so I didn't ask for details.

"Jake Stillwell worked here at the hatchery a few years ago. He used to hear me complaining about Fish and Game all the time. I guess he felt safe telling me things. Jake still comes by the hatchery, every once in a while, to ask questions or brag about something he's shot. I listen, but I don't approve of what these guys are doing. When I read the newspaper article, I knew that had to be them."

"We want to prosecute these guys for killing the eagle and writing the threatening note," I explained. "Without your testimony we may not be able to do that."

"My bosses think these guys will poison the fish or do something to harm the hatchery," said Hollis. "I told them about this and they don't want me to get involved any further."

"Maybe we can talk to them," I offered. "Who are these guys?"

"I'm sure you guys know one of them," replied Hollis. "He's Dennis Woodhall. The other one is Dick Marshall."

Szody and I immediately recognized one of the names—Dennis Woodhall. He was a retired Fish and Game officer who had worked in the area for many years.

"You mean to tell me that Woodhall won't allow you to testify," I asked, incredulous, "in a case like this, where a warden's life has been threatened and a bald eagle has been shot?"

"Yeah, he feels pretty strongly about it," replied Hollis, sounding apologetic.

"How about letting us talk to Woodhall and Marshall? Maybe we can convince them how important this is."

"You guys do whatever you can, but they were pretty adamant."

I thanked Hollis for meeting with us and advised him that we would be in touch. Driving away, Dave and I shook our heads in disbelief. Both of us were thoroughly disgusted by what we had just heard.

It was a week or so later, in early March, when I was finally able to arrange a meeting with retired Fish and Game Officer Dennis Woodhall and his business partner, Dick Marshall. Dressed in civilian clothing, Dave Szody and I met the two private fish hatchery owners at a Red Bluff coffee shop. Woodhall had put on a ton of weight since retiring, but still had a shiny bald head and a jaw that never stopped flapping.

After initial greetings, Woodhall came right to the point. "Dick and I don't want Michaels to testify."

I was taken aback by Woodhall's extremely negative attitude, considering the fact that he had been a wildlife protection officer for thirty years.

"This guy, Stillwell, is as bad as they come," I explained. "He killed a bald eagle and threatened the life of one of our wardens. I just talked to a man who said Stillwell shoots hawks and deer all the time, just for the fun of it."

My attempt to shame Woodhall into changing his mind fell on deaf ears. It was clear that he and Marshall had already made up their minds and were only concerned about the money they had invested in their fish hatchery. Although Woodhall had a reputation for being able to talk the hump off a camel, he had only this to offer: "You guys will get them again for something else." Szody and I were insulted by Woodhall's statement and refused to dignify it with any kind of response. While Woodhall tried to justify his case with a barrage of self-serving BS, I wondered, *How could this guy take an oath to enforce the law, then retire and turn his back on the whole thing?* Our silence spoke volumes.

After thanking Woodhall and Marshall for the meeting, Szody and I left the restaurant.

Nearly two months passed. Dave and I continued to look for anything we could use to break open the case. We went by and talked to Al Hollis two or three more times, but got the same response. I was about ready to cut our losses and file charges against Stillwell and Davis for the prosecutable offences when we finally got the break we needed.

One afternoon, at the end of April, Al Hollis walked into the Redding Fish and Game office. I happened to be there at the time and led Hollis into the squad room.

"Have a seat, Al. What's on your mind?" I asked.

Hollis sat there for a minute or two before responding. I could tell he wanted to tell me something, but was hesitant to get it out. "I have decided to testify if you still need me," said Hollis. "I might end up losing my job if those guys wreck the hatchery, but I have to do the right thing. I guess in my heart I'm still a game warden."

My mind immediately began processing Al Hollis's surprising statement. "I can't tell you how much I respect you for your decision," I said. "You know, with all the evidence we are going to throw at these guys, they may well plead guilty and you won't have to testify anyway."

I thanked Al Hollis several more times before the courageous former warden left the office. I wondered what had motivated him to change his mind. Too many years had passed for him to have any chance of getting back on the job. Hollis knew that. He hadn't even brought it up. This guy may have had a drinking problem, but he still had the heart and the guts of a real game warden.

The remainder of my work day was spent typing up formal criminal complaints against Jake William Stillwell and Mitchell Wayne Davis. Most of the narrative had already been written up in case we got lucky.

My original complaint, submitted May 1, 1985, charged Stillwell and Davis with the following crimes:

1. Threatening a public officer—felony.
2. Take and possess endangered bald eagle— misdemeanor.
3. Take and possess mountain lion—misdemeanor.
4. Possess fully protected ring-tailed cat— misdemeanor.
5. Possess protected furbearing mammal (fisher) or parts thereof— misdemeanor.
6. Take or possess fully protected bird (golden eagle) or parts thereof —misdemeanor.
7. Maintain steel leg-hold traps within thirty feet of exposed bait— misdemeanor.
8. Trap furbearing or nongame mammals without a trapping license—misdemeanor.
9. Sale of raw furs of furbearing or nongame mammals without a trapping license (seven counts)—misdemeanor.

Once the criminal complaints had been approved by the district attorney's office, warrants were issued for the arrests of Stillwell and Davis. Arrangements were made for them to turn themselves in to Fish and Game on May 25, 1985.

Prior to Stillwell and Davis arriving at the Fish and Game office, I telephoned one of the deputy district attorneys I had been working with on the case. I asked if there was any legal problem with secretly recording the two arrestees while they were in custody and sitting in the back of a marked enforcement vehicle. As expected, the deputy district attorney confirmed that there was no legal expectation of privacy under those circumstances. Always looking for ways to strengthen the case against Stillwell and Davis, I figured a conversation between the two wildlife outlaws might produce an admission of guilt or additional evidence. Just before their arrival, I placed an active tape recorder under the front seat of the marked patrol car that would be used to transport them to the county jail.

Stillwell and Davis arrived just before noon, as expected. They were immediately handcuffed and placed in the backseat of a green, Department of Fish and Game patrol car, marked with the standard DFG logo and equipped with red light and siren. I was just about to sit down in the driver's seat when Warden Szody popped his head out the back door of the Fish and Game office.

"You have a phone call," he said.

"You guys sit tight, I'll be right back," I said, as I stepped out of the vehicle and walked back into the office. Of course there was no phone call. Szody and I watched from a nearby window while Stillwell and Davis carried on a five minute tape-recorded conversation. We then returned to the patrol vehicle and transported the two outlaws to the county jail, where they were promptly booked.

III

Stillwell and Davis would not be scheduled for trial before July or August. During the weeks that followed, I set out to build an even stronger case against them. I contacted a handwriting expert with the Federal Bureau of Investigation (FBI), and received instructions on how to conduct handwriting exemplars. Stillwell and Davis were ordered by the court to submit to the exemplars, which I administered on July 10, 1985.

As the FBI expert had advised, I instructed Stillwell and Davis to use a black felt-tip pen. Davis's exemplar was of no consequence, as expected. Jake Stillwell, on the other hand, left no doubt that he had written the threatening note to Warden Hatcher. The completed exemplars and several other handwriting samples were submitted to the FBI on July 11, 1985. Results were received on July 22, 1985. Jake Stillwell was identified, by the FBI, as the person who had written the threatening note.

All eight times, Stillwell spelled Hatcher's name, "Hather," just like in the note. Davis, on the other hand, spelled it correctly every time. Regardless of how slowly I dictated the text, Stillwell wrote in a fast, scribbling manner. Davis printed slowly and deliberately. Stillwell consistently left words out of the text. He continued to use cursive form and run letters together, in spite of being repeatedly instructed to print. Davis took his time, printed neatly and did not leave words out. Stillwell avoided the use of any punctuation. Davis placed punctuation marks in obvious places. Stillwell refused to print the alphabet in lower case, claiming he did not know how.

Early in the investigation, I had asked a Redding veterinarian to X-ray the bald eagle carcass at the center of our investigation. Although a bullet had passed completely through the bird, the vet determined from the size of the hole that it had come from a .22 or slightly larger caliber firearm. Now that we had filed criminal complaints against Stillwell and Davis, I decided to call my friend, Jim Banks, at the Sacramento Fish and Game Forensics Lab, to see if they had come up with anything further.

Banks had transported the bald eagle to San Francisco's Chief Medical Examiner's Necropsy Department. These skilled professionals were accustomed to solving human murders, but welcomed some variety in their normal routine. The fact that someone had killed our national bird and threatened a peace officer was also a motivating factor. According to the medical examiner's necropsy report, conducted on July 19 and 20, 1985:

> Multiple fragments of lead were present about the bald eagle's body. A through-and-through gunshot wound passed through the eagle's liver. The eagle appears to be an immature female. Based on the trajectory of the bullet through the body and the position necessary to align the wing wound to the body, the eagle was most likely shot while on the ground. The point of fire appears to be slightly higher than that of the eagle. Finding fresh food in the crop supports a recent feeding. The meat and hair found in the crop suggested deer.

The medical examiner's report left no doubt as to how the bald eagle had been killed. I telephoned Dave Szody to run my theory by him. "Here's what I think happened," I said. "Jake Stillwell killed a deer to bait in the eagle. The eagle was feeding on the deer carcass when Stillwell shot it from his car window."

"Without a doubt," said Szody. "He shot the deer out there off Platina Road, away from the pavement. They let the deer lie, knowing that eagles historically winter out there around Cottonwood Creek. All they had to do was keep an eye on the carcass until an eagle started feeding on it. *Bang!* They have their bird."

I remembered what Fred Hoffman had said earlier in the investigation: "Jake Stillwell was always shooting hawks and the further away the better." At the time of this investigation, Dave Szody and I each had about eleven years on the job. We had come across a lot of serious poachers but we both agreed Jake Stillwell was by far the worst.

Back in July, I had told Al Hollis he would probably never have to testify— Stillwell and Davis would be faced with a mountain of evidence and their attorneys would try to make some kind of a plea bargain. As worried as Hollis was about possible retaliation and the prospect of losing his job, he stuck to his word and was ready to testify when the original trial date arrived. I was duly impressed when the former Fish and Game warden walked into the courthouse wearing a suit and tie. As it turned out, Stillwell and Davis had no interest in facing a jury of decent, reasonable citizens. Their attorneys must have convinced them of how badly they would look, because sometime in November, 1985, they both finally entered pleas of guilty.

A sentencing hearing was held for Mitch Davis on December 4, 1985. He brought his attorney, his whole family, several friends of the family and nine letters, all testifying to his outstanding character. According to Davis's character witnesses, this fine, upstanding, Sunday school-teaching young man was as pure as the wind-driven snow. They blew so much smoke at the judge, it's a wonder the courthouse didn't catch on fire.

Then it was our turn. The assistant district attorney made the following statement: "Your honor, we have a tape recording that was made on the day Mr. Davis and his partner, Jake Stillwell, were booked into Shasta County Jail. It is a recording of the conversation that these two men had while they were handcuffed and sitting in the backseat of a marked patrol car."

With the judge's permission, I placed a tape recorder in front of the bench and turned it on. The voices on the tape were clearly those of Mitch Davis and Jake Stillwell. Instead of sounding concerned about their impending incarceration, the two men spent most of the five minute recording laughing and making fun of the situation they found themselves in. Although there were no clear admissions of guilt, nearly every other word out of Davis and Stillwell's mouths was of the four-letter variety.

"I've heard enough," announced the judge. After listening to the recording, the judge gave little or no credence to anything else that Davis or his character witnesses had to say. Since Jake Stillwell had already pled guilty to killing the bald eagle and writing the threatening note, Mitch Davis was stuck with all of the trapping and protected species-related crimes. He was sentenced to serve 266 days in Shasta County Jail and ordered to pay a fine of $5,950. Davis was placed on three year's summary probation; during such time he was to obey all laws, submit his person, property and vehicle to warrantless search and not hunt, trap, or be in the field with anyone else who was hunting or trapping.

Jake Stillwell was finally sentenced on January 31, 1986. He was found guilty of threatening a public officer—a felony—and killing an endangered bald eagle—a misdemeanor. Stillwell was sentenced to serve 365 days (one year) in the Shasta County Jail, fined a total of $6,120 and placed on five years' formal probation. During the period of probation, Stillwell was to have no contact, in any manner, with Mitch Davis. Subject to warrantless search, he was not allowed to hunt, trap, or accompany any other hunters or trappers. As a convicted felon, Jake Stillwell could never again legally possess a firearm in the state of California.

Desert Rats

I

I first met my longtime friend and working partner, Dave Szody, in 1973. I was pursuing a master's degree at Sacramento State University and had signed up for an upper division zoology class that turned out to be half classroom work and half field experience.

One day the professor sent us all out to the Yolo Bypass, where we spent several hours seining fish in one of the irrigation canals. Two of us were on one end of the seine and two others on the opposite end. Carefully, we maneuvered the seine into the shallows, where we discovered what had to be a pretty good sample of every freshwater fish species in the Central Valley. Over half the captured fish were thread-fin shad, but there were also bullhead catfish, channel catfish, hardhead minnows, carp, bluegill, sunfish, smallmouth bass and even a few fingerling salmon and steelhead.

After documenting our catch, we released the fish and I struck up a conversation with the student on my end of the net. It turned out we were both about the same age and had similar career goals—Fish and Game warden if at all possible, park ranger if that didn't work out. At the end of the semester we went our separate ways, not expecting to cross paths again. Little did we know that our careers would progress in virtual lockstep. I became a park ranger for Sacramento County, and he became a park ranger for Monterey County. A year and a half later, I was appointed the rookie Fish and Game warden for the Earp Patrol District. Six months after that, he was named the rookie Fish and Game warden for the adjoining Blythe/Palo Verde Patrol District.

II

One of the high points of my life happened in September of 1974, when I finally got the news I had been waiting for. An old Fish and Game inspector named Ellis Berry telephoned me from the California Department of Fish and Game headquarters in Sacramento: "Your number has come up on the hiring list. If you want the job, we have one for you in Earp." I had no idea where Earp was and didn't care. Being a Fish and Game warden was my career goal and I would go wherever they sent me.

Berry made the position sound pretty good by saying that the current deputy director of the Department of Fish and Game had begun his career in Earp. It turned out that Earp was nothing more than a post office and a gas station on the west edge of the Sonoran Desert, just across the Colorado River from a small Arizona town called Parker. This isolated spot had been home to the legendary Wyatt Earp, back in the early 1900s. The famous lawman did some mining in the nearby Whipple Mountains and apparently stuck around long enough to have a post office and a gas station named after him.

It would be a few months before I could begin my new adventure on the Colorado River. First, as required by law, I would have to complete my peace officers training (POST) at the Riverside Sheriff's Academy. When I entered the academy I was twenty-six years old, stood six feet tall and weighed a hundred and eighty pounds—eventually filling out to my career weight of two hundred and twenty pounds.

Just out of the academy and rarin' to go, I arrived in Earp just before Thanksgiving. The first order of business was meeting my new supervisor, Captain James A. Reynolds. Captain Reynolds lived in Blythe, which bordered the Colorado River and was located about fifty miles downstream from my new patrol district in Earp. Reynolds's entire Fish and Game career had been spent in the desert, with the exception of a short stint in Ventura. Jim immediately revealed his passion for his beloved desert: "Years from now," Reynolds said, "after you've transferred to some place up north, you'll look back on the time you spent here in the desert as the best years of your career." He went on to describe the Colorado River as a jewel in the desert, teeming with fish and wildlife.

At the time of our first meeting, Captain Reynolds was approaching sixty and had worked almost forty years for the Department of Fish and Game. His work day usually began at 5:00 a.m. with a two-mile run at the nearby park. Jim was fairly thin, standing about five feet ten and weighing approximately one hundred and sixty pounds. His skin had been prematurely aged by decades in the desert sun. After his workout, Captain Reynolds would tend to the day's business in his home office—listening to the Fish and Game radio, performing necessary paperwork and monitoring his squad of wardens: Dave Fry (Needles), Jim Worthington (Blythe North), Paul Menard (Winterhaven) and me (Earp). This self-described desert rat had a reputation for being hard-headed, fair, and unfailingly supportive of his men. You never had any doubt about what was on Jim Reynolds's mind; he would tell you in no uncertain terms.

My indoctrination to Fish and Game law enforcement was actually pretty simple: Captain Reynolds handed me a stack of citation books and told me to go get 'em. Fortunately, I already knew a little bit about the job. Being the son of a Fish and Game warden, I had ridden on patrol several hundred times during my childhood. While at the sheriff's academy, I had studied the Fish and Game Code and all the relevant Colorado River hunting and fishing regulations, so I felt confident and well prepared for what was to be the first day of my life's work—protecting California's fish and wildlife resources.

The warden that I replaced had transferred north almost a year earlier and there had been no fish and game enforcement in the Earp Patrol District since he left. It didn't take me long to figure out that my new district had become what Fish and Game wardens refer to as a "cherry patch": Every place I looked there were violations—fishing without a license, multiple fishing lines, over-limits, limb lining, quail hunting during closed season, waterfowl hunting during closed season, killing of protected nongame birds and an incredible amount of littering.

By littering, I mean violation of Fish and Game Code Section 5652—"disposing of refuse in or within one hundred and fifty feet of state waters." During the warmer months, a steady stream of cars and trucks towing boats would leave the Los Angeles area every Friday afternoon for a weekend of waterskiing and serious beer drinking. Many of these fun-seekers had never been schooled in environmental ethics. Or if they had, they forgot about them somewhere out around Twenty-nine Palms. Highway 62 was littered with thousands of empty cans and bottles. When these so-called recreationalists finally reached their destination, they naturally assumed that the Colorado River and Lake Havasu were also refuse disposal sites. Some would simply throw their empties overboard; the sneaky ones would dangle a hand in the water, all the time letting the air out of an empty can or bottle. Upon release, the container would sink to the bottom and not be visible to anyone who might object. I did object and so did the local judge. During my first year on the job, I made over three hundred and fifty cases—a third of them were litter related.

The one negative about my new patrol district was the heat. It lasted for about seven months out of the year, from mid-April to mid-October. An average summer day would hover around one hundred and fourteen degrees, cooling down to a hundred at night. I learned that in spite of extremely high daytime temperatures, the dry desert air was actually tolerable when the sun went down. During the hot months, I generally patrolled early in the morning, in the evening, and late at night. The remainder of the year was quite pleasant and as Captain Reynolds had promised, there was no shortage of wildlife.

Thousands of waterfowl occupied the river's sandbars and backwaters. Quail and doves were plentiful and during the monsoon season, the riparian zone along the river became a bird watcher's paradise. Most of the deer stayed in the riparian zone, but I occasionally saw a big buck or two up in the desert washes. They were a large, isolated subspecies called burro mule deer. You wouldn't think the desert could produce trophy-sized bucks, but some of the largest deer I have ever seen came out of that hot, dry country.

III

My district included ten thousand square miles of open desert and four small, low-elevation mountain ranges: the Riversides, Whipples, Old Woman and the Turtles. A small population of desert bighorn sheep lived in the Turtle Mountains, near Mopah Spring. The only time anyone ever saw these elusive animals was during the summer months when extreme conditions required them to stay near a water source. I became so protective of my little band of bighorns that I often braved the elements and made regular patrols into the tiny, isolated spring that sustained them.

The road into Mopah Spring was barely passable, even with four-wheel drive, so I found it necessary to walk the last half mile. That rocky footpath was occupied by a healthy population of western diamondbacks. I learned a lot about these fascinating reptiles during my three and a half years in the desert. A grown man could walk past a diamondback with or without a reaction. The unpredictable coontail, as they are sometimes called, might retreat without the pedestrian even knowing it's there. If the snake feels threatened, it will likely begin its characteristic buzzing and scare the daylights out of the intruder. A western diamondback will usually head for cover, but it is not unusual for one to stand its ground or even crawl in the direction of a perceived threat. During the heat of the day, its primary concern is getting out of the hot sun. It was my experience that a dog couldn't come within ten feet of an active diamondback without setting it off.

On two different occasions, Molly, my faithful Labrador, prevented me from being bitten when I was in imminent danger. Both times, the rattlesnake started buzzing twenty feet before Molly even got close. Not being an expert in ethology, I figured it had something to do with a long history of encounters between *Crotalus atrox* and *Canis latrans*.

Mopah Spring was really nothing more than a washtub-sized pool of water, shaded by several mature desert fan palms. It sat at the base of Mopah Peak, a majestic mass of jagged rock that could be seen from miles away. I would methodically scan the peak with my binoculars, looking for any sign of movement. Bighorns blended so well with the surrounding background that only a keen, experienced eye could spot them. Any sheep that were sighted were usually ewes or immature rams. Only once, during the three and a half years that I patrolled the Turtle Mountains, was I lucky enough to spot a mature ram. That magnificent, full curled specimen stood on the edge of a cliff as if posing for a painting.

California's bighorn sheep have been fully protected since the 1870s. A few years before I was hired by the Department of Fish and Game, a famous undercover case was made by agents of the U.S. Fish and Wildlife Service. It involved a Southern California taxidermist who portrayed himself as a conservationist and staunch advocate for bighorn sheep. He and some of his associates helped build guzzlers (water sources) for bighorns living in Anza Borrego State Park and other isolated desert locations. Greed apparently set in, because this man began using his knowledge of bighorns to substantially enrich his bank account. He and his employees were guiding wealthy hunters from all over the United States and Canada on expensive bighorn ram hunts. His lust for money caught up with him in 1970, when an undercover U.S. Fish and Wildlife agent signed on as one of his clients. I had no tolerance for those who illegally profited from wildlife and often referred to this now infamous case for inspiration. Interestingly, after paying for his crimes, this former taxidermist became a successful wildlife artist. His favorite painting subjects were bighorn sheep.

IV

Early in July, 1975, Captain Reynolds advised me that they had finally filled the vacant Blythe/Palo Verde warden's position. He said the new warden was a young man named Michael David Szody; at the time, I didn't place the name.

One hot afternoon, Reynolds sent the new rookie up to work with me on Lake Havasu. It took a few minutes, but I finally recognized our new warden as the student from my Sacramento State zoology class. Szody had been a long-distance runner for most of his high school and college years, while I had played baseball. Along with our common interest in sports, Dave Szody and I were totally dedicated to protecting wildlife. It didn't take long before we became good friends and working partners.

Wanting to arm ourselves with every possible edge against those who would harm California's natural resources, we became self-taught students of the Fish and Game Code, Title 14 (California Administrative Code), the California Penal Code, the Health and Safety Code and every federal regulation that had anything to do with fish or wildlife. If one of us didn't know a particular regulation or law, the other one did. We viewed ourselves more as wildlife detectives than game wardens, making outstanding cases as a matter of routine.

For a while, Captain Reynolds set strict limits on the amount of time Dave Szody and I were allowed to work together—he maintained the old school attitude that each warden should stay within the boundaries of his own district. That lasted about six months until Reynolds realized that he couldn't argue with success: every time Szody and I worked together, something good happened.

Squeaky

Warden Dave Szody was so enthusiastic about his new career as a Fish and Game warden that he worked practically nonstop during his first year on the job. He quickly formed a healthy network of informants and put a significant dent in his district's unlawful hunting and fishing activity. Like the Earp Patrol District I had inherited, the Blythe/Palo Verde Patrol District had not been worked for several months and the outlaws knew it.

One of the more popular illegal activities was limb lining. The Colorado River, downstream from Blythe and all the way to Yuma, was a limb liner's paradise. This was particularly true in and around Picacho State Recreation Area. That stretch of the river boasted a species of catfish that literally grew as long as a man's leg—a fifty pound flathead catfish was not considered unusual. Flatheads were very difficult to catch by legal means: California law requires a closely attended rod and reel with hook and line attached; the fish must voluntarily take the hook in its mouth and not be snagged or netted.

There were some very crafty characters living down along the river in trailer parks and fishing camps. These outlaws had little or no respect for California regulations and chose to use fishing methods commonly practiced in southern states like Oklahoma, Louisiana, and Arkansas. One of those outlaws was a scrawny little character that the locals called Squeaky. No one along the river knew his real name.

Squeaky was in his late fifties but looked seventy. Exposure to the sun and heavy drinking had taken their toll. When Squeaky wasn't fishing, he was usually drinking. That meant he was bragging about his illegal fishing activities. "I've been limb linin' around here for a long time," he was overheard to say. "No game warden has ever caught me and no game warden ever will."

One July evening, Warden Szody received a telephone call. He didn't recognize the voice, but it sounded like any number of older gentlemen who lived down along the river.

"Have ya ever heard of a guy they call Squeaky?" asked the caller, in a slow, deep voice.

"Yes," said Szody. "I've heard that name mentioned a few times."

In actuality, Warden Szody had heard all about Squeaky from his friend, Wade Somers. Somers was the proprietor of a four hundred square foot retail establishment in the heart of downtown Palo Verde—population one hundred and twenty-three. Bowman's Bait and Tackle was the only store in town and Somers specialized in selling beer, booze, cigarettes, soft drinks, junk food, bait, and a few hooks and sinkers. Most of Wade's inventory was sold to busloads of farm workers who stopped in after a hard day's work. The backroom of this little gold mine was always stacked to the ceiling with cases of beer, which Somers turned over every forty-eight hours.

Wade Somers was a big, easygoing, twenty-six-year-old entrepreneur everyone seemed to like. He had discovered the river while on vacation, liked the slow, easy lifestyle, and decided to stay. When Bowman's Bait and Tackle went up for sale, Somers bought it and went into business. His friendship with Dave Szody was sealed the day a customer tried to walk out the door without paying for a pack of cigarettes. Szody happened to be approaching the store at the time and chased the guy down. Wade became a good friend and a great source of information.

Nothing happened within ten miles of Palo Verde that Wade Somers didn't hear about. Squeaky was buying beer in the store one day when Szody walked in. "That's the guy I was telling you about," whispered Wade. Warden Szody took a mental photograph of the little outlaw and stored it away for future use.

"Squeaky lives here in Miller's Camp," the caller continued. "I'm sick of hearin' him brag about all them big catfish he's catchin'. Everybody down here knows he's limb linin'."

"Do you know where he's doing the limb lining?" Szody asked.

"Down by Picacho. That's where all them big flatheads are," replied the caller. "He usually goes out before daylight and comes back about noon. He'll always have a couple rods with him to make it look like he caught 'em legal, but he ain't caught nothin' legal in years."

"Is there anything else you can tell me?"

"No, that's about it."

"Can I get your phone number in case I need to call you?"

"I'd rather not get any further involved. Good luck. I hope ya catch him," the caller concluded.

Warden Szody immediately telephoned me at my residence near Earp.

He asked if I would like to come down and do an all-night stakeout. I said that sounded like fun and asked where we were going. Szody said down by Picacho State Park, where one of the local outlaws was limb lining flathead catfish. I was excited about the opportunity to see my first flathead. Those primitive-looking monster catfish were never seen north of Blythe. We agreed to meet at 2:00 p.m. the following afternoon at Szody's Blythe's residence.

July was the hottest month of the year down along the Colorado River. Dave and I packed our gear into his little tri-hull patrol boat and headed for Picacho about 3:00 p.m. The temperature hovered around one hundred and twelve degrees that day. We had traveled an hour downriver when Szody cut the motor and pulled into one of the backwaters. "It's time for a *Nestea plunge*," he said, referring to a TV commercial popular at the time.

Both of us dropped our gun belts to the deck and removed our boots. In full uniform, we jumped over the side, immersing ourselves in the cool, refreshing river water. Having temporarily escaped the relentless heat, we climbed back into the boat and proceeded downriver. Within minutes, our uniforms were completely dry.

It was about 5:00 p.m. when we approached Picacho State Recreation Area. That section of the Colorado River—located about twenty-five miles upstream from Yuma, Arizona—was heavily vegetated. Salt cedar (tamarisk) thickets were so dense that limbs reached all the way to the water. The highly invasive North African exotic had displaced most of the native willows and cottonwoods. I hated that bully of the plant world and often referred to it as the "tree from hell." Tamarisks were choking the life out of riparian areas throughout the arid Southwest, but in this particular location they shaded the deep eddies along the California side of the river and provided limited habitat for large channel cats and monster flatheads.

"He's supposed to be operating somewhere around here," said Szody, as he slowed the motor and headed toward the California side of the river. Limb liners would often mark the location of their illegal sets with a rag, a beer can, or some type of clearly visible object. The more sophisticated operators would place the marker a certain distance up or down stream, so as not to give away the actual location. Squeaky's system wasn't evident, so we had to find his lines the hard way, by trial and error.

I picked up a six-foot metal pole with a hook on the end. As Szody maneuvered the boat close to shore, I began working the pole back and forth through the water, under the overhanging branches. We soon located the first limb line. A length of monofilament was tied to the end of a salt cedar limb. At the other end was a hook, baited with a live goldfish. "We know it's active," I said. "The bait is still alive." After marking the location of the first limb line, we continued downriver. It didn't take us long to find several more lines, all rigged and baited the same way.

With the blazing sun still a dominating factor, Szody and I decided to take another *Nestea plunge*. We were just about to jump over the side when our boat drifted into a shaded area immediately below a hundred-foot rock cliff. "Pull in here. I think I see something moving," I said.

Szody steered the boat closer to the cliff where we immediately spotted a salt cedar limb bouncing in and out of the water. I reached under the water with my bare hand and felt a line that was tied to the limb. As I pulled up on the line, whatever was on the other end came very close to pulling me overboard. "Hello!" I said. "We have something big on the other end of this line."

Bracing myself, I again pulled up on the heavy test monofilament line. Suddenly, a giant dinner plate-sized mouth appeared out of the dark water. "Look at this thing!" I said, as the fish turned and bolted back into the darkness. "It's a big flathead." Szody cautioned me to be careful and not allow the giant catfish to escape. We would leave the big fella right where he was and find a place to hide.

It was 6:30 p.m. when we hid our boat in a backwater downstream from the large flathead. Sweating profusely, Szody and I gathered our overnight gear, an ice chest, two water jugs, binoculars, and two spotting scopes. One of the scopes was a standard-issue spotting scope and the other was a night vision starlight scope that Szody had borrowed from the Department of Justice. He was familiar with starlight scopes, having used them extensively in Viet Nam. Sometime after 7:00 p.m., we reached a lava rock plateau overlooking the shaded eddy where the catfish was located. From that vantage point we could see a mile upriver and would be able to spot any boat long before it reached us.

As evening wore on, Szody and I continued to bake in the incredible heat that radiated from our exposed position. The blazing sun finally began to recede about 8:00 p.m., but the temperature remained in the triple digits. That's about the time the first mosquito began buzzing in my ear. "If there's a mosquito within three miles, it will find me," I complained. One mosquito was followed by another and another and what seemed like a thousand more. "My favorite creatures on this earth are bats, swallows, and nighthawks," I said, "because they eat those blood-sucking little parasites."

The pesky insects continued to drive us crazy until it turned pitch dark around 10:00 p.m. As if someone had flipped a switch, the mosquitoes disappeared and a welcome peace returned to the desert night. By then we had begun questioning our dedication. Unable to sleep, Szody and I occupied our time by testing the starlight scope. "There's a great-horned owl sitting in that big cottonwood," Szody said, as he handed me the scope. "Make sure you never look into a light when you're using that thing. You can really damage your eyes."

By midnight the temperature had dropped into the high eighties, with a cool breeze off the river. It was completely quiet except for the booming territorial calls of the great-horned owl across the river and an occasional bull frog billowing in the backwater. We took turns trying to sleep on the hard lava rock, with no success.

As day dawned, our previous enthusiasm had given way to absolute misery. To make matters worse, the mosquitoes returned and stuck around until about 7:00 a.m., when the scorching desert heat drove them away. There had been no sign of Squeaky or anyone else. My disillusioned partner and I wanted to pack up and go home, but something told us that Squeaky would show up any minute. An hour passed and Squeaky had still not come, so we waited one more hour and then another.

By 10:00 a.m., the temperature had climbed to a hundred degrees and was quickly rising. We felt like a couple of eggs, frying on a hot rock.

"Where are you, Squeaky?" asked Szody, groggy and beaten down by the elements.

"Do you hear something?" I asked, reaching for my binoculars.

Szody picked up his spotting scope and pointed it upriver. The faint sound of a distant outboard motor teased our ears. At first we thought we were just imagining things; then the hum of the motor grew slightly louder. A big smile spread across Szody's face as a small boat came into view. "Is that you, Squeaky?" he wondered aloud.

The tiny skiff continued to make its way downriver. There appeared to be one man aboard, wearing a big straw hat and a light colored shirt. We dropped to the prone position, failing to acknowledge the 130 degree rock we were lying on. Szody continued to watch with his spotting scope and I with my binoculars.

The slow-moving skiff eventually reached the first limb line and pulled in close to the bank. The operator reached over and pulled up the line. Apparently there was nothing on it, because he dropped it back down and proceeded to the next line. Szody and I had seen enough to make a case but it would be so much better if we could catch the violator with a fish in his possession. The small boat finally reached the base of the cliff and the location of our large flathead catfish. Like excited kids, we scampered to the edge of the rock just in time to see the object of our all-night vigil remove the trophy-sized flathead from his hook. With the fish flailing from side-to-side, it took all of the strength the diminutive boatman had to wrestle it into a large ice chest. Once the catfish was secured, he re-baited the hook with a live goldfish and dropped it back in the water. Hanging off the bow of the skiff were two heavy duty fishing rods with reels attached. These were obviously props, as Szody's informant had described.

This must have been the last of his limb lines, because the sneaky little outlaw turned his boat around and headed back upriver. Szody and I knew we could easily overtake the slow moving skiff, so we gathered our gear and headed across the plateau. Like mountain goats, we traversed the back side and made our way to the state boat.

Once underway, it only took us about five minutes to catch up with the limb liner's slow moving ten-horse outboard. The boat's operator, oblivious to our presence, was steering from the stern seat when he casually peered over his right shoulder.

"Hello Squeaky," said Szody, in a voice that only I could hear. Squeaky clearly saw us but failed to slow down or change course. Szody pushed the throttle forward and, in a quick burst of speed, pulled the Fish and Game boat alongside. I stood up and motioned with my hand for Squeaky to cut his motor. Squeaky finally complied and both boats immediately began drifting backwards in the swift current.

"Pull your boat over to that shore," I shouted, pointing to the California side of the river. We kept a keen eye on the cunning little man, making sure that he didn't throw anything overboard as he followed instructions and beached his boat. The state boat pulled in beside him.

Believing this to be a routine license check, Squeaky pulled out his California Fishing License and handed it to Warden Szody.

"That's great that you have a fishing license," said Szody. "Now I need to see a driver's license."

"What for?" whined Squeaky. "I ain't done nothin' wrong."

I reached over and opened Squeaky's ice chest. Suddenly subjected to the bright sunlight, the twenty pound flathead inside began flopping violently. As expected, Squeaky swore up and down that he had caught the fish legally, with one of the fishing rods in his boat. Szody reviewed, in minute detail, every move that Squeaky had made in the last hour. Every time Squeaky would start to bend the truth, Szody countered with what had really happened.

Normally, we would never have argued or carried on a heated conversation with someone we were in the process of busting. This time, however, there was a method to our madness. Squeaky became so convinced that two of his associates had squealed on him that he returned the favor by hinting about a current camp just upriver. This was a common ploy—*the real bad guys went thataway*—which Szody and I easily recognized.

Because Squeaky had opened the door, Szody cleverly seized the moment to press him further about what might be going on upstream. There was no need for a Miranda warning, since we were not questioning Squeaky about his own violation. We had just witnessed that one firsthand.

While Squeaky described the camp upriver to my partner, I attended to the big catfish—still alive and flopping around in his ice chest. I opened the lid and photographed the fish for future evidence purposes. Grabbing the ice chest by both handles, I carefully lifted it out of Squeaky's boat and carried it to the water's edge. I could hear Squeaky trying to recant what he had just said from the shade of a cottonwood tree, about ten yards away.

"Squeaky, you lying son of a bitch!" said my exasperated partner. River water rushed into the ice chest as I tipped it forward and brought the dehydrated catfish back to life. With a few flips of its tail, the whiskered predator was back in the river, out of sight, and headed for the bottom.

By the time Warden Szody finished his field interrogation, Squeaky had offered up a detailed description of where his two associates were camped, where their limb lines were located and what each man had eaten for breakfast. Szody issued Squeaky a much-deserved citation. As the outmatched catfish poacher stood on the riverbank with his mouth hanging open, we headed upriver to find out if anything Squeaky had told us was actually true. Telling the truth wasn't something that came easily for Squeaky, but retribution can sometimes bring out the best in people.

Surprisingly, everything we found was pretty much as Squeaky had described it. Two middle-aged men were sitting at the water's edge, drinking beer. The heavier man wore a swimsuit and a black tank top with the name of some bar written across the front. He covered his head with a straw hat. The other man wore nothing but cutoff jeans and had the typical, dark brown river-rat tan.

"How are you guys doing?" I asked, as Szody beached our patrol boat next to their twelve-foot aluminum skiff. "Are you catching any fish?"

"We caught a couple," replied the shirtless man.

By then Szody and I were a finely coordinated team. While I continued my conversation with the laid-back fishermen, Szody quietly looked around. "Where are the fish?" I asked. The shirtless fisherman pointed toward a line that was tied off the stern of their boat. Szody had already spotted the suspected stringer, but continued to survey the camp. Lying across a small, portable table were several limb line sets, probably prepared for use that evening. Szody gathered them up and carried them to the state boat.

Two heavy-duty lines hung over the side of the aluminum boat. Szody carefully stepped onboard and pulled up the first one. At the other end was a plastic bait box, filled with live goldfish. The second line was tied to a metal stringer containing three large channel cats and a fifteen pound flathead. I inspected the men's fishing licenses and asked to see their driver's licenses, which confirmed that they lived in the same trailer park as Squeaky. I advised them that Warden Szody and I would be keeping their identification until we returned.

"We'll be back," said Szody, as we climbed in the patrol boat and headed upriver. About a quarter mile from the campsite, we came to the small island Squeaky had described. One by one, I began pulling in baited limb lines. Each line had a live gold fish attached and was set up exactly the same way as the ones found in camp.

Warden Szody and I returned to the camp and confronted the two fishermen with what we had found. "These limb lines we just pulled are set up exactly like the ones my partner found on your table over there," I explained. "They're freshly baited with live goldfish, just like the ones in your bait box."

"Who told you where them lines were?" asked the man with the hat.

That question, alone, was as good as an admission. Confronted with a few more details, the fishermen came clean and admitted that they had put out the limb lines. All their equipment and the catfish were seized into evidence. The catfish were photographed and released. I refused to tell the two violators who had tipped us off, but they already had a good idea. Before heading back upriver, we returned to Squeaky's baited limb lines and carefully pulled each one.

The next day, Dave Szody walked into Bowman's Bait and Tackle and was greeted with a standing ovation. Several of the local fishermen were in the store, thrilled that three of the Colorado River's worst fish poachers had been caught and would finally receive their just desserts. Squeaky paid a couple hundred dollars for his violation and lost his fishing privileges for one year. We heard he couldn't handle not being able to fish, so he moved back to Oklahoma.

Dove Opener

I

September first was generally the busiest day of the year for California Fish and Game wardens working down along the Colorado River. Throngs of hunters traveled from big cities like Los Angeles and San Diego to bag those fast-flying gray birds that congregated by the thousands in cultivated fields and mesquite thickets near the small desert town of Blythe.

Mourning doves were the most numerous of the three native species found there. The slightly larger white-winged doves usually hung around for a few days after the opener before heading south into Mexico. Mexican ground doves—about half the size of the other two species—were far less common; though protected by law, this solitary member of the dove family seemed to end up in more than a few game bags. There was really no excuse for shooting a Mexican ground dove: a flash of red appeared when these tiny birds were in flight—ample warning for any discriminating sportsman.

II

Early one September morning in 1975, I was patrolling south on State Highway 95, between Vidal Junction and Blythe. I had spent the previous two days working my first dove opener. Most of the dove hunting activity was in the cultivated fields south of Blythe, so we had concentrated our enforcement effort in that area. On this particular morning I was basically mopping up—seeing if there were any hunters still around and checking out a few of the fields overlooked during the opener.

I was about twenty-five miles north of Blythe, when I turned east onto a dirt road leading across a large, fallow field. There were still a few doves around. Small groups of four and five birds would burst out of the low-lying vegetation as I slowly passed by.

Most of the well-traveled, unpaved roads down along the Colorado River were covered with a layer of fine, powdery dust. This dust could be up to a foot deep in places, depending on how often the road was used. The first thing I learned when I came to the river was, never drive faster than five miles per hour on these roads unless you want a thirty-foot-high dust cloud to announce your approach to anyone within five miles—not to mention the fact that any equipment stored in the back of your patrol rig would end up buried in the stuff.

I stopped and walked around until I had reached the field's midpoint. Every few minutes a gust of wind would come up and scatter tiny, gray down feathers in my path. Judging from the large number of expended, number eight shotgun shells lying on the ground, the previous two days of hunting had been very good.

Eventually I reached the far end of the field and what appeared to be a shaded campsite. Someone had raked and cleared the brush under a grove of mature mesquite trees. I couldn't fail to notice several fresh vehicle tracks and human footprints throughout the area. It appeared that a large group had camped there within the past twenty-four hours; a warm fire pit confirmed my suspicions.

Looking around, I noticed two well-trod foot trails leading out into the thick patches of seven-foot-high arrow weed that grew between the campsite and the river. One of the trails led to a makeshift restroom site. The other was less obvious, extending for about thirty yards and leading to a small clearing.

There before my eyes was a three-foot high by four-foot wide pile of carcasses and dove feathers. Ants had already begun working on some of the carcasses. I began sifting through the pile, wondering just how many doves these people had killed. With more than half of the pile still left to count, I reached two hundred.

"Damn!" I said. While I had been busy working another patrol district during the opener, somebody was having a field day up here in my district. As I drove back across the field and out to the highway, I said to myself: "They got away with it this time, but next year will be a different story!"

III

All winter and into the following summer, I thought about what had happened whenever I drove by that particular field. August finally came around and with it, what the locals referred to as the Sonoran Desert monsoon season. The weather was not only hot, it became humid and sticky. Tropical thunderstorms turned dry desert washes into raging torrents in a matter of minutes. For a short time, the desert turned green and teemed with life. The riparian zones along the river hosted bird species I had never seen before—cardinals, blue grosbeaks, vermillion flycatchers—some coming up from Mexico and others from the east.

Doves arrived by the thousands. Mourning doves had always been more plentiful than the larger white-wings, but during August of 1976, white-winged doves seemed to be everywhere.

As this year's season opener approached, doves flocked by the hundreds into the field where I had discovered the abandoned hunting camp. I brought Dave up from Blythe to show him the incredible concentration of game birds. We figured there had to be a thousand birds or more feeding on seeds from the various plant species growing in that fallow field.

There was no way I was going to let those scofflaws repeat their performance from the previous dove opener. "If they show up this year, I don't want them to even know we're around until late the second day," I explained to Dave. "When they're packed up and getting ready to leave, we'll give them the surprise of their lives!"

On the morning of August 31, 1976, I left Earp and headed for the annual pre-season dove opener meeting in Blythe. Instead of taking Highway 95 on the California side of the river, I drove across the Parker Bridge and went south by way of Arizona. My plan was to give my field a wide berth in case the group from the previous year showed up early.

As was usually the case, wardens and warden supervisors from all over southern California were brought in to work this annual, two-day event. There were no lieutenants back then, so the meeting room was filled with wardens and a few captains. Captain Reynolds was in charge of the meeting, but he let the two Blythe area wardens, Jim Worthington and Dave Szody, do most of the talking. Everyone was given an assigned area to work and provided with maps and court information. Dave didn't have much to say, but Jim kept us sitting there for a good hour, discussing some of the local outlaws and good places to eat.

Jim Worthington was a very large, barrel-chested man with a booming voice to match. Dave Szody and I used to say that Warden Worthington could be telling a joke at one end of a crowded restaurant and people sitting at the other end would be able to repeat the punch line.

As Jim continued his lengthy presentation, a slight smile crept across my face. My mind wandered to an incident that had happened the previous December. It was about 5:00 a.m. and Jim and I were getting ready to work duck hunters downriver in Warden Worthington's twelve-foot, aluminum Jon boat. While I retrieved some equipment from my truck, Jim climbed into the boat and began revving the little ten-horse outboard motor. I was returning to the boat when Jim shifted the motor into gear and slowly turned the throttle. With two hundred and eighty pounds sitting in the stern of the boat and virtually no weight in the bow, it's not difficult to imagine what happened next—the bow of the boat flew into the air and continued right over the top of Warden Worthington. A few seconds later, he popped his head out of the water—unhurt, but more than a little embarrassed. It looked like something out of a Laurel and Hardy movie.

That evening, several hours after the dove opener briefing, I headed north on Highway 95. It was just getting dark when I passed my field. Without slowing down, I glanced eastward and saw exactly what I had anticipated: several pickups were parked at the far end of the field and a fire was burning. "Yes!" I shouted, continuing north. "Welcome back boys."

"They're here, Dave!" I exulted over the telephone. "I saw three or four rigs parked at the far end of the field when I drove by." Dave and I knew that our group would hunt at least two days, with a morning and an evening shoot each day. We decided to stick to our plan and leave them alone until late in the afternoon of the second day.

It was just before 4:00 p.m., on September 2, 1976, when Szody and I pulled off the highway and hid our patrol truck in a wash just south of our suspects' field. It was like entering a warzone. Shotguns were blasting away in rapid succession. We found shade under a palo verde tree and continued to watch and listen until about 6:00 p.m. Convinced that the group had finally finished hunting and would soon be hitting the road for home, Dave and I plotted a course of action.

The field was surrounded on three sides by thickets of mesquite, salt cedar, and arrow weed. I would approach the camp on foot, concealed by heavy vegetation. When I reached the camp, I would signal Dave, who would drive the patrol truck four hundred yards across the field to the campsite. Our intention was to get a feel for what was going on before we made contact and so prevent the hunters from destroying or hiding any evidence after they spotted the approaching Fish and Game truck.

With the patrol vehicle well out of sight, Szody hunkered down behind some brush and watched the campsite through his binoculars. I carefully began working my way through the dense vegetation at the south edge of the field. The early evening temperature was well over one hundred degrees. Conditions reminded me of a time when a high school friend and I had crashed our way through poison oak, hiking into Chico Creek Canyon to go trout fishing. Poison oak didn't grow in the desert, but one could step on a rattlesnake. These weren't the Pacific rattlesnakes I was accustomed to seeing in Northern California; they were western diamondbacks, some of them reaching seven feet and as big around as the arm of a good-sized man. Wading through classic diamondback habitat was a little risky, but I was experienced enough to know where to put my feet. If I encountered a snake, I would simply say hello and give it plenty of space. I had never killed one of those rodent-eating machines and hoped I would never have to. Diamondbacks are very much a part of the desert's mystique and natural beauty. As a young wildlife protection officer, I understood and respected that.

By the time I finally approached the hunters' camp, my uniform shirt was soaked with sweat and I was completely covered with debris. My mouth tasted like cotton and was so dry I could barely swallow. I knew I was getting close, because I could hear laughter and the occasional sound of a truck door slamming.

"Anybody ready for another beer?" came a voice from the camp.

"What do you guys want to do with this extra food?" shouted another voice.

With stealthy footsteps, I entered the back side of the camp, nearest the river. Four newer model pickups were parked between me and the group. From my hiding place, I counted eight adult males. Five were sitting in lawn chairs. The other three appeared to be in the initial stages of breaking camp. Several large ice chests were on the ground and one was perched on the edge of a tailgate.

I stepped into the open and signaled Warden Szody, who immediately spotted me and signaled back. The hunters still had not seen me, so I returned to the rear of the camp. About five minutes later, a green Dodge Power Wagon headed our way from across the field, a thirty-foot-high wall of dust in its wake. The men in the lawn chairs were suddenly quiet, no longer joking about the day's hunt. One of them jumped up and ran toward the ice chest on the tailgate. He pushed it into the bed of the pickup and threw a tarp over it.

"We would appreciate your leaving everything where it is," I said, stepping into view. No one said a word. It was as if I had just hit a "pause" button. Szody pulled up about ten yards from the camp. He stepped out of the patrol truck and walked toward me. I asked him to keep an eye on things while I checked something out. Following the same well-worn trail that I had discovered the previous September, I walked straight to the clearing. The old pile of carcasses had decomposed long ago, but right beside it was another pile, just as high and just as wide. "These have to be the same guys," I muttered to myself. I walked back into camp and pointed the path out to Szody. He followed the trail to the massive pile of feathers and dove carcasses, while I kept a close eye on the hunters.

"That's one big pile of carcasses," said Szody, returning to camp. "Looks like they were too lazy to pick 'em completely, so they just breasted 'em out."

"I'm tempted to bust these guys for waste of game, along with the over limits," I said.

Shotguns, game bags, ice chests, and hunters were spread out all over the camp. With hundreds of doves to count and eight hunters to keep an eye on, Dave and I instructed the men to sit down in their lawn chairs while we conducted our business.

Seven of the hunters cooperated, but as is so often the case, one of them tried to shove his weight around. This time it was the older man in the group, about sixty years old and posturing like some kind of supervisor. "I have permission to hunt and camp in this field," said the man. "What right do you have to come in here and bother us?"

I have to admit, the first thing that popped into my head was something I had recently heard one of the local deputy sheriffs say, down at Ox Bow Lake. I looked over at Warden Szody, with a barely detectable grin on my face. He knew exactly what I was thinking. Without going into a long dissertation, I explained that California Fish and Game wardens had legal justification to enter private property anywhere in the state where hunting was going on. We had been watching them blast away for the last two hours, so they were clearly hunting.

"You gentlemen have obviously killed a lot of doves," I explained. "We are here to inspect them and check your hunting licenses. First we're going to take a look at your shotguns to make sure there are no plugs missing. This process may take a while, so please sit back and relax." I tried to be as cordial as possible, considering the verbal assault we had just received from their elderly leader. All the shotguns contained plugs, as required by law, and all eight hunters possessed valid California Hunting Licenses.

Szody opened the first ice chest, which was sitting on the ground close by. It contained food and drinks, but no evidence of game. The second and third ice chests were the same. A fourth chest was completely empty. I remembered one of the hunters pushing a large ice chest into the bed of his pickup and covering it with a tarp. Removing the tarp, I pulled the chest out onto the tailgate. Inside, I found several rows of one gallon milk cartons. Each carton was filled to the top with skinned-out dove breasts. "We're going to have to do some counting," I explained, as Szody brought over a large plastic bag to lay the birds on.

I proceeded to count dove breasts while Warden Szody tabulated the findings. An hour later, after going through two additional ice chests, we completed our count—328 dove breasts, six of which were too small to be anything but Mexican ground doves. The possession limit was twenty doves per hunter and there were eight hunters, making anything over 160 doves an over-limit. These hunters were in possession of 168 doves over the legal possession limit.

It turned out that all eight hunters worked for the same power company out of San Diego. Most of them had hunted this same field every dove opener for the last several years. I didn't let on that I had found evidence of their previous year's hunt. When I told them that they would all be charged with joint possession of 168 doves over the legal possession limit, the leader of the group spoke up again. He claimed that two members of their group had left earlier. This was a common ploy, for which Warden Szody and I were well-prepared. I explained that we had been watching them since 4:00 p.m. and no one had left during that time. We asked for the names and addresses of the hunters they claimed had left. That way we could have wardens contact them as they arrived home—probably carrying additional doves. Instead of eight, ten people would be charged for the obscene over-limit. When the men realized that their ruse had failed, they recanted and admitted that there were only eight of them involved.

The illegal 168 doves were seized as evidence, along with all eight shotguns. Surprisingly, not one of the hunters volunteered any type of excuse for their significant breach of the law. Based on what they had gotten away with during previous years, I figured they counted themselves lucky. In addition to a substantial fine, we would request forfeiture of the shotguns and revocation of hunting privileges for three years.

"Did you run into any snakes?" asked Szody, as we drove away.

"No," I replied, "but next time, I drive the truck and you go wading through the brush. Have we got any water left?"

Swans for Thanksgiving

I

Captain Reynolds had not exaggerated: the Colorado River was a virtual jewel in the desert back in the 1970s. During the August monsoon season, a bird watcher could expand his life list with species seldom seen north of the Mexican border or west of the Colorado River.

An avid birder myself, I was thrilled to spot vermilion flycatchers, summer tanagers, cardinals, and blue grosbeaks for the first time. Every winter thousands of waterfowl and shorebirds crowded the river's shallow sandbars. The most noticeable of those birds were the magnificent and graceful whistling (tundra) swans, which usually arrived in November and December. On a quiet day, you can hear them coming from miles away.

II

It was 2:00 p.m. on Thanksgiving Day, 1975, when the phone rang at Warden Dave Szody's Blythe residence. Dave's wife was getting ready to take a turkey out of the oven and Dave was setting the table. The weather was clear, reaching into the mid-seventies. "I'll get it," said Dave, as he walked into the other room and reached for the phone. Wardens who worked out of their homes in those days had only one phone line, which had to be used for personal and work-related calls. On this particular day, Dave Szody figured it was relatives, the neighbors, or worst case scenario, the sheriff's dispatcher calling. Had it been any other day, Szody would have welcomed a violation report and pounced on it like a chicken on a grasshopper. It was Thanksgiving, however, and guests from next door would be ringing the doorbell any minute.

"Hello," said Szody, hesitantly. He could hear the familiar beeping in the background that let him know it wasn't relatives on the other end of the line.

"This is Riverside County Sheriff's Dispatch. Is this Warden Szody?"

"Yes."

"We have a report of hunters shooting swans on the Colorado River."

"Do you have a specific location?"

"The gentleman who reported the violation said it took place about a half mile south of Blythe, on a sandbar. The shooters were reportedly two older men in a small aluminum boat. I have the Arizona boat registration number and address information if you're ready to copy."

"Go ahead with the information," replied Szody. "When did this happen?"

"The reporting party said the two men shot at least six swans and were retrieving them at approximately 9:00 a.m. He apparently just came off the river and couldn't get to a phone before this. I asked for a callback number, but he wanted to remain anonymous."

Szody looked at the clock and calculated that over five hours had elapsed since the incident. The dispatcher provided an Ehrenberg, Arizona address, which included a Space Number 12. Ehrenberg is located just across the river from Blythe. The space number indicated some kind of mobile-home park. Normally anything on the Arizona side of the river would fall outside of a California Fish and Game warden's jurisdiction. Whistling swans, however, were protected under the federal Migratory Bird Treaty Act. California Fish and Game wardens were deputized by the U.S. Fish and Wildlife Service to handle situations such as this, when no one else was available. In this case, there were no federal agents or Arizona Game and Fish officers within sixty miles.

Dave Szody wasn't about to let anyone get away with killing swans in his patrol district. As he buttoned his uniform shirt and adjusted his holster straps, the dedicated young warden could hear their neighbors, Bill and Debbie, walking through the front door. "Pour them a glass of wine," said Szody, "I'll be back as soon as possible."

A few seconds later, a beat-up dark green AMC Matador, with Fish and Game insignias on the side, roared out of the driveway and headed for Interstate 10. It took only ten minutes for Szody to reach the highway, cross the river into Arizona, and head north into the tiny desert community of Ehrenberg.

A man walking his dog provided directions to the only trailer park in town, which was about five minutes farther down the road. Once inside,

Warden Szody spotted an aluminum boat at the end of the first row of mobile homes. The boat was mounted on a trailer and attached to a Chevy pickup. Szody counted the space numbers as he slowly drove up the road. He stopped his patrol car in front of Space Number 10 and decided to go the rest of the way on foot.

With no search warrant or means of contacting the informant, Szody hoped to find some kind of physical evidence before knocking on the door. He peered into the boat, looking for any possible indication that swans had been killed. The deck was cluttered with empty beer cans, fishing tackle, a gunny sack full of duck decoys, and several expended twelve gauge shotgun shells.

Reaching in, Szody picked up one of the expended shotgun shells. It was a BB load, smelling as if it had recently been fired. At the stern, lying next to a red removable gas tank, was the item Szody had been looking for: one snow-white down feather had lodged itself between the gas tank and the side of the boat. *If this guy was trying to hide the evidence, he missed this one*, thought Szody, as he picked up the feather and placed it inside his shirt pocket.

Unable to find any further evidence inside the boat, Szody slowly approached the residence. On his way to the door, he picked up eight more wispy white down feathers and noted a dozen or so blowing across the carport. It was fairly obvious that someone had recently been plucking swans.

Szody climbed the porch steps and knocked on the door. A sixty-plus-year-old woman answered, wearing a cloth apron and holding a glass of red wine in her right hand. Through the doorway, Warden Szody could see a portly, gray-haired man sitting at the kitchen table, drinking a beer. He was still wearing camouflage overalls from the morning's hunt. Judging from the puzzled look on the woman's face, she had no idea why this uniformed officer was standing on her doorstep. Apparently her husband had failed to tell her that the giant white birds he had brought home were federally protected and could not be killed or possessed.

"My name is Dave Szody. I am a California Fish and Game warden and a federal deputy. I'm here for the swans."

"Chester, are you gonna to take care of this?" said the woman, giving her husband an angry stare.

"I guess we're in some kinda trouble?" said Chester, as he set his beer on the table and stood up—his overalls splattered with blood and a tiny white down feather sticking to his left boot.

"You and another man reportedly killed at least six swans this morning," said Szody. "I'm going to need all of them."

"Two of 'em is out back and one is right there in the oven," replied Chester.

"And the other three?"

"Ya need ta ask Bob, next door, about them."

Chester's wife started to pull the swan out of the oven, when Warden Szody told her to leave it there for the time being. He asked Chester to lead him to the other two swans in the backyard. Chester led Szody to a clothesline pole where two twenty pound swans were hanging in the shade. With their massive webbed feet dragging the ground and necks outstretched, the giant white birds were almost five feet long.

Chester took the swans down, grabbed them by their long necks and followed Warden Szody into the front yard. Szody asked to see identification and a current hunting license. Chester pulled out an Arizona Drivers License and an Arizona Hunting License. To his credit, he did have the appropriate state and federal duck stamps. Szody took the documents and advised Chester, whose last name was Claypool, to stand by while he went next door to pay Bob a visit.

Bob and his wife were just about to sit down to a swan dinner when Warden Szody knocked on their door. This time the bird was actually on the table when the door opened. Bob was four or five years older than Chester and had shaved and cleaned up since bringing the swans home. His expression quickly changed from elation, having just watched the Oregon Ducks score a touchdown on TV, to bewilderment and uncertainty. "Ah, we was just about ta eat," he said. "Would ya like ta join us?"

Szody smiled and explained the situation.

"I already picked and cleaned 'em," Bob said. "They're in the freezer. I'll fetch 'em for ya." He followed Warden Szody out to the patrol car.

"I'm going to need to see your driver's license and your hunting license," said Szody. Bob, whose real name was Robert Wayne Tanner, brought out an Oregon Drivers License and a Non-resident Arizona Hunting License. Tanner and his wife were snowbirds, from Eugene, who came down from Oregon every year to escape the rain. Bob had also purchased the appropriate state and federal duck stamps.

Szody copied each of the men's identification information and explained: "This is what's going to happen. Technically I am seizing six unlawfully taken swans into evidence and returning one back to each of you. That is only because they have been cooked and would go to waste if I took them now. A U.S. Fish and Wildlife agent will receive my report and sometime in the next few months you guys will be notified to appear in federal court. That will probably be in Yuma or Phoenix."

Szody might have taken a little more time to discuss the matter with the two men, but he was on a mission. He put the four swans in the trunk of his patrol car and drove away. The hungry warden raced back across the river to Blythe, making a quick stop at Captain Reynolds's house to store the swans in an evidence freezer in the captain's garage. Captain Reynolds invited Szody to stay for a "horn of corn," but Szody knew that guests were waiting so he thanked him and continued on his way.

One hour and fifteen minutes after leaving the house, our hero walked in the front door and was handed a glass of wine by his wife. Everyone had plenty to talk about over dinner and the phone didn't ring again for the rest of the day.

The next morning, Warden Szody mailed his report to Selden Wright, the veteran U.S. Fish and Wildlife Agent, in Yuma. Agent Wright, whom Captain Reynolds jokingly referred to as "Seldom Right," was more than happy to file a good swan case with the federal prosecutor.

Crowley Trout Opener

I

The last weekend in April marked the opening of trout season in California's Eastern Sierra Mountains. This annual spectacle rivals the Mardi Gras in New Orleans or spring break in Palm Beach.

Highway 395 out of the Los Angeles basin was jammed with a steady stream of cars, trucks, motor homes, and trailers, all the way to Bridgeport. Every motel in Lone Pine, Bishop, Mammoth Lakes, Lee Vining, and Bridgeport was booked and every campsite was full. What Christmas is to department stores, trout opener was to businesses in the Eastern Sierras. Fish and Game wardens from all over Southern California were commandeered to leave their own manageable districts and spend three days in virtual chaos.

Late one April in the mid-seventies, Warden Dave Szody and I were chosen to participate in this annual spectacle. It was an experience we'll never forget.

"Who's that on the radio?" I asked.

"It sounds like Bob Perry from up in Ventura," Szody said, turning on his left blinker and preparing to pass one of a thousand slow-moving vehicles on its way to the Eastern Sierras.

"He seems to be doing some kind of travel log on the car-to-car setting of his radio."

"Bob likes to talk. There's probably some rookie warden following him."

"Not to change the subject, but how do you like this new patrol rig?"

"I can finally go off the pavement without getting stuck," replied Szody, as he again turned on his left blinker and prepared to pass a motor home. "I'm not going to miss the Matador."

"That's Mount Whitney Hatchery on the left," boomed Warden Perry over the radio. "It was built in 1916 and was the first state trout hatchery in California. You should go in there on your way back. The old buildings are beautiful."

"Unbelievable!" I said, laughing out loud. "What a character!"

Warden Szody and I continued north through Lone Pine, Independence, Big Pine, and eventually into Bishop. We reached Bishop Friday afternoon, the day before trout opener. As we rolled into town, we heard the Inyo County Sheriff's dispatcher come over the radio asking for any Fish and Game unit in the area of Lake Sabrina—located about fifteen miles southwest of Bishop.

"Let's wait and see if any of the local guys answer up," I said. "We don't want to step on any toes."

There was another call for assistance. According to dispatch, a group of three individuals were jumping the gun and taking stringers of trout near the south end of the lake. They were driving an older model blue station wagon with a white top. No license plate was given. Using our radio call numbers, I advised dispatch that Warden Szody and I would be responding. We had located Lake Sabrina on the map and by the time I hung up the microphone, Szody's new Dodge Power Wagon was already headed up Highway 168.

About a mile before we reached Lake Sabrina, we saw a blue station wagon rounding the corner. "That has to be them," said Szody. "The driver's eyes looked like saucers when he saw us."

Szody quickly turned the patrol truck around and headed back down the mountain. Within minutes we were bearing down on the car with our red spotlight clearly visible in the driver's rearview mirror. Two men appearing to be in their early twenties were seated in front, with a third man, about the same age, in back. Several fishing rods were visible through the back window. The station wagon slowed and continued down the highway until it came to a wide spot and pulled over.

Szody approached from the driver's side and I held back a little, standing next to the right rear of the suspect vehicle. My partner pointed to the registration sticker on the rear license plate, which had expired. In our experience, if a person failed to keep his vehicle registration up to date, he was more likely to commit minor Fish and Game violations. We both noticed a red-and-white ice chest in the back section of the station wagon and exchanged a knowing look.

"Have you guys been fishing?" asked Szody.

"No, we were just checking out the lake for tomorrow," replied the driver, whose sunburned face told another story. His pale skin had turned a bright shade of pink from overexposure to the high altitude sunlight.

Szody and I always enjoyed a little game of cat and mouse, especially with a trio of brain surgeons like these guys. We asked a series of questions aimed at leading to the closed-season trout we were looking for.

"Do you all have your fishing licenses?" asked Szody.

"We weren't fishing," repeated the driver, "but I have a fishing license."

The young man pulled out his fishing license and handed it to Szody. His two friends, expressions blank, did not reply.

"Do you guys have any fish in the car?" I asked.

"No! I told you we haven't been fishing," insisted the driver.

The driver's nervous tone and the group's body language were dead giveaways. "We'd like to take a look in your ice chest," I said, pointing at it through the back window. "Please pull it out for us."

The driver exited the car and walked around to the back. He pulled out the ice chest and emphatically pointed out that it was, in fact, empty.

The man in the backseat, who had been quiet up until that point, was apparently feeling more confident. "He told you we haven't been fishing," he said. Ignoring the sarcastic comment from the backseat, I reached into the ice chest and ran my finger along the wet slime on the bottom. My finger smelled unmistakably of fish. These characters had either thrown the fish out the window after seeing us pass by or hidden them somewhere in the car. The fact that the man in the backseat had not moved was particularly suspicious.

"Would you please step out of the car," said Szody, pointing to the man in the backseat. Ignoring my partner's instructions, the young man leaned back slightly, his boots firmly tucked under the front passenger seat. "I'm going to ask you one more time to step out of the car," commanded Szody, this time with more authority. The man reluctantly climbed out of the car. I escorted him to a spot on the side of the road where the driver was already seated.

"What do we have here?" Warden Szody leaned through the back door, reached under the front passenger seat and pulled out a metal stringer. Attached to the stringer were nine twelve-inch brook trout. Szody subsequently walked to the other side of the car and reached under the driver's seat. He pulled out a second stringer containing five more brook trout, all the same size.

During the days leading up to the trout opener, the Department of Fish and Game had stocked many of the area lakes and streams with catchable-sized trout. Lake Sabrina's allotment was a load of beautiful brookies, raised and planted by the Mount Whitney Trout Hatchery. These three San Bernardino residents had somehow found out about the fish planting and decided not to wait until Saturday. They were each charged with joint possession of fourteen trout during closed season. The trout and all their fishing gear were seized as evidence.

"That was a pretty good start," I said, as we pulled onto the highway and headed for Bishop. "I have a feeling this is going to be a busy weekend."

II

Warden Szody and I arrived back in Bishop just in time for the orientation meeting. Ken Brown, the Bishop Patrol Captain, advised us that we would be assigned to the north end of Crowley Lake for the weekend. I had worked that area the previous year and was familiar with it. "Let's check into the motel, get something to eat, and run up to Crowley this evening," I suggested, as we walked out of the Bishop Fish and Game office. "We have to be up at the crack of dawn, so we don't want to be out too late."

It was just after dark when Szody and I approached Crowley Lake. Driving up Highway 395, we crossed over Crooked Creek, one of the lake's many tributaries. This small stream flowed through a large culvert, allowing the water to pass under the highway and eventually into the lake. "Why is that car parked there?" I asked, pointing toward the north side of the highway. Szody eased the patrol truck off the highway and onto a wide spot near the suspicious vehicle.

Gently closing my door, I walked over to a small, dark-colored sedan. "The hood is still warm," I whispered, as Szody approached. I shined my flashlight into the car, which appeared to be empty, except for two pairs of shoes on the front floorboard. I pointed out that the occupants of the car had apparently changed their shoes, but my voice was barely audible over the roar of cars and trucks passing by.

"Did you hear that?" asked Szody, pointing toward the culvert. "Somebody's in there." We walked to the north end of the culvert, where the stream flowed outward in the direction of the lake. A peek inside revealed a flickering light at the other end.

"There's one—get it," said an excited voice, followed by the sound of two or more people splashing through the water. "Throw me the net!"

Based on what we had just heard, there was little doubt as to what the people on the other end of the culvert were up to. Szody and I clambered over the north shoulder of the highway and headed down the steep bank on the other side. We could see the silhouettes of what appeared to be two male adults climbing up the hill in our direction. Szody and I hunkered down and waited for the figures to approach. The man in the lead was within a few yards of us when Szody shined a flashlight in his face and said, "Trick or treat."

The startled fish poacher immediately dropped the dip net he was carrying, fell backwards and tumbled ass over tea kettle all the way to the bottom. His surprised partner, halfway up the hill at the time, watched him roll by. Lying on the ground were three large German brown trout that had freed themselves from the dip net and begun flopping their way back toward the stream.

We climbed down the steep embankment and instructed the two violators to sit tight while I tended to the three trout. The man at the bottom was shaken but unhurt. One of the eighteen-inch trout had apparently just been captured. I held it upright in the water for a few seconds before it slithered out of my hand and darted upstream. The other two fish were too far gone and never recovered. We retained them as evidence, along with the dip net that had been used to capture them.

We walked the two men back to their car, where they were rewarded for their efforts with a pair of citations. Both were charged with unlawfully taking three trout in closed waters and illegal method of take—using a dip net.

III

When the sun began to rise on opening morning of trout season, Dave Szody and I were perched on a bluff overlooking Crowley Lake. "You have to see this," I said, handing Szody a pair of binoculars. "There must be a fishing rod every three feet all the way around that lake. How would you like to check all of those fishing licenses?"

By this time in our careers, Dave Szody and I had learned that checking fishing licenses on a crowded lake could be chaotic. This large Eastern Sierra lake was as crowded as anything we had ever seen. Teamwork would be absolutely essential. From a distance, we watched people fish and looked for clues: Who was catching all of the fish? Were they putting their fish on individual stringers or community ones? Were they running fish up to their camps and returning?

Some Fish and Game wardens would simply walk along the bank of a crowded lake like this, checking licenses as they went. They might scratch out a few citations, but the recipients were usually misinformed people and not the deliberate violators. With such a large crowd to deal with, working that way often led to confusion and more than a few arguments.

When it was finally time for an approach, we decided that one of us would make the contacts while the other watched to see who suddenly reeled in his line, cut his line, or walked away from his fishing gear. With nowhere near enough wardens to check everyone on the lake, a certain amount of gamesmanship and strategy was necessary. By mid-afternoon, we had issued a dozen or so fishing license citations and were ready to sink our teeth into something more substantial.

Earlier we had run into a fish planting truck from the nearby Hot Creek Trout Hatchery. The driver, a Fish and Game employee, told us that someone had entered the hatchery the previous night and taken several of the brood stock. Brood stock were the large trout used to provide eggs for the hatchery. Most of them weighed five pounds or more. These valuable fish were maintained in separate ponds from the "catchable" trout that were planted in lakes and streams.

The intruders had not only stolen trout, but they had also broken into one of the hatchery buildings, taken a long-handled dip net off the wall and used it to capture the fish. "We found the net lying by the brood stock ponds this morning," said the driver. "Next to it were fish eggs scattered all over the ground."

Warden Szody and I were on a roll, having already caught several early season violators and a couple of individuals with over-limits. The possibility of catching somebody stealing trout from the state fish hatchery was too good to pass up. Both of us had brought our sleeping bags, so our plan was to spend the night on the cement floor of the hatchery building. We would take turns sleeping, allowing one of us to stay awake and watch out the window.

It was about 9:00 p.m. when we arrived at Hot Creek Hatchery. Arrangements had been made for us to sleep in a room connected to the main hatchery building. From that vantage point, we would have a clear view of the brood stock ponds. With all lights off, we settled in. We kept our uniforms on, in case it was necessary to move quickly, but removed our gun belts and boots.

Both of us had been up since 4:00 a.m., so staying awake would be a challenge. Particularly for me. By 10:30 p.m. I was in dreamland, leaving Szody to take the first watch. He was too keyed up to sleep anyway, having drunk half a pot of coffee.

A little after midnight, Szody heard a metallic thump coming from the adjacent hatchery building. The walls were metal and the slightest contact with a hard object produced a thump that resounded clearly in our building next door. Seconds later, he saw the silhouettes of two men walking outside near the brood stock ponds. One of them was carrying a long-handled dip net. "That guy just went into the building next door and got a dip net," whispered Szody. "Steve, there's somebody out there!"

Szody quickly put his boots on, and without lacing them, jumped to his feet. I had opened my eyes and was still trying to figure out where I was when my partner raced out the door. As I climbed out of my sleeping bag, I heard Szody's voice coming from the brood stock ponds outside: "On your knees, you sons o' bitches or I'll blow your heads off!"

Brave talk for someone who had left his gun belt lying on the hatchery building floor. A second adult male voice cried out, "Don't shoot."

Running to the window, I was just in time to see two men drop to their knees and put their hands in the air. With both gun belts in one hand and my boots in the other, I bolted for the door. When I arrived at Szody's side, the two fish thieves were on their knees next to a long-handled dip net and a flopping five-pound trout.

"Did you forget something?" I asked, as I handed Szody his gun belt. In stocking feet, I walked over and carefully placed the stressed-out trout back into one of the fish ponds.

We turned our attention to the two petrified fish thieves who were still on their knees with their backs facing us. Szody instructed them to produce identification.

The taller of the two was Bruce William Preston, twenty-five years old, from San Bernardino. His partner in crime was Mark Douglas Crooker, twenty-six years old, also from San Bernardino. They both worked out of a pipe fitter's union in the Los Angeles area.

"What did you guys think you were doing?" asked Szody.

"We're sorry," replied Crooker. "We just wanted to take home a couple trophy-sized trout."

I explained that they could go to jail for burglary and grand theft. Those large egg-producing fish were worth a lot of money to the State of California. Szody asked where they had gotten the net, although he already knew the answer: the long-handled dip net the thieves had used was exactly like the ones hanging on the wall inside the next building. Crooker admitted that they had gone inside the hatchery building and taken the net.

"We're sorry," said Preston, repeating what his buddy had said.

"Where are you guys staying?" I asked.

"We're camped at Crowley Lake," answered Crooker.

"How many people are in your camp?"

"Just the two of us. We have a camp trailer."

"Okay, boys, we have your identification and we know where you work," I said. "Now we're going to follow you back to your camp."

Our fish thieves already seemed worried, but telling them that we were going back to their camp put them in panic mode. They were terribly concerned about something, and Szody and I were pretty sure what it was. These were very likely the same misguided characters who had raided the hatchery the previous night.

"Let's go," said Szody.

We gave the two men a ride to their pickup, which they had parked a half mile down the road from the hatchery. I asked who owned the pickup. Crooker said it was his. "Then you drive," I said. "Your buddy can ride with us."

By keeping the two men apart, they would not be able to compare stories or plan some kind of subterfuge. It took about fifteen minutes to arrive at the camp trailer. I jumped out of the patrol vehicle and met Crooker before he had time to enter. We did not want to give him a chance to hide evidence.

A medium-sized ice chest was sitting outside, near the front door of the trailer. Inside the ice chest I found two limits of twelve-inch rainbows, seemingly identical to the hundreds of Crowley Lake trout that Dave and I had inspected earlier that day. When Szody and Preston joined us, I instructed Crooker to lead us inside. Opening the door to the refrigerator, I found two five-pound rainbows; both were carbon copies of the brood fish I had just seen flopping on the bank of the hatchery pond.

I pulled out my Miranda card and instructed Preston and Crooker to sit down while I said, "I want you guys to listen carefully. Please don't say anything until I'm finished. 'You have the right to remain silent. Anything you say can and will be used against you in a court of law. You have the right to talk to a lawyer and have him present with you while you are being questioned. If you cannot afford to hire a lawyer, one will be appointed to represent you before any questioning, if you wish. You can decide at any time to exercise these rights and not answer any questions or make any statements.' "

Crooker looked scared to death. Their big adventure had turned into a nightmare.

"These fish obviously came from the hatchery," I continued. "We can easily have someone from the hatchery identify them." Resuming the Miranda warning, I asked, "'Do you both understand each of the rights I have explained to you?'" Both men answered in the affirmative. I finished reading from the Miranda card: "'Having these rights in mind, do you wish to talk to us at this time?'" I paused and stared straight into the eyes of the two men—it was clear that I meant business.

Crooker and Preston looked at each other and decided that they would waive their rights and talk to us. The first one to speak was Crooker. "We didn't take those fish in the refrigerator. They were given to us."

"Who gave them to you?" asked Szody.

"We would rather not say," replied Crooker.

"You guys are in possession of those fish and you are going to be held responsible. Suit yourselves," I said.

After mulling over their choices, Crooker turned and pointed to the pickup parked next to their trailer. A camper was mounted in the bed and there were no lights on inside. Little did Szody and I know that two more pipe fitters were watching us through the back window of that camper.

"What are you trying to say?" asked Szody.

"Those guys are the ones who took fish from the hatchery last night," said Crooker. "They came back with five fish and gave us two of them. They're the ones who told us how to do it."

I instructed Crooker and Preston to remain in their trailer until we returned. Szody and I walked over to the pickup and knocked on the camper door; we could hear movement inside so we knew someone was there. A few minutes later, a light came on and the door opened.

"Department of Fish and Game," I announced. "We would like to talk to you. Would you please step outside?" Two men stood at the camper door, both about the same age as Preston and Crooker. The taller of the two had greasy, bleached-blond hair, tied in a pony tail. He cringed as his bare feet hit the cold ground.

"Dude, hand me my shoes before you come out."

"Where are they," asked his partner, beginning to turn around and re-enter the camper.

"Never mind the shoes, I said, "stay out here where we can see you. Your buddies told us about you two going into the hatchery last night and taking a bunch of fish. We're going to search anyway, so please make it easy on everyone and show us where the fish are."

The barefoot man looked down at a tarp that was covering something. When my partner pulled the tarp back, we discovered a large ice chest, containing two individual limits of Crowley Lake trout. At the bottom of the ice chest, under several inches of ice, we found what we had been looking for—three trophy-sized brood fish, all placed in individual plastic bags.

"We thought it would be neat to take home a few big fish," the barefoot man explained. "I guess that wasn't a very good idea."

With all four men identified, Szody and I seized the five stolen trout as evidence. "Here's what is going to happen," I said. "Formal criminal complaints will be filed with the local district attorney's office. All four of you will be charged with unlawful removal of fish from a state fish hatchery. We will discuss the matter with the Hot Creek Hatchery manager. He and the DA will decide whether or not you will also be charged with burglary or grand theft."

It was 2:00 a.m. when Szody and I left Crowley Lake and headed for the motel. We were looking forward to a few hours of sleep before Sunday's weekend finale.

"That was a good case," said Szody, yawning.

"We could have been satisfied with just busting the first two guys," I said. "That's why I'm always talking about following the trail to the absolute end. It's hard enough to catch 'em. When we do, we need to shake 'em until everything falls out of their pockets. You know what I mean?"

"I know exactly what you mean," said Szody. "Let's go by the hatchery tomorrow and see what the manager wants to do with those idiots. We need to pick up our sleeping bags anyway."

"They'll pay a couple hundred bucks each and that will be that," I said, leaning back in the seat and closing my eyes. "The hatchery manager won't want to take it any further."

We decided to skip Sunday morning and sleep in. It was almost noon before Szody and I arrived back at Crowley Lake. The sky was clear and it was going to be a beautiful, fifty-five degree afternoon—one of those times when the air was so comfortable that I forgot how intense the Eastern Sierra sun could be. By the end of the day my face would be fried and beet red. Some of the camps were already packing up to leave and everywhere we looked people were cleaning fish. The perfect time to find out who had gotten greedy over the weekend.

Friendly conversation was not only good public relations, it was a great way to find things out. Conscientious, law-abiding fishermen generally don't like it when somebody near them is taking home more than his fair share of fish. If provided with a convenient opportunity, they will usually tell enforcement officers about it.

We practiced our communication skills all afternoon, slowly driving through campsites, showing the colors and stopping to talk to people. Many of them were only too happy to provide us with information about the people in the next camp who had failed to stop at the legal limit. By dark we had added sixteen over-limit cases to an already productive weekend.

Metro Wardens

I

On January 1, 1978, I was promoted to patrol lieutenant and assumed my new supervisorial duties in the metropolitan areas of Riverside and San Bernardino. The next three years would bring more animal adventures than I had ever dreamed of.

"Metro" wardens, which I would supervise, not only worked hunters and fishermen, they enforced laws dealing with exotic mammals—African lions, tigers, wolves, leopards, apes, and even elephants. Native and exotic reptiles—from king snakes to king cobras—were also part of the job, along with regular inspections of pet shops, airport shipping docks, and falconry facilities.

I still recall the first day of my new assignment. I had arranged a meeting with Warden John Slaughter, one of the officers I would supervise. Ten years older than I, Slaughter was a former ballplayer who had grown up in Riverside and knew the area like the back of his hand. The six-foot-two-inch southpaw had been scouted by the pros but settled for a job with the Highway Patrol, before lateraling over to Fish and Game. With much in common, this character and I would share a lot of laughs over the next three and a half years.

As I approached Slaughter's vehicle, I received instantaneous on-the-job training: there, in the bed of his patrol truck, lay a nine-foot alligator with its mouth and legs bound. Slaughter had just seized the huge reptile from a local resident and was in the process of transporting it to a city animal-control facility.

Laughing, Warden Slaughter slapped me on the back and said, "Welcome to Riverside, Lieutenant!"

What is there for a game warden to do in the city? You might be surprised. During the late 1970s there were more captive African lions in the Los Angeles basin—including Riverside and San Bernardino Counties—than there were wild lions in Africa. For several decades, birds, mammals, fish, reptiles, and amphibians had been imported into California with very few restrictions.

Metro wardens were responsible for enforcing a set of relatively new laws and regulations dealing with the importation, transportation, and possession of restricted, live wild animals. Some species were restricted because if they escaped, they could become established and compete with or destroy native wildlife. Others were restricted because they could pose a threat to California's multi-billion dollar agriculture industry. Species such as large carnivores and poisonous snakes were restricted for public safety reasons. All live wild animals, imported or possessed, were subject to strict regulations regarding their general welfare and humane treatment.

A permit system was established to make allowances for people in the entertainment industry, zoological institutions, educational facilities, and people who possessed these animals before the laws came into effect. Wildlife protection officers referred to this part of their job as "Animal Welfare."

Animal Welfare permits were issued based on specific cage and enclosure requirements. These requirements were designed to prevent escape and ensure the humane treatment of each animal. Some species, particularly poisonous snakes, were strictly prohibited, and permits were issued only under special circumstances. Animal Welfare generally amounted to about one fourth of a metro warden's duties, but keeping track of big cats, wolves, monkeys, chimps, snakes, and alligators—to name a few—was time consuming and extremely complicated.

II

There were three large operators in the Riverside/San Bernardino area and probably hundreds of people with individual wild animals. The big operators maintained small compounds, surrounded by ten-foot-high fences to keep the animals in and the neighbors out. Their menageries of exotic animals were ostensibly kept for the entertainment industry, but we suspected that offspring were regularly sold and traded illegally out the back doors.

Shortly after arriving in my new district, I conducted an inspection at the compound of a man named Lundberg. Mr. Lundberg was a little guy who kept a lot of very large African lions on his property. Most of these lions were females, but he had one male I would not soon forget. I asked to see Mr. Lundberg's veterinary certificate, which was supposed to be renewed annually. A tiny smirk appeared on the lion owner's face. "It's right over there," he said, pointing to a framed document hanging on a nearby wall.

In order to examine the certificate, I had to brave an eighteen-inch-wide pathway between two chain link cages, each containing a lion. A lioness occupied the cage on the left; she was sleeping on top of a wooden box. Inside the cage on the right was the largest lion that I had ever seen. It appeared to be a young male, with little or no mane. The giant feline had a head the size of a basketball and must have weighed well over five hundred pounds. This lion also appeared to be sleeping.

As I traversed the pathway and began reading the veterinary certificate, the massive cat slammed against the chain link fence, mere inches from where I was standing. With its thunderous growl he announced his intention of ripping me to shreds and eating me for lunch. I stared into a huge orifice, sporting four five-inch canines that looked more like sabers than teeth. Shuffling sideways, I quickly exited the pathway. Warden Slaughter, who had witnessed this spectacle, told me later that I had been so concerned with the male lion, I had failed to notice the full grown female trying to get at me from the opposite cage. Lundberg, vastly amused, obviously knew exactly what was going to happen when he sent me over there.

I eventually regained my composure and finished the inspection. Later that day, Slaughter and I shared a good laugh. I told him I was glad it had happened. I'd learned a valuable lesson about wild animals; they are completely unpredictable and have the strength and speed to end your life in the blink of an eye. That is particularly true of the big cats—African lions, tigers, leopards, jaguars, and mountain lions—and mature chimpanzees. Those cute little chimps, like the one that Tarzan used to pal around with, grow up to be five times stronger than the average man and extremely dangerous.

A few years later, after I had transferred to Northern California, Lundberg's luck with big cats finally ran out. While throwing meat to one of his adult African lions, he got careless and exposed his right arm. As a house cat would grab a dangling rubber mouse, the lion sunk its massive teeth into Lundberg's arm. Slamming him against the outside of the cage, the lightning fast and incredibly strong animal tore his arm off at the elbow.

III

One November day, we received an anonymous tip about a man in Fontana who was keeping a leopard in his garage. Warden Slaughter and I made a house call. Before ringing the doorbell, we noticed an unattached garage at the east side of the house. Both the front and side doors were closed.

A burly, middle-aged man wearing a three-day-old beard answered the door, The TV was blasting, and beer cans and a pizza box littered the coffee table behind him.

"We're with the Department of Fish and Game. It has come to our attention that you are in possession of a leopard," said Warden Slaughter.

"Just a minute," said the man, a perplexed look on his face. "Let me turn the TV down. Who told you I had a leopard?"

The man's expression was a dead giveaway.

"I don't know anything about any leopard!"

I asked to see his identification. He produced a California Commercial Drivers License. "Are you a truck driver, Mr. Wycoff?" I asked.

"Yeah, I am. What difference does that make?"

"Would you mind if we take a peek inside your garage?"

"All right, I'll tell you the truth," said Wycoff. "I was in Texas and I ran into a guy who owed me money. Instead of paying me he gave me this young leopard that he had in the back of his rig. He said he bought it from some carnival."

Wycoff rattled on with another five minutes of BS before I interrupted and asked if the cat was inside his garage.

"Yes," he finally admitted.

"Do we have your permission to look?"

"Yeah, go ahead." He sighed and looked at the floor.

My earlier experience with Lundberg's lions stood me in good stead. With Warden Slaughter standing behind me, I partially opened the side door of the garage and peeked inside. Sunlight penetrated across the cement floor and lit up the building, but I saw no sign of a leopard. Taking a half step inside, I immediately got the feeling I was being watched: out of the corner of my left eye I could see two large greenish colored eyes staring down at me. The half-grown leopard had jumped from the garage floor, eight feet into the air and perched itself on one of the crossbeams. I carefully backed out of the garage and closed the door.

Wycoff was charged with unlawful possession and importation of a prohibited species. The juvenile leopard was later transported to a Los Angeles area wild animal care facility; all the zoos were filled to capacity and unwilling to permanently house any of the confiscated big cats. This was particularly true of African lions, which seemed to breed like rabbits in captivity.

IV

I ran into many more "animal people" during my three and a half years in Riverside/San Bernardino. Several of them lived in the Perris area, a few miles south of Riverside. During the late seventies, Perris was still fairly rural, providing owners of exotic animals with the opportunity to put an acre or two between themselves and their closest neighbors. It was not unusual to drive out to Perris and see a variety of unusual animals grazing or lolling about in the fields—exotic deer, mouflon sheep, ostriches, emus, and bison. There were also wolves and a host of exotic cats, maintained in cages and enclosures.

One Perris resident, affectionately known as the Tiger Lady, had installed a twenty-foot-high chain-link fence all the way around her little one-acre patch of heaven. Sultan, her five-hundred-pound Bengal tiger, had the complete run of the place, inside and outside the house. He even slept with his owner in her king-sized bed.

One day I was standing in the Tiger Lady's front yard, inspecting her Animal Welfare Permit, when I felt a vice-like grip on my right thigh. I looked down to find Sultan's enormous maw wrapped around my leg. Sultan's little game ended when his owner zapped his hindquarters with a cattle prod—apparently standard equipment for tiger handlers. The tiger released my leg, but my thigh was black and blue for several weeks afterwards. Sultan's canine teeth had been removed. I was not in favor of this procedure, but in this case it had worked out well for me. Besides, how many people can say they've been mauled by a five-hundred-pound Bengal tiger and lived to tell about it?

Before leaving, I jokingly asked the Tiger Lady if she had any problem with burglars or uninvited guests. Not surprisingly, she answered, "No."

Most people didn't like the idea of big cats moving into their neighborhoods, so we often received calls. An anonymous tip led Warden John Slaughter and me into the strange world of Whitley Milton. According to our source, Milton had recently acquired a leopard and kept it at his new house in Perris. The house was way out at the end of a gravel road.

As we pulled up in front of the house, Warden Slaughter commented that it looked like some contractor had just slapped the thing together, graded a ten-foot path around it and left it sitting out in the weeds.

Although no cars were present, Slaughter and I decided to knock. The doorbell didn't work so Slaughter tapped lightly on the picture window next to the front door. Sheets covered all of the windows; fortunately the sheet covering the front picture window had fallen partially down. Warden Slaughter peered inside and noticed that the living room was completely devoid of furniture. The floor seemed to be made of dark-colored tile.

As Warden Slaughter was about to tap on the window a second time, a five-foot monitor lizard shot across the living room floor and down the hall. The tile floor was so slippery that the giant reptile had spun out.

"Did you see that?" asked Slaughter.

I laughed. "Unbelievable!" I said. "How would you like to clean that house?"

We left and returned several times over the next few days before finally finding Milton at home. A fortyish dark-skinned man wearing a pink Hawaiian shirt answered the door.

"We are with the Department of Fish and Game," said Warden Slaughter. "Are you Whitley Milton?"

"Yes, I am," answered Milton, a puzzled look on his face.

"Would you mind if we come in and talk with you for a few minutes?" asked Slaughter.

Neither of us really wanted to go inside the house, imagining what it might smell like, but we figured it would provide us with an opportunity to look around. Milton asked us to wait a minute while he put his lizard in another room. He finally led us into a dimly lit den, furnished with a couch and a few chairs. A large bird cage containing a scarlet macaw hung at one end of the room.

"That's a beautiful bird," said Slaughter, hoping to gain Milton's confidence with a little friendly chit chat.

"Oh, thank you," said Milton. "That's Reggie; I've had him for over twenty years. Please sit down. Can I get you gentlemen something to drink?"

Slaughter and I politely declined the drink offer. We sat down on the couch and began asking general questions about the monitor lizard. During the conversation, a jet black house cat was playing with one of my boot laces. "We received a report that you recently acquired a leopard, Mr. Milton." I tried to pull my foot away, but the cat was quite insistent. "Can you tell us about that?"

"I had a leopard for a few days," Milton said, "but I shipped it back east. I wanted to get a permit and have a cage built."

Before either Slaughter or I could respond, Milton began asking a series of hypothetical questions, each one beginning with, "Answer me this, Lieutenant Callan." Animal Welfare regulations required a certain amount of interpretation by the officers enforcing them. It became obvious that Milton was trying to pin me into a corner on requirements for the possession of big cats. I tried to interpret the regulations fairly and as they were intended, but deep down I deplored the idea of private individuals keeping these magnificent wild animals in backyard cages.

Milton droned on for five or ten more minutes before I noticed something unusual about his kitty—its extremely large paws. The determined little feline was still busy chewing on my right boot.

"Wait a minute!" I said, interrupting Milton in the middle of a sentence. "I think we've found our leopard." John and I had been looking for a typical yellow and black animal, not one in the melanistic black phase. We hadn't paid much attention to the playful little kitten on the floor. Upon closer examination, we realized that this little black kitty with the oversized paws was actually a very young black leopard cub.

Milton had purposely kept the shades closed, so there was very little light in the room. I picked up the cat and carried it to the window. When I pulled the shades back, the light poured in and exposed the characteristic leopard spots through the animal's shiny black fur. We might have been concerned about Milton lying to us, but John and I were a little embarrassed about not recognizing the leopard in the first place.

Charges were filed against Milton for unlawful possession and importation of a prohibited species. No zoos or legitimate facilities were willing to take the leopard so it was eventually shipped back east to its original owner.

V

The most ferocious felines I ever came across were inside a small cage at the Los Angeles International Airport. I was working with Warden Lon Whiteside that day, a metro warden in the truest sense of the word. Whiteside was a tall, thirty-six-year-old lateral from state police with fifteen years of law enforcement experience under his belt. His previous experience dealing with hardened criminals and big city problems served him well in his Los Angeles area patrol district.

There was no hunting activity in Warden Whiteside's district and freshwater fishing was limited to a couple urban reservoirs. Lon seldom had the time or the inclination to work these inner city mud holes and I really didn't blame him. Most of the adult fishermen chose to buy beer and cigarettes rather than the required fishing license. If a warden pulled into the parking lot, word quickly spread and everyone scattered.

Although Warden Whiteside's patrol district was about as urban as it could get, his daily work schedule could be quite interesting. It generally involved airports, pet shops, wild animal facilities, and arrest warrants. Our first stop was Los Angeles International Airport (LAX). Wild animals from all over the world were commonly shipped in and out of this massive facility.

Strict regulations governed the importation of exotic species. The law required that each shipment container be accurately labeled. Sometimes boxes and containers were intentionally mislabeled, making the job of an inspector hazardous and possibly life-threatening: An unsuspecting enforcement officer could open a crate of parakeets and find himself face to face with a spitting cobra or a black mamba.

In this instance, two bobcat kittens had been unlawfully shipped from the southern United States. No bigger than your average house cat kittens, these little guys had the dispositions of full-grown wild animals. As Lon and I approached their small cage, both kittens began growling and aggressively hurling their bodies in our direction. Whoever named them wildcats knew what he was talking about.

Warden Whiteside contacted the addressee by phone and advised him that his package had arrived and was ready for pickup. When the suspect arrived and took possession of the cats, we came from around the corner and confronted him. As was usually the case, this person did not have a permit to import or possess the animals. He was issued a notice to appear in court and the kittens were shipped back to their point of origin.

After saying goodbye to those sweet little kitties, we began checking a series of downtown pet shops. Armed with legal justification, we methodically searched every aquarium, terrarium, and bird cage. It didn't take me long to figure out which shops were more likely to be in violation; without exception, it was the smelly ones. The cleaner the shop, the less likely it was to contain prohibited species.

Warden Whiteside drove our patrol car into a seedy-looking area in the heart of downtown LA. I noticed bars on all the shop windows and graffiti spray painted on most of the walls.

"This is a nice area," I said, facetiously.

"There's a little pet shop on the next block that I have been meaning to check out for some time," said Whiteside. "I want to surprise 'em, so we'll park here and walk up."

"Will the car still be here when we come back?" I asked. Whiteside shrugged.

As we stepped inside the shop, a tiny bell hanging from the front door announced our presence. The shop was small and dimly lit, with terrariums and fish tanks stacked in rows near the entrance. Parakeets were chirping in back and the unpleasant odor of rodent urine and wet sawdust filled the air.

We began slowly walking through the display room, looking for clawed frogs, snakeheads, piranhas, native reptiles, or any number of other species that were illegal to possess or sell. A thin, gray-haired little man with a cigarette hanging out the side of his mouth came around the corner.

"Can I help you gentlemen?" he said.

"We're just conducting a routine inspection," said Warden Whiteside, peering into a terrarium filled with green iguanas.

"I'm the owner and you won't find anything illegal here."

The phone rang and the shop owner left for a few minutes. "If this guy isn't dirty, I'll buy you lunch," I said.

We reached the rear of the shop and still hadn't found anything illegal or suspicious.

"I told you guys you wouldn't find anything," said the shop owner, reappearing from the cash register area.

"What's in that room?" I asked, pointing to a closed door.

"That's the store room," said the shop owner. "Nothing in there but empty aquariums, bird seed, and cardboard boxes."

If the shop owner had been clever enough to say the door led to his living quarters, Whiteside and I might have had problems. Instead he told us the truth—half the truth, that is: the store room also contained an aquarium filled with twenty-three six-inch alligator gars. These voracious fish from the southern United States can reach over eight feet in length and weigh as much as three hundred pounds. Should they become established in California waters, they could wreak havoc with game fish populations. All of the gars were seized into evidence and the store manager was issued a citation for unlawful possession and sale of prohibited species.

The furious shop owner claimed that the gars were not for sale—that's why they were in the back room. I pointed out that gars were also illegal to possess and if he had not intended to sell them, why did he have a ($19.95 each) price tag pasted to the side of the aquarium?

That afternoon we managed one Animal Welfare inspection before attempting to serve an arrest warrant that Whiteside had been working on for some time. The permittee owned a large, gray, timber wolf, which he maintained inside a two-hundred-square-foot chain-link cage. I admired this magnificent animal's long legs, oversized paws, huge head, and piercing yellow eyes. In spite of being born and bred in captivity, these restless canines remain wild in spirit. This one never stopped pacing back and forth the entire time we were there.

Our last stop of the day was in Baldwin Park. Baldwin Park is just one of many communities that occupy the Los Angeles basin. To me they were all the same—cars, houses, shopping centers, industrial parks, factories, and that foul, gray stuff that everyone calls smog.

Arrest warrants from all over California were sent to Warden Whiteside for service. It was his job to locate Los Angeles area residents who had received hunting or fishing citations elsewhere in the state and had failed to pay their fines or appear in court. It took a considerable amount of investigative skill to track some of these people down, but Warden Whiteside had become quite proficient at it.

Whiteside had been searching for a particular individual for several months and had recently obtained a new address from one of his many information sources. Upon arrival we found, parked in front of the house, a car registered to the person named on the warrant. Warden Whiteside went to the front door and I walked around back. As he knocked on the front door, the man we were after climbed out one of the rear windows. "Here, let me help you," I said, as I slapped the cuffs on him.

VI

Oak Glen is one of the nicer areas of San Bernardino County. In the seventies it was a small, lower elevation mountain community where citizens of San Bernardino and Riverside could go to buy a box of farm-raised apples or just escape from the hustle and bustle of city life.

Warden John Slaughter and I were patrolling through Oak Glen one day, in 1978, when Slaughter said he had someone he wanted me to meet. He pulled into a long driveway, leading up to a beautiful, rustic, A-frame house. The front deck had been built around a giant oak tree and every architectural feature of the house was designed to blend in with its oak woodland surroundings.

Slaughter and I climbed out of the patrol truck and were immediately greeted by an avian orchestra: cranes, swans, geese, and ducks from all over the world were squawking in unison. A fifty-five-year-old man with a butch haircut and wearing a white T-shirt walked out to greet us. Slaughter introduced me to his long-time acquaintance, Ray Farber. Farber invited us up to the deck, where we sat and talked for some time. I must have had a puzzled look on my face. Before I could ask about the bird sanctuary on the lower half of the property, Warden Slaughter told me that Farber did have a Domesticated Game Breeder's License. He had worked with wild animals for most of his life. Years earlier, Farber had been a wild animal handler for some of the early true-life adventure features.

Over the next two years, I would drop by Ray Farber's ranch whenever I was in the area, partly because of my interest in the many bird species this man possessed, but mostly because he was a wealth of information. I was particularly interested in his previous relationship with a man named Glen Steele. Having made every effort to protect a small band of desert bighorn sheep during my three and a half years in the desert, I wanted to learn everything I could about the 1970 criminal conspiracy case against Steele and his associates. Farber and Steele had apparently been partners in a private museum, located just south of Farber's Oak Glen ranch. According to Farber, Glen Steele was an exceptional taxidermist and his work was on display in the museum.

One day when I dropped by to see a new pair of fulvous tree ducks, Farber already had a visitor at the ranch. He introduced me to a Native American woman named Rose. As the three of us sat on Farber's deck, the conversation got around to the infamous bighorn sheep case. Unknown to me, Rose had worked for Glen Steele at the time of the bighorn sheep investigation and was prosecuted along with Steele and his other associates.

I asked Rose how she got involved in that mess. She said she had worked in Steele's taxidermy shop and was a professional skinner. "You wouldn't believe how fast Rose could skin an animal," Farber interjected.

"Rose, did you go on any of the illegal bighorn sheep hunts with Steele and his rich clients?" I asked.

"Lots of 'em," Rose replied.

"What was your role?" I asked.

"I skinned out the rams the clients killed," replied Rose.

"Where did they find all of those trophy rams?"

"Most of them were killed in the park."

"What park was that?"

"You mean you don't know? Anza-Borrego."

"The sheep were killed inside Anza-Borrego State Park?"

"Most were killed in the park. A few out by the Mexican border."

Anza-Borrego is the largest state park in California. I asked if they had been concerned about being caught by the park rangers. Rose laughed.

"That park is huge! You could drive all day and not run into anybody."

According to Rose, Glen knew where all the sheep were—from his work on the guzzlers he had helped install there. Guzzlers are man-made structures that capture water from rainfall. He and his associates would drive the clients out in the park, walk a distance to the sheep and simply tell their customers which ones to shoot.

"Kinda like shootin' fish in a barrel?" I asked.

"We could skin out a ram head and cape in a few minutes and be on our way," Rose said.

I asked, a second time, if they were concerned about running into the rangers. Rose said they did have one close encounter. "We were driving out on this dirt road and saw a park truck coming toward us. The horns and cape of a sheep we had just killed were on the front floorboard, under the client's legs. I was sitting in the middle of the front seat, between the client and Glen. We pulled up alongside the ranger's truck and spoke to him for about five minutes, through the window. He never got out of his truck."

Rose's story bothered me. What did the ranger think these three people were doing, miles out in the park, in one hundred and fifteen degree heat?

Rose described another interesting encounter that occurred about a year before Steele and his gang were caught. She and Glen were working in the taxidermy shop when the local game warden showed up unexpectedly. According to Rose, Glen was working on one of the bighorn ram heads at the time. He shoved it under the work bench just before the warden came in the door. The warden stood there and talked with Glen for twenty minutes, then left.

"He never even looked around," said Rose. "Another ram head was buried in the salt pile on the floor."

I learned a great deal from the Steele Bighorn Sheep Case, particularly about taxidermists. Over the next twenty-three years I would inspect dozens of taxidermy shops; some taxidermists were honest and others were opportunists, just like Steele. Money, after all, is what got this once respected taxidermist and businessman into trouble. Faced with wealthy hunters willing to pay big money for trophy desert bighorns, he saw his conservation ethic go right out the window. Steele and his associates could rationalize all day about the need to cull the old rams, but their motivation for breaking the law and depriving California's public of the sight of those magnificent animals was unquestionably money.

Sidewinders

I

As a kid growing up in San Diego, I had spent much of my time exploring the nearby canyon and catching snakes and lizards. I appreciated how interesting and beautiful these creatures were and learned to identify every species.

Unlike birds and mammals, reptiles tend to be out of sight and out of mind. As Southern California's human population has grown, more desert lands, canyons, hillsides and open spaces have been buried under asphalt, houses, and shopping centers. Much of the limited reptile habitat that remains has been exploited by individuals wildlife protection officers refer to as "herpers"—taken from herpetology, the study of reptiles and amphibians. These were the reptile collectors, whose main purpose in life was to find snakes and lizards to sell, trade, or add to their personal collections.

Some collectors began with native species, like rosy boas and mountain king snakes, and graduated to exotics, like pythons and giant monitor lizards. The real screwballs kept poisonous snakes, most of which were illegal. Of the dozen or so species of rattlesnakes found in the western United States, some—particularly the small Arizona species—are quite rare. A serious herper might go to great lengths to add a rare species to his collection.

II

My first experience dealing with herpers came in 1978. West of Palm Springs, near a place called White Water, the Mohave Desert transitions into a Southern California chaparral and chamise—both types of evergreen shrub—landscape. This transition zone was occupied by a significant variety of reptile species, particularly snakes. Sometime in the early seventies, a housing development was planned in this area; a whole labyrinth of roads, with street signs included, was paved and laid out. Apparently the developer ran out of money because that was as far as he got. Some herper discovered that these paved streets were magnets for reptiles trying to maintain their body heat on cool nights. The word got out and collectors came from all over the country to pillage this fragile resource.

One fall evening, Warden John Slaughter and I were on stakeout a short distance from the unfinished development near White Water. From our vantage point, we could see the headlights of any vehicle working the roads.

Shortly after 10:00 p.m., two cars headed into the collecting area; they appeared to be working together at first, then split off and traveled in different directions. It was clear what they were up to because each vehicle was driving slowly and making periodic stops in the middle of the road. Every time they stopped, dome lights came on and doors opened and closed.

"Let's give these people time to hang themselves," I suggested. "We'll catch them coming out." As the two suspect vehicles worked their way up the hillside, Slaughter and I slowly headed toward the entrance to the development. Our headlights were turned off and the switch on Warden Slaughter's patrol vehicle was set so the brake and backup lights would not come on.

We waited near the entrance for about two hours before the first vehicle came down the hill. It was a beat-up blue utility van with no rear or side windows. The second vehicle was still up the hill and out of sight. Warden Slaughter turned on his red spotlight and quickly turned it off when the van came to a complete stop. We did not want the occupants of the car still up the hill to see the red spotlight and ditch anything illegal they might have.

As the van stopped, I stepped from behind a bush and identified myself to the surprised driver. His window was down so I told him to turn off his motor and keep his hands away from the CB radio. I could see a five-gallon bucket on the passenger side floorboard and several pillow cases on the passenger seat, along with a set of snake tongs.

"Looks like you've been out collecting," I said. "Would you please step out of the vehicle?"

With an audible sigh, the reptile collector opened his door and stood next to his van. Although his skin was weathered by the elements, I guessed his age at mid-thirties. He was reed thin and tall—about six foot three—and sported a scraggly red beard. Dressed like a typical herper, he wore a filthy white T-shirt and cutoff Levis, the threads dangling over his knees. His left hand was bandaged.

"What happened to your hand?" I asked, as Warden Slaughter approached. The man remained silent until he saw Warden Slaughter reach for the snake tongs.

"I got bit by a sidewinder last night," he said.

"And you're back out collecting tonight?" blurted Slaughter.

"I've been bit before," said the man, with a careless shrug.

"Do you have some identification?" I asked.

"It's in my glove compartment," the man replied.

Due to the late hour and the potentially dangerous situation, Warden Slaughter peeked inside the glove compartment before allowing the reptile collector to reach in. Seeing no visible firearms, I told the reptile collector to go ahead and retrieve his identification. Again, I advised him to keep his hands away from the CB radio.

The man produced a Nevada Driver's License, indicating that he was from Las Vegas, so I asked to see his Non-resident California Fishing License. He gave me a blank stare. I advised him that a California Fishing License was required to collect reptiles and in his case, he would need a non-resident license. At that moment, a voice came over the suspect's CB radio.

"Crotalus to Sidewinder."

"No need to answer that, Mr. Sidewinder," I said. "You just sit down on that rock right over there while we conduct our business."

Warden Slaughter jumped into his patrol truck and backed it around the corner and out of sight. The beam of approaching headlights lit up the road behind Sidewinder's van. An older-model sedan stopped behind it and a small, slender man got out.

"What did you find?" shouted the man, as he walked around the van in our direction. His voice was gruff and high-pitched.

"Department of Fish and Game," I announced. "Please come over and join us. You must be Crotalus."

Crotalus looked like a five-foot-six-inch version of Sidewinder, very thin and also sprouting a scraggly beard. I wondered, *Do all reptile collectors look alike? This guy sure picked an appropriate CB handle.* Crotalus is the genus for American pit vipers (rattlesnakes).

While I kept an eye on the two herpers, Warden Slaughter examined the sedan. Snake tongs were lying on the front seat and the backseat contained three five gallon buckets. Warden Slaughter returned and asked Crotalus for his driver's license and California Fishing License. Crotalus produced a Nevada Driver's License, showing a Henderson, Nevada address. Like Sidewinder, he did not have a California Fishing License.

While the two suspects continued to slouch despondently on a nearby rock, I opened the side door of the van and prepared to search the contents. I counted seven five gallon buckets, including the one in the cab, all bearing lids. Not anxious to be bitten by a rattlesnake, I tapped on the side of each bucket before carefully loosening the lid and shining my flashlight inside. Bucket number one contained four desert iguanas. These large, fairly common desert lizards were found in washes and sandy areas. California pet shops were full of them until regulations changed and the sale of native species was prohibited. Desert iguanas are diurnal, an indication that Sidewinder and Crotalus had been collecting elsewhere.

Bucket number two contained one chuckwalla, another diurnal species. Chucks were harder to find since they never strayed far from a protective rock crevice. Collectors sometimes resorted to using crowbars to pry them out, causing considerable damage to their habitat. This large and very interesting lizard was also prominent in the pet trade. It became clear to me that these guys had been collecting all over the country and not just there at White Water.

Bucket number three contained a shovel-nosed snake and two rosy boas. Rosy boas were probably the most sought-after species of native California snakes. Prior to the regulation change, they were widely sold in pet shops. This beautiful and completely docile Southern California species was being seriously exploited.

Bucket number four contained a half-grown desert tortoise. Take or possession of a desert tortoise was strictly prohibited. Like countless others, this one was probably found crossing a desert highway. Over the years, hundreds of desert tortoises have been picked up by people traveling through the desert. Thinking that these slow moving reptiles would make interesting pets, they transport them back to their homes, located in cooler and damper climates. Their new "pets" generally survive on lettuce and backyard vegetation, but soon contract pneumonia or some type of respiratory ailment. The symptoms include a discharge coming from their nostrils. Desert tortoises are burrow diggers by nature, able to wreak havoc with a typical backyard. Some dig under fences and escape, later to be run over by cars. Others may be injured by domestic animals or picked up by someone else, beginning the process all over again. Bottom line—leave them in their native habitat where they belong.

When I tapped on bucket number five, the response was a loud buzzing. That bucket was put aside for more careful examination later. Bucket number six offered a faint, barely audible buzz; it was also put aside. Bucket number seven was empty. Under the seats were two cloth bags. One contained a half-dead pair of California king snakes, the other, a tiny ring-neck snake. Of all the reptiles found in Sidewinder's possession, the ring-neck snake bothered me the most. This harmless, beautiful little reptile would have surely died before reaching anyone's collection.

Crotalus was lucky. He had apparently been transferring whatever he caught to Sidewinder's van. Only two reptiles were found inside his vehicle, a gopher snake and a common king snake. He was charged with unlawful collecting without a California Fishing License.

All of the reptiles were seized into evidence. A later examination of the two buzzing buckets produced a six-foot red diamond rattlesnake and a sidewinder. The red diamond was collected in the San Diego area, probably in or near Anza Borrego State Park. The eighteen-inch sidewinder could have been found anywhere in the desert where sands have accumulated. Apparently this little rattler didn't appreciate being handled and bit his namesake. A formal complaint was filed against Sidewinder, better known as Jerald Phillip Hicks. He was charged with unlawful possession of protected reptiles, over-limits, and collecting without a California Fishing License. All of the seized reptiles were eventually released back into their native habitats.

Saving Lake Mathews

In 1939 Franklin Roosevelt was midway through his twelve-year presidency. Hitler was pushing his way across Europe. Baseball fans said good-bye to Lou Gehrig and Joe Louis was the heavyweight champion of the world. It was also in 1939 that the Metropolitan Water District of Southern California dedicated Lake Mathews. Located six miles from the city of Riverside, Lake Mathews would provide drinking water for Southern California.

This thirty-two hundred acre reservoir, with twenty-six hundred acres of surrounding land, was fenced and literally cut off from the outside world. As the years went by, Riverside County changed from a semi-rural county of orange groves, rolling green hillsides, and vast, unoccupied deserts to one of the fastest growing areas in the United States. Most of the rolling green hillsides have since been buried under housing developments and shopping centers. The once thriving citrus industry is now remembered in the form of California Citrus State Historic Park, inside the city of Riverside.

Like an island spared the effects of time, Lake Mathews and its surrounding lands remained virtually untouched in the late 1970s. Its undisturbed grassland plant community contained hundreds of native plant species, many of which were difficult, if not impossible, to find elsewhere in Southern California. Every spring the entire enclosed area was blanketed with wildflowers, reminiscent of days long past. Thousands of ducks and geese flocked into the lake during winter months, followed by as many as thirty southern bald eagles. With an abundance of fish, waterfowl, and small mammals to prey on and virtually no human interference, golden eagles, ospreys, prairie falcons, and a dozen other species of hawks and owls were commonly seen there. Reptile populations that had been decimated throughout Southern California still thrived within the confines of the perimeter fence.

In 1979, the Metropolitan Water District of Southern California signed a memorandum of agreement with the California Department of Fish and Game designating 2,565 acres of land surrounding Lake Mathews for wildlife mitigation purposes. This was intended as partial compensation for wildlife losses from the massive State Water Project. According to this agreement, "any use of these lands that would impinge upon the maintenance of wildlife populations would not be allowed." Aware of the rare and priceless value of this oasis of life amidst an ever-growing metropolitan area, my squad of wardens and I patrolled Lake Mathews on a regular basis in an effort to hold back the tide of human encroachment.

It seems like nothing good lasts forever, particularly when it comes to our natural resources. Someone always comes along wanting to change things, or as developers like to say, make them better. I have never believed that man can improve upon nature and Lake Mathews was no exception. In January of 1981, the director of the California Department of Parks and Recreation announced plans to turn Lake Mathews into another recreational lake, open to public waterskiing and fishing. He offered to pay a substantial sum for Metropolitan Water District lands outside the Lake Mathews perimeter fence in return for the right to open and develop the area inside the fence.

When I heard about this plan, I was outraged. My wardens and I had protected this special place for several years and were not about to give it up without a fight. I contacted biologists from the Department of Fish and Game's Wildlife Management and Fisheries branches, intent on heading off this idea before it gathered steam. We formed a committee, including local educators and representatives from nearby conservation groups. Everyone agreed that opening this precious area to recreational uses would drive away its birdlife forever. Instead of poppies, lupines, daisies, lilies, horned lizards, king snakes, rosy boas, and Stephen's kangaroo rats (a threatened species), there would be cars, boats, pollution, erosion, litter, beer, and loud parties. The healthy fishery that eagles and other birds depended upon would be depleted within weeks.

Our aim was to permanently designate Lake Mathews and its surrounding lands as an ecological reserve, under the protection of the California Fish and Game Code. I gave slide presentations all over the county and gained the support of every major conservation organization in Southern California. In our meetings we agreed that the Lake Mathews area should be opened only to carefully supervised nature study and educational tours. Local university professors referred to the area as a "natural museum."

On March 14, 1981, we met with the Director of the California Department of Parks and Recreation. The room was filled with conservationists and educators—all expressing their concerns about losing this precious resource to recreational use. After all, three water-oriented recreational areas already existed in the Riverside area—Lake Perris, Lake Elsinore, and Lake Skinner. The State Parks Director was clearly not expecting so much opposition. Rather than give up, he formed an ad hoc committee to evaluate the resources of Lake Mathews and make recommendations. Dr. Wilbur Mayhew, of the University of California, Riverside, was appointed to head the committee.

On May 9, 1981, Dr. Mayhew and six prominent scientists presented their findings—based on firsthand knowledge and published studies—to the State Parks director, in the form of a five-page letter. Speaking for the committee, Dr. Mayhew stated, "We are unanimous in our strong opposition to any attempt to open Lake Mathews to boating and fishing." Dr. John Moore, world-famous professor of biology and member of the National Academy of Sciences, submitted the following written statement:

> Some decisions set in motion a train of events that cannot be reversed or remedied easily. Such would be the decision to make Lake Mathews freely available to the public. Every body of water that the public has touched has been ecologically degraded and polluted. Lake Mathews is the last fully protected large body of water in Southern California. It is the only remaining true sanctuary for thousands of waterfowl that spend their winters with us. It supports the largest winter population of the bird that is our national emblem. Is it unreasonable to ask that this small bit of nature remain inviolate? It is surely immoral if we do not.

Shortly after this meeting, the plan to develop Lake Mathews was dropped and the area designated as an ecological reserve.

When I retired in 2002, I looked back on the thousands of cases I had worked on during my thirty year career. The accomplishment I was most proud of was my role in saving this special place.

Redding

In September of 1981, a lieutenant's position opened up in Redding. Redding is located in Shasta County and sits at the north end of California's Great Central Valley. I had grown up an hour south of there, in Orland, so this would be as close as I would ever come to going back home.

I had hoped to secure a position with lots of open space and plenty of waterfowl, but those lieutenants' districts were already occupied by senior lieutenants with no interest in changing locations or retiring. Activity in Shasta County would center on Shasta Lake, the Sacramento River, lots of tributary streams and mountains full of deer. September was a great month to jump right into the action: the fall salmon run had just begun and deer season was in full swing.

They didn't exactly roll out the red carpet on my first day in Redding. After meeting my new supervisor, Captain Jack Weaver, at the regional office, I asked about my patrol vehicle. Weaver handed me a set of keys and said my Dodge Power Wagon was parked somewhere out in the back parking lot. The truck was a wreck; the windows were clouded over with dust and the battery was dead. Apparently this worn-out pile of metal, with a hundred and twenty-five thousand hard miles on it, had sat there all summer in the hundred-degree Redding heat.

It was 4:00 p.m. by the time I replaced the battery and got the old clunker running. The Sacramento River, which ran right through town, was full of spawning salmon, and there was enough daylight left to make my first salmon case. I had already mastered the local regulations and felt quite at home in my new surroundings. After all, I had spent my teenage years sixty miles down the road and paid my way through college working summers at a nearby state fish hatchery.

Most of the Redding-area fishermen were after Sacramento River trout, which were legal to catch as long as no more than three were taken and restrictions on hook size were observed. The upper Sacramento River contained some of the most beautiful trophy-sized rainbow trout in the country. Sections of the river above and below Redding were legally classified as "salmon spawning areas—fishing for salmon was strictly prohibited." Any salmon that was hooked had to be returned to the water immediately, unharmed.

There were people who chose to ignore the law and take salmon anyway. Some rigged their lines for trout, knowing they would "accidentally" hook salmon. The illegal fish were usually hidden in the weeds until the violator could make a safe getaway. Serious salmon poachers didn't bother with bait or a lure. Instead they used large, weighted treble (three-pronged) hooks. As salmon swam upstream through the shallow riffles, poachers would cast these fist-sized hooks across the fish's path. It usually took a couple hard yanks on the rod before one of the sharp hooks sank deep into the flesh of a spawning salmon, usually in the back or tail region. People who engaged in this activity were referred to, by Fish and Game wardens, as "salmon snaggers."

Driving through downtown Redding, I decided to check out a few streets that dead-ended on a bluff overlooking the Sacramento River. My first stop was at the end of East Street. Parking my patrol rig away from the bluff, I walked to the edge with binoculars in hand. As luck would have it, East Street ended directly above a popular spawning riffle. I immediately noticed a fisherman below and ducked behind a nearby blackberry bush. Focusing my binoculars, I zeroed in on a dark-haired man of medium build wearing a white, V-necked T-shirt. Instead of rubber hip boots or waders, he wore blue jeans and tennis shoes. I wasn't quite sure about the man's age, but his lack of appropriate footwear and his ability to withstand the extremely cold water led me to believe he was in his twenties or early thirties.

Standing knee-deep in the river, the fisherman held a heavy-duty fishing rod that seemed better suited for tuna or marlin than trout. I directed my binoculars toward the end of his line as he retrieved it. Even from forty yards, I easily recognized a very large, silver, spoon-type lure. *No self respecting trout is about to bite on that damn thing*, I thought.

I watched several large salmon working their way upstream. All but one appeared to be male, displaying the striking deep red spawning coloration on their back and tail regions. The fisherman made nine or ten casts across the riffle before finally hooking a fish. It was a large male, weighing thirty pounds or more. The fish was hooked in the back, just above the adipose fin. Rather than allowing the salmon to put up a fight, the man horsed it toward the north shore and up on the rocks. Glancing in several directions, he walked into some high grass along the edge of the river and stashed his ill-gotten prize. I made a mental note of the hiding place and watched as the violator returned to the river and began the process again.

Scanning the area, I decided on the best way to approach the salmon snagger: I would need to cross the river and head downstream. A trailer park was located directly north of the violator, about one hundred yards away. *That's probably where this guy came from and where he'll be taking the fish,* I thought. Returning to my truck, I headed for the Market Street Bridge, a couple of blocks away. The first road on the north side of the bridge led to the trailer park.

Once inside the park, I maneuvered my dark green Power Wagon through several rows of older mobile homes. It didn't take long before I attracted an audience. A group of older men sitting in the shade of a carport were particularly interested. "What are ya lookin' for?" one of the men called out. I smiled and waved as I went by. Finally reaching the south boundary of the trailer park, I locked my truck and walked toward the river.

When I had gone about a hundred yards, I spotted the salmon snagger. It was the same man I had watched from the bluff, busy reeling in yet another salmon. Just as before, the salmon was foul-hooked in the back and horsed onto the rocks. "You can go ahead and carefully release that one," I ordered, walking toward the salmon snagger. The startled suspect turned toward me, eyes wide and jaw slack with fright. Without missing a beat, he attempted to block my view and pull the large treble hook from the salmon's back. "That won't be necessary," I said. "I saw where you hooked the fish. Now carefully return it to the water without injuring it any further."

Before the snagger could think of any more evasive actions, I reached for his fishing rod and secured the treble hook to the tip. I asked to see his fishing license and identification. Both documents indicated that the man's name was Ronnie Charles Webb.

"Now lead me to the salmon you hid in the weeds," I said.

"I don't have any salmon hid in the weeds," he replied.

"Come with me," I said.

We walked directly to the spot where I had seen the man stash his salmon. There I discovered not one fish, but three. All three salmon were still wet— one began flopping when I touched it. Bloody gashes covered their backs. I tried to save the flopping salmon by placing it back in the river, but it had been out of the water too long. After enduring a three-hundred-mile journey from the ocean, this fish was completely spent. By the time these exhausted travelers reach the upper Sacramento River, they are usually dark, covered with abrasions, and pretty beat-up—not likely to be very good for human consumption.

Many Fish and Game officers would have issued a citation for such a violation and delivered it directly to the court. I preferred to handle significant cases by submitting typed, long-form complaints through the district attorney's office. That way I could do a thorough job of presenting the case, justifying the charges and documenting the evidence. This method would not only gain the respect of the district attorney's office, it would ensure a more suitable disposition (fine/sentence). Professionalism was and is very important to me and I wanted to set a positive example for the wardens I would soon be supervising. My formal complaint charged Webb with the unlawful take and possession of three salmon in a salmon spawning area and with unlawful method of take—snagging.

Over the twenty-one years following that first incident, I made hundreds of similar salmon cases. I often asked myself, *Am I really making a difference chasing violators around at all hours of the day and night?* While my crew and I were saving a few salmon here and there, millions of these valuable fish were being destroyed every year. Fingerling salmon and steelhead were being diverted into irrigation ditches and out into fields. Water diversions were robbing streams of enough cold water to sustain fish. Dams and other manmade obstacles were cutting fish off from traditional spawning grounds. Pollutants were pouring into rivers, streams, and the Pacific Ocean from a thousand different sources. A juvenile salmon has a one in a thousand chance of making it from a hatched egg, downstream to the Pacific Ocean and, three or four years later, back upstream to spawn. I felt that if one of those incredible fish somehow made the 300-mile journey back from the ocean—past all the predators, the obstacles, the pollutants, and the legal fishermen—it deserved a chance to spawn and perpetuate the species. That's if some outlaw didn't snag it, net it, spear it, shoot it, club it, or hit it with a rock.

All biological, statistical, and practical reasons aside, I had to do what I could to increase each fish's chances of survival, no matter how inadequate my efforts.

Assault with a Deadly Salmon

I

Dave Szody eventually tired of 115-degree summer days and the smell of cotton defoliant drifting from the nearby fields. A warden's district opened up at the other end of the state, where cool fog dripped from forests of redwoods and Douglas firs. Instead of bone-dry washes, there were rivers and streams filled with native salmon and steelhead. In 1980, when Dave arrived at his new Fortuna Patrol District, the local wardens regaled him with a tale so incredible, it had to be true.

It happened on the Eel River during the late seventies. At that time, the Eel River was producing some of the best Chinook salmon runs in memory. Salmon weren't just plentiful; they were big, averaging over twenty-five pounds each. Word spread like wildfire and every outlaw in the country converged on this famous spawning stream.

In those days, Bob Taylor was the area Fish and Game warden. During the spawning season, he had his hands full covering not only the Eel but several other anadromous streams that flowed through his busy North Coast patrol district. One of the most popular poaching spots was the "Box Car Hole," located just outside the city limits of Fortuna. Railroad tracks along the north bank of the river were threatened by erosion, so the railroad company buried a string of old box cars along the track to hold the bank together. The railroad's erosion control plan created a couple of very deep pools at the base of the box cars, providing an ideal stopover for migrating salmon. Salmon will swim the riffles and shallower parts of a stream and stop to rest in the deeper pools. In this case, large concentrations of fish stacked up in the Box Car Hole and became targets for both legal and illegal fishermen.

During daylight hours, the Box Car Hole was usually crowded with "legal" anglers who did a pretty good job of policing themselves. If someone foul-hooked a fish, the other fishermen kept a keen eye on that person until he released the fish unharmed. After sundown it was a different story. The legal fisherman would go home, leaving the outlaws with the entire river to themselves. Like roaches scurrying from under the kitchen sink, dark silhouettes would surface along the riverbank. Instead of six legs, this particular species had two—each man carrying a rod and reel—outfitted with heavy-test monofilament line. Attached to that line would be a fist-sized three-pronged hook, weighted with a wrap-around pencil sinker. Wardens referred to this illegal setup as "snag gear."

One moonlit night, Warden Taylor was out working his district's spawning streams. He decided to check out the Box Car Hole before going home. It was approaching midnight when Bob grabbed his binoculars, locked his patrol truck, and began walking the narrow foot path that led to his observation site. Once there, he began scanning the riverbank below.

"Oh no, not him again," whispered Taylor, as he trained his binoculars on a pickup with a camper shell, parked at the water's edge. Warden Taylor immediately recognized the pickup as belonging to a local poacher named Alvis Musser. Most of the Eureka-area law enforcement officers were very familiar with this stereotypical Humboldt County dope-growing outlaw. Musser was a short, stocky, thirty-five-year-old with a three-inch scar on his right cheek. He wore the scar like a badge of honor, claiming he got it in a knife fight. In actuality, Musser had snagged himself in the face one night while carelessly casting a large treble hook. This pint-sized troublemaker had a big mouth and a huge chip on his shoulder. Ready to fight at the drop of a hat, Musser was always in trouble. Wardens would say, "If Alvis Musser put as much effort into doing things legally as he does doing things illegally, we would be reading about him in *Forbes Magazine*." He was a thief, a dope-grower, and a world-class poacher. When Musser wasn't poaching deer or salmon, he was stealing redwood burls and shake bolts from the timber companies.

Musser and two other men stood knee-deep in the river. Taylor wasn't able to identify the other two, but they were all attempting to snag salmon. "Here we go again," mumbled Taylor. He recalled an incident that had taken place several weeks earlier, on a remote sandbar downriver. As was usually the case, Taylor was working alone that day with no backup available. He caught Musser and three of his outlaw buddies in the act of snagging salmon. Warden Taylor gathered identification from each man and began to issue citations. Dealing with four loudmouthed recalcitrants who have been drinking beer all afternoon is no easy task. Keeping one eye on the citation book and the other on the violators, Taylor continued to write. Meanwhile Musser and his three buddies became argumentative and increasingly belligerent.

"I'm going to seize your equipment and your fish as evidence," announced Taylor, as he finished issuing the last citation. "It will be up to the judge whether or not you get your gear back."

With that, the easily agitated Musser went into orbit, following Taylor to his patrol vehicle, shouting expletives every step of the way. The five-foot-ten inch, one hundred and sixty-five pound warden wanted to place Musser under physical arrest, but taking all four of these drunken Humboldt County hooligans into custody was out of the question. "If you ever mess with me again, it will be the last thing you ever do!" shouted Musser, as Taylor climbed into his patrol vehicle and drove away.

Warden Taylor considered his options as he continued to watch the three salmon snaggers in the river below. Given the late hour and what had happened during his last encounter with Musser and his associates, Bob decided to play it safe and request backup before moving in. The Box Car Hole being less than a mile from the Fortuna Police Station, he asked the dispatcher to try Fortuna PD first. Dispatch came back a few minutes later and advised Taylor that it was against Fortuna Police Department's policy to respond to anything outside of the city limits.

Humboldt County Sheriff's Deputy Phil Eastman was working graveyard shift that night and overheard the radio traffic. "I will be responding from Eureka," said Eastman. "My ETA (estimated time of arrival) is thirty minutes." Warden Taylor knew Deputy Eastman and considered him one of the best deputies to have at his side, should anything go wrong. A few years earlier, Eastman had responded to a call regarding a 5150 (psycho) and found himself staring into the business end of a twelve gauge shotgun. A cool head and years of law enforcement experience prevailed. Deputy Eastman was able to talk his way out of the situation and arrest the man without any shots being fired. Joining Deputy Eastman as backup for Warden Taylor was Patrolman Frank Chapin from the nearby Ferndale Police Department. Tiny Ferndale had only one officer and Chapin just happened to be on duty.

While Warden Taylor waited for his backup to arrive, he watched Musser and his companions land several salmon and stash them inside Musser's camper shell. Meeting the two officers back at his patrol car, Taylor filled them in on the situation—explaining how Musser had threatened him a few weeks earlier. He advised them to be ready for a fight. Both Eastman and Chapin had dealt with Musser before and understood the potential danger. Eastman was an average-sized officer, standing about six feet tall and weighing 185 pounds. Chapin stood about five-foot-nine and, like so many small-town police officers, had become too fond of donuts and sweet rolls. He tipped the scales at 275 pounds and had a reputation for busting out the seat springs in patrol units.

As the three officers approached, Deputy Eastman focused on Musser while Taylor and Chapin confronted the other two poachers. "Department of Fish and Game," announced Warden Taylor. "You are all under arrest for unlawfully taking salmon." Taylor instructed the three subjects to hand over their illegal fishing gear. As Deputy Eastman reached for Musser's fishing rod, the unpredictable Musser suddenly jerked it out of Eastman's hand. They tussled over the rod for a few seconds before Musser released his grip, turned around, and ran into the camper shell.

"He's got a gun, he's got a gun!" shouted Eastman, as Musser reappeared in the doorway of the camper shell, brandishing a loaded .25 caliber semi-automatic pistol. Deputy Eastman drew his revolver and aimed it at Musser: "Drop the gun and come out!"

Warden Taylor couldn't see Musser from where he was standing and immediately assumed that all three subjects were armed. He and Officer Chapin drew their revolvers and ordered Musser's two companions to drop to the prone position and not move. Meanwhile, Deputy Eastman and Musser seemed to be at a standoff—both pointing their weapons at each other. "Drop your weapon and come out of the camper!" shouted Eastman. "I'm not going to tell you again."

The hammer of Deputy Eastman's revolver was millimeters from reaching its apex and beginning its downward trajectory when Musser finally put his gun down and stepped out of the camper. "Turn around and place your hands behind your back," instructed Eastman. Musser began to comply, then wheeled around and attempted to overtake the officer. With the other two poachers still lying prone on the ground, Taylor and Chapin ran to assist Deputy Eastman. Musser proved to be as strong as he was stupid: He was squealing like a stuck pig when Officer Chapin placed his right knee in the small of Musser's back, applying the full force of his massive torso. Musser gasped for breath and quit resisting long enough for Eastman and Taylor to force his arms behind his back and apply the cuffs.

After all three poachers had been safely secured in the caged section of Deputy Eastman's patrol unit, Eastman, Chapin, and Taylor stood nearby.

"Damn!" exclaimed Chapin, brushing the sand off of his rumpled uniform. "You fish cops have a dangerous job."

"That was just routine," replied Taylor, laughing. "We do that every night." Warden Taylor was just kidding, but contacting potentially dangerous subjects while working alone was very much a part of a Fish and Game warden's job. This time backup had been available, but that wasn't always the case.

Alvis Musser watched from the rear window of Deputy Eastman's patrol car as Warden Taylor unloaded several unlawfully taken salmon from Musser's camper shell. As Eastman pulled away, Musser couldn't pass up the opportunity to show everyone how tough he was: "I'm gonna get you, Taylor!" Musser squeaked in his high pitched, irritating voice.

"Shut up Musser, you blithering idiot," responded Deputy Eastman. "You're in enough trouble already."

Alvis Musser was charged with resisting arrest and felony assault on a peace officer. He was eventually tried, convicted, and sent to state prison for several years. The other two subjects, who had not been armed and had cooperated with the officers, were charged the fishing violations, ordered to pay their fines, and released.

II

Shortly after moving to the North Coast, Warden Dave Szody met Rio Dell Police Sergeant Pat White. Although White worked for the local police department, he cared deeply about preserving natural resources and frequently worked with Fish and Game on important investigations. While still in his early twenties, White had volunteered to go undercover and help take down a large commercial deer poaching ring. He proved so credible as an undercover operative that Fish and Game used his services again about a year later: this time Pat played the role of a sleazy sturgeon poacher. He was able to infiltrate a group of Klamath River commercial sturgeon poachers, leading to their eventual arrest and conviction.

White was born to be a backwoods cop. He worked on the family ranch, became an accomplished horseman, rode bulls in the rodeo, and learned to fix anything with a wrench and a screw driver. Pat never went to college, but compensated for his lack of formal education with natural street smarts and an uncanny ability to read people. Standing five feet nine inches tall and weighing 160 pounds, this cop was tough as nails—the kind of officer you wanted with you in case of trouble. Dave Szody described White as being "steadfastly loyal." "When you work with Pat White," Szody would say, "you never have to worry about your back."

During the fall of 1981, Sergeant White responded to a domestic disturbance report of a woman being beaten by her boyfriend. The victim, Mary Heath, told the dispatcher that her boyfriend—none other than Alvis Musser—had assaulted her. Heath was the classic fishwife, 185 pounds of piss and vinegar. She had such a foul mouth that the neighbors could hear her cussing from clear down the street.

"That son of a bitch hit me with a fish," Heath shouted over the phone—her voice so loud that the dispatcher had to remove her earphones.

As White entered the house, the overwhelming stench of cigarette smoke reminded him of the bar fight he had broken up the night before. He immediately noticed that Heath had been beaten to a pulp: her face and head were black and blue, covered with dried blood. One of Heath's lower teeth was missing, but White remembered that from the previous time he had responded to a call at her residence.

"Are you all right?" asked White.

"I told him I was gonna turn his ass in this time," replied Heath.

Heath led Sergeant White through the house to a freezer on the back porch. She opened it and pointed to a large frozen salmon inside.

"That's what he used to beat me with," Heath said.

"That must've hurt," said White, as he noticed a meat saw hanging from the wall.

"Hell, yes, it hurt!" replied Heath. "How would you like ta get hit in the head with a ten-pound frozen fish?"

A closer look revealed fresh blood and tissue on the blade of the meat saw. It was also covered with hair, which White—an avid hunter—recognized as deer.

"This ain't the first time he hit me," said Heath.

"This looks like deer hair," mumbled White, not paying attention to Heath's ceaseless blabbering.

"That's from that doe that Alvis brought home the other night. He skinned it out and butchered it on the patio in back."

"Is this venison here in the freezer?"

"That's all from the same deer."

Sergeant White radioed his dispatcher and asked her to contact Warden Szody. Szody happened to be on patrol in the area and responded to Heath's Rio Dell residence within minutes. Mary Heath and Sergeant White met Szody at the front door. "I think we have something you might be interested in," said White.

White and Heath led Szody to the back porch, where he examined the meat saw and identified the deer hair. Sergeant White then pointed out the deer meat in the freezer and led Szody to the backyard, where someone had recently skinned out a deer. In addition to the homemade gambrel—a frame used to hang game by the legs during the butchering process—there were scattered bits and pieces of deer hide, tissue, dried blood, and hair.

"I'll start bagging this stuff up if you want to put out a BOLO (be on the lookout) on Musser," said Szody.

"You got it," replied White.

Just as Sergeant White and Warden Szody were leaving the Heath residence, Alvis Musser came driving up the street. Right behind Musser was a Rio Dell police unit that had responded to the BOLO and recognized Musser's rusted-out old pickup. The officer, assisted by White and Szody, dropped Musser face down on the pavement and applied the cuffs without incident. Musser was charged with assault with a deadly weapon (ADW)—not a gun this time, but a frozen salmon.

Musser, still on parole, was sent back to prison for a minimum of ten years and never heard from again.

Big Night at Bull Creek

Sometime during the fall of 1982, Warden Dave Szody planned an all-night stakeout for deer poachers on Bull Creek Road, in Humboldt County. He was accompanied by his friend, off-duty Rio Dell Police Sergeant Pat White.

On this particular evening, Warden Szody picked up Sergeant White at the Rio Dell Police Station, just after White had finished his eight-hour shift. Pat was still wearing his police uniform when he climbed into Szody's patrol truck. The county road that Szody decided to stake out that night was in a remote area of Petrolia, near the Mattole River. It was commonly used by poachers and internationally known for illegal marijuana cultivation.

About 11:00 p.m., the officers found a suitable place to hide their patrol vehicle, just off a logging road, behind some dense vegetation. The truck came to a stop on a downhill grade, far enough from Bull Creek so the rushing water wouldn't drown out the sound of possible gunshots. Planning on a long night, Szody and White had brought along plenty of coffee and a giant-sized bag of unshelled peanuts. They kept awake during the first couple of hours by talking about many of the cases they had been involved in. When it came to police work, Pat White had a photographic memory: he could provide the name and physical description of every person he had ever arrested.

By 2:00 a.m., all traffic on the road had ceased, the floorboard of the patrol truck was covered with peanut shells and both officers were ready to head for home and a soft bed.

"Let's give it five more minutes and get the hell out of here," said Szody, as he stifled a yawn. Pat, whose eyes had been closed, was temporarily startled by Szody's voice.

"That sounds good to me," White replied.

Just then a loud report from a high-powered rifle echoed from the hill just above the two officers. "That was close!" said White. "It came from right behind us."

The shot had actually come from a half mile away, but the sound was amplified in the quiet night air. A few minutes later, a pickup drove past the hidden patrol vehicle, headed downhill on the county road. With lights blacked out, Warden Szody put his green Dodge Power Wagon in gear and inched onto the county road behind the suspect vehicle. There was just enough moonlight to prevent the sleepy warden from driving off the road and crashing into a redwood tree.

Szody and White followed the vehicle for about a mile before deciding to stop the suspected deer poachers and avoid any possibility of their getting away with an illegal deer. Szody activated his red spotlight and lit up the back of their pickup with an overhead light that was mounted on the roof of his patrol truck. The suspects rolled for another quarter mile before finally pulling over to the right side of the road.

Through the rear cab window, Warden Szody and Sergeant White could see three heads. There were two rifles visible in the gun rack mounted to the inside of the cab. Szody radioed the stop to dispatch and White waited for him at the right front bumper of the patrol vehicle. They made their careful approach. White stopped at the right side of the tailgate and Szody focused on the driver from the westbound lane. Although both officers had done this many times before, there was always an element of anxiety—not knowing what to expect.

Sergeant White saw that the bed of the suspects' pickup was filled with freshly harvested marijuana plants and advised Warden Szody by loudly calling out, "11357." Section 11357 of the California Health and Safety Code provided criminal sanctions for the unlawful possession of marijuana.

The scene had turned into a felony stop. Warden Szody drew the .357 Magnum revolver from his holster. With a flashlight in his other hand, he ordered the driver out of the truck. As the driver stepped out of the pickup, hands in the air, Szody could see a rifle resting on the driver's seat with the barrel pointed toward the floorboard.

"There's a rifle. Cover me!" Szody said.

White provided cover while Szody cuffed the driver and instructed him to sit on the ground at the side of the road. When the driver was secured, White directed his attention to the passenger in the right-front seat. "You, on the passenger side of the pickup, come out with your hands in the air where I can see them!" shouted White. The man did as he was told. White cuffed him and ordered him to sit at the side of the road, next to the driver.

Both officers turned their attention to the man still sitting in the middle of the cab. In spite of all the noise and confusion, he appeared to be asleep or passed out. They had one more concern—this man was huge. They guessed the giant Samoan's weight at well over three hundred pounds and, unless he had unusually short legs, he was at least six feet six inches tall.

Nothing is easy, thought Szody, as he pondered what to do next. *This guy could very well be faking and waiting to grab one of us.*

The behemoth was slumped over in the seat and snoring loudly, so Szody took a chance and poked him with his baton. Like a bear roused from its lair, the man grunted and opened his eyes. Without turning his head, he directed his eyes toward the uniformed officer who was standing in the doorway, a baton in one hand and a flashlight in the other.

Szody motioned with his finger for the man to slide across the seat and step out of the truck. Without a word, the man followed Warden Szody's instructions; he was so stoned he could barely function. Somehow the officers managed to get him seated on the ground next to his buddies. The man's wrists were so large that traditional handcuffs would not fit. Luckily, Szody kept plastic flex cuffs in a box behind his seat. They would have to do.

With all three of the suspects sitting on the ground between the two trucks, Warden Szody and Sergeant White began searching their vehicle. They started with the pickup bed, where White had already identified a large number of marijuana plants. A very large four point buck was lying between the side wall and a muddy ATV. It was warm to the touch and still oozing blood. This deer had been the target of the recent shot Szody and White had heard.

"You guys have been busy," said Szody, as he discovered two more freshly killed bucks lying under some camping gear and a mountain of marijuana stalks. "Pat, I'll keep an eye on these guys if you want to search the cab."

"Whoa!" exclaimed White, as he stuck his head inside the cab. Even with both doors wide open, the overwhelming stench of marijuana permeated the truck's interior. "No wonder these guys are messed up."

Sergeant White removed three fully loaded rifles, with live rounds in all three chambers. He gingerly unloaded the weapons and placed them inside the Fish and Game patrol truck. Returning to the deer poachers' pickup, he looked under and behind the bench seat. "Looks like we've got some bud here," said White, as he uncovered another forty pounds of marijuana. A spotlight, which had obviously been used to take the three deer, was still hot to the touch and lying on the floorboard.

When all the evidence had been inventoried, Szody and White shook their heads in disbelief.

"All three of 'em are stoned," Sergeant White said. "That big guy must have smoked pounds of the stuff to be as messed up as he is."

Warden Szody radioed dispatch and requested that a caged sheriff's unit join them to transport the three suspects to the county jail in Eureka. A tow truck was also dispatched to transport the poachers' pickup to the Fish and Game yard for storage and further inventory.

By the time Szody and White headed home, it was almost daylight. Both officers were exhausted, but adrenaline still coursed through their veins. "You know what those idiots did?" said White, as he began analyzing the situation. "They were out poaching deer when they stumbled onto someone else's marijuana grove. After dark, they came back to steal the plants. I wouldn't be surprised if they broke into a cabin or a barn to get at the dried stuff."

Their conversation continued until daylight, when Szody and White reached the Rio Dell Police Department. Szody dropped White off in the parking lot, where his personal pickup was still sitting. "Good thing you're off today," said Szody. "Be careful going home and thanks for everything."

The next morning, Warden Szody filed formal criminal complaints against the three deer poachers. They were charged with felony possession of marijuana, unlawful take and possession of three deer, and having loaded rifles in their vehicle while on a public thoroughfare. No one ever reported a cabin break-in, for obvious reasons.

Because the subjects did not have prior criminal records, their sentences were minimal. One of them received a year in the county jail and the other two did six months.

Apparently the driver, Ronald James Limacher, liked jail so much that he wanted to go back. A year or so later, he saw Pat White driving through town in the Whites' family car— took several shots at him—hitting the car several times. The off-duty policeman wheeled around and chased after Limacher, who fled the scene in his pickup. Although Limacher escaped at the time, he was eventually arrested, convicted in court, and sent to state prison.

Night Patrol on Lake Shasta

Having spent a few years in the damp, marijuana-infested forests of Humboldt County, Warden Dave Szody saw an opening and took it. He applied for a recently vacated warden's position in my lieutenant's district. Szody's new patrol district would cover the mountainous southeast portion of Shasta County, fulfilling a lifelong dream he and his wife had of living in the mountains. They moved to the small mountain community of Shingletown in September of 1983.

It had been almost five years since Warden Szody and I had worked together. We took up our friendship where it had left off, although I was now officially Szody's supervisor. One warm fall evening we hopped into the Shasta Lake patrol boat and headed east on California's largest reservoir. This mammoth body of water is fed by three major rivers—the Sacramento, the McCloud, and the Pit. Several smaller year-round streams and hundreds of ephemeral streams also flow into the lake.

Deer season was open and it was not uncommon for someone to go out in a boat and spotlight a nice buck. Deer were all over the shore and they had become accustomed to house-boaters feeding them everything from peanut butter sandwiches to ice cream bars.

Szody and I managed to patrol the Dry Creek arm and a portion of the main lake before dark. We contacted a few fishermen, but saw no one who had killed a deer or looked as if they intended to. By the time we reached the confluence of the Pit River and Squaw Creek, the sunlight had disappeared and a partial moon peeked over the treetops. The lights of Jones Valley Marina were visible to the south, and we saw nothing but a half mile of glassy smooth water in all other directions. I cut the engine and we came to a stop in the middle of the lake. With all lights turned off, Szody and I would sit and wait for the telltale sound of gunshots in the distance. On a still night such as this one, the slightest sound would carry across the water and be heard for miles.

All we heard during the first two hours of our all-night stakeout were our own voices. It was about 11:00 p.m., when we noticed the running lights of a small skiff coming out of Jones Valley Marina. Instead of heading up the Pit River or the Squaw Creek arm of the lake, the boat came to a stop about two hundred yards from the south shore—a good half mile from where we were sitting. The operator of the boat cut the motor; the silence was interrupted by the splash of an anchor being dropped over the side.

Bored from the inactivity, Szody and I focused our binoculars on these recent arrivals. That particular night, we did not have a night vision scope, which turned out to be a good thing. The brilliant beam of an overhead lantern suddenly lit up the distant skiff. Anyone watching with a night scope could have sustained serious eye damage.

"It looks like four people are on board," whispered Szody. "They're getting ready to do some fishing." Although the boat was lit up like a Christmas tree, the occupants would not be able to see anything outside the immediate glow of the lantern. We were looking for deer poachers, but watching these fishermen would at least keep us awake until something more exciting came along.

Szody and I continued to watch the four fishermen. Based on the high pitch of some of the voices we heard and all the giggling, we guessed that two of them were women. As midnight approached, a slight breeze caused our boat to drift ever closer. The only sounds on the entire lake seemed to be raucous laughter coming from the lit-up skiff. When we drifted within a hundred yards, their voices came through loud and clear. Szody and I were finally ten yards outside the beam of their lantern when we heard one of the women say, "You know Nancy and I don't have fishing licenses. What happens if a game warden catches us?"

"You think a game warden is going to be out here at this time of night?" replied the man sitting next to her, laughing.

"The game wardens are all home in bed," offered the man at the opposite end of the skiff.

"I hope you're right," said Nancy.

All four subjects were holding fishing rods, with lines in the water, as we finally drifted into the beam of their overhead lantern. The man in the stern of the boat was in the middle of a joke when he noticed the two uniformed officers watching him from ten feet away. His jaw dropped as Warden Szody said, "How is everybody doing?"

No one responded. The men stared in disbelief and the women directed angry looks at their respective boyfriends.

"Do you all have your fishing licenses?" asked Szody. Of course he already knew the answer to that question. As expected, the two men produced current licenses and the two women just sat there, eyes flashing daggers. The tension was thick enough to cut with a knife, when a distant shot rang out. The resonating report of a high powered rifle echoed across the water.

Szody and I swiveled our necks toward the Pit Arm of the lake, where the shot had come from. "I hope you folks have learned your lesson," I said. "Game wardens never sleep." I turned the ignition key and dropped the patrol boat into gear. In seconds we were headed east and out of sight.

The shot seemed to have originated in Clickapudi Inlet, a half mile up the Pit Arm of Shasta Lake. As we approached the mouth of the inlet, I cut the motor. From that point forward, we would black out and drop the running speed to a barely audible level. It was 1:00 a.m. and a half moon lit the way, preventing the patrol boat from running aground or hitting one of the many tree snags that filled the inlet at low water.

For the first quarter mile, there was no sign of activity. We rounded the second bend and still saw no light and no other boat. I was concerned that we had misread the direction of the shot and wasted valuable time investigating the wrong inlet. Just then, Szody tapped me on the shoulder and whispered that he heard something up ahead. I maintained the boat's current speed for a few more yards and completely cut the engine. Our forward momentum carried us toward the east shore.

Szody and I climbed out of the boat and quietly tied the bow to a nearby snag. On foot, we crept toward a point overlooking the end of the cove. As I had done many times before, I cautioned Szody to step carefully and watch out for snakes. It was still warm enough for rattlers and the driftwood that littered the shoreline made ideal habitat.

A man's voice resounded in the quiet night air. "Bring me a rag."

I directed my binoculars toward the voice and could barely make out a human figure at the water's edge. About thirty yards to the right, the beam of a flashlight moved in the direction of the human figure. "I think that guy is gutting a deer," I whispered. We decided to be patient and let things play out.

Twenty minutes went by and the man at the water's edge began washing his hands. Both subjects grabbed whatever it was that they had been working on and dragged it across the ground in a westerly direction. I suspected it was a deer, but it could have been a pig, a young elk, or even a mountain lion. I had recently arrested three men for shooting a mountain lion on Backbone Ridge, about a mile to the south. "One, two, three," commanded a voice in the darkness. We heard the thud of a heavy object landing on the deck of a boat. "Throw that tarp over it," said the same voice.

Szody and I listened for a few more minutes before heading back to the patrol boat. As we climbed in, we heard the sound of a distant boat motor kicking over. "That's it," I whispered. Szody grabbed a powerful handheld spotlight and I started the engine.

Before the suspects' boat could pull away from shore, we were bearing down on them. "Department of Fish and Game," shouted Szody. "Turn off your motor and stay right where you are!" With the intense beam of our spotlight in their eyes, both men froze like the proverbial deer in the headlights. These spotlighters were ironically getting a taste of their own medicine. The deer, or whatever it was that they had just killed, probably saw much the same thing seconds before a bullet ripped into its body.

I ordered the two men to sit in their boat while Warden Szody climbed aboard. Unlike the local dirtbags that we might expect to encounter at that time of night, these forty-plus-year-olds were dressed like city slickers— Roughneck jeans, Filson coats, and brand new $150 hunting boots.

Dave had to step over an assortment of fishing rods and a large object covered with a tarp. As Szody and I suspected, beneath the tarp was a freshly killed deer—a nice little three point buck. It came as no surprise that a deer tag had already been attached to the deer's antlers. I looked at my watch and noticed that it was 1:45 a.m. The tag had been filled out to show the deer being killed at 6:30 a.m., later that same morning and after daylight. I noticed a spotlight much like ours lying in the bow section of the boat. Things were becoming increasingly complicated for the two poachers.

Our two spotlighters had Sacramento addresses. Because they weren't locals, there had to be a houseboat nearby. The man who shot the deer finally admitted that they had come from a houseboat anchored up the Pit Arm, a few miles away. I said we would follow them and make sure they got back all right, although their well-being wasn't exactly my primary concern—if they had poached one deer, there might be others. We had one of the men ride with us and the other operate their boat. Keeping the suspects separated would prevent them from coordinating stories, should we find additional evidence at the houseboat.

Operating in the dim moonlight, we took almost an hour to arrive at the houseboat. As we pulled alongside, I noticed a second skiff tied to the bow, with several fishing rods leaning over the gunnels. Now Szody and I knew that others were involved. Szody jumped onto the deck while I tied us off.

After we were aboard the houseboat with our two suspects, lights came on inside the cabin and two more middle-aged men appeared—eyes as big as saucers and features slack with shock. "I told them they were gonna get caught," mumbled one man under his breath.

"We are tired and in no mood for shenanigans," I said. My partner and I would like you all to sit here in your deck chairs while we search the boat for more deer. The sooner we complete our task, the sooner we get out of here and you guys can get some sleep."

Based on the crimes we had already witnessed, we had no shortage of probable cause, giving us legal authority to search the boat and its contents.

I found several bass in one of the outside ice chests and a few more in a metal box-stringer hanging off the side of the boat. That discovery paled in comparison to what I found in the cabin refrigerator. When I opened the refrigerator door, a huge pile of bass spilled out onto the deck. Each licensed fisherman was allowed to possess one legal limit of five bass. These guys had a total of sixty-three, an over-limit of forty-three bass for the entire group.

The two deer poachers would be charged with possession of an unlawfully taken deer—during closed hours and with a spotlight. The owner of the deer tag would also be charged with license fraud—making false statements on a deer tag. All four men were charged with joint possession of forty-three bass over the legal limit. The deer, the rifle that was used to kill the deer, and forty-three bass were seized into evidence.

As Szody and I maneuvered the patrol boat into our Bridge Bay Marina slip, the sun was just coming up.

"Not a bad night," said Szody.

"Yeah," I replied, stifling a yawn. "We made a good deer case, a good bass case, and scared the daylights out of that group that was fishing. Why don't we drop the deer at the rescue mission on the way through town. There's usually somebody up all night."

"I'll take the fish to Mrs. Farmer tomorrow," said Szody. "That eagle she's rehabbing will have bass to eat for two months."

Gill Netters

Man has devised many ingenious tools for catching fish. The simplest and best known is the hook and line. According to California's freshwater fishing regulations, the only way a person can legally catch a fish is with a closely attended hook and line. That doesn't mean people won't try other methods, particularly when a profitable catch is the result.

Back in 1987, it wasn't that difficult to knock on the back door of a north coast fish market or restaurant and sell a freshly caught twenty-pound salmon for fifty dollars or more. One of the more effective but highly illegal methods of catching salmon and steelhead is with a centuries-old invention called a gill net.

Modern day commercial gill nets are generally made of transparent monofilament fiber that is difficult, if not impossible, for fish and non-target animals to see under water. The mesh size depends on the species of fish the fisherman is trying to catch. The object is for the fish to poke its head in the mesh but not be able to fit its entire body through. When it tries to back out, its gills get stuck, hence the name "gill net."

Some gill nets, such as the one referred to in this chapter, may be a hundred feet long or shorter. Such a net would be manageable from the shore or a small boat. Longer gill nets, such as those used by commercial fishing fleets all over the world, can extend for hundreds of miles.

II

California's north coast is blessed with some of the most beautiful and productive salmon and steelhead spawning streams in the country. Sportsmen come from all over the world to fish the Klamath, Smith, and Eel Rivers. Just as productive, but not so well-known are the Mattole, Van Duzen, and Madd Rivers. The Madd River, fifteen miles north of Eureka, is reputed to offer some of the largest steelhead on record—and that's where this story begins.

Our hero is California Fish and Game Warden Nick Albert. Nick was a member of the North Coast Squad, working out of Eureka. Like me, Albert had been hired by the California Department of Fish and Game in 1974. While I had drawn Earp as my first patrol district, Nick ended up in a significantly larger community called San Francisco, a few miles up the coast from his hometown of Monterey. Warden Albert was no stranger to law enforcement. He had been a patrolman for Seaside Police Department before being hired by the Department of Fish and Game. Seaside was a bedroom community for Fort Ord—one of the U.S. Army's largest training centers—and had its share of enforcement problems. At five feet nine and 170 pounds, Nick Albert wasn't a big guy, but this former high school wrestler was the kind of officer you wanted with you if an arrest had to be made.

San Francisco proved to be an ideal training area, with a little bit of everything: commercial fishing, sport fishing, fish markets, water pollution, stream alteration, animal welfare, falconers, pet shops, and waterfowl hunting. Every day was a new adventure and the first two years flew by like a flock of canvasbacks racing across the bay. After two and a half years in the crowded Bay Area, Nick had experienced enough of big city life. He transferred to Humboldt County, the land of salmon filled rivers and trees that reach for the clouds.

On November 28, 1987, at 6:15 a.m., the telephone rang at the Eureka home of Warden Nick Albert. Nick already knew it was a work-related call when he answered the phone. At that time of morning it had to be the Humboldt County Sheriff's dispatcher or a private individual reporting a violation—someone poaching a deer, spearing a salmon, or operating a bulldozer in one of a thousand spawning streams.

"Department of Fish and Game," answered Albert.

"Yeah, I was walking upstream from the Hammond Trail Bridge when I saw a net stretched across the river," said the adult male caller. "There was a little orange boat on the opposite bank, near the end of the net."

"Are we talking about the Madd River Bridge, downstream from Highway 101?"

"Yes, I live not too far from there."

"How far from the bridge was this?"

"Are you familiar with the Piling Hole, where those cement pilings are sticking out of the water?"

"Yes, it's about two hundred yards up from the bridge, isn't it?"

"That's right. The net is right there."

"Did you see anyone around?"

"No, but there was a green pickup parked under the bridge. I didn't get close enough to see if there was anybody in it."

"Can I get your phone number in case I need to call you back?"

"I would kinda like to stay out of this. There are some scary people around here and I live nearby."

"I understand," replied Albert, about to walk out the back door and climb into his patrol truck. "We appreciate the call."

Just upstream from the Madd River Estuary was the so-called "Piling Hole." The river deepened as it approached the estuary, slowing the current and creating ideal conditions for the operator of an illegal gill net. Many of the local outlaws were well aware of this situation and willing to risk going to jail for a pickup load of fresh-run salmon or steelhead. There were hundreds of places like this on North Coast rivers and streams, but only a handful of wardens to patrol them. Reports from private citizens were critical to the enforcement effort.

Warden Albert cut his headlights and slowed his patrol vehicle as he approached the Hammond Trail Bridge. It was still dark, but there was a glimmer of light in the eastern sky. He parked about fifty feet back and continued toward the bridge on foot. Just as the informant had described, a green Ford pickup was parked under the bridge, next to one of the south pillars. Albert made a cursory inspection of the pickup, which had no license plates in front or back. Inside the pickup bed he saw an upside-down wheelbarrow and a pair of brown, Hi-Tec boots.

Warden Albert decided to cross the bridge and approach the Piling Hole from the north bank. The thick riparian vegetation on that side of the river would provide ample cover, allowing him to survey the area without being seen. His heart pounding from the adrenaline rush, he continued a slow jog and then a fast walk upstream.

Through the leafless alders at the edge of the river, Albert could see the partially submerged pilings. He methodically scanned the area with binoculars and spotted a line of white, telltale gill net floats, stretched across the entire channel. The north end of the net was tied to a piling and the south end was anchored to something near the opposite beach.

"There's that little orange boat," mumbled Albert, continuing to scan the south shoreline. "And what do we have here?" Lying near the boat was a human figure inside a sleeping bag. "Did you get a little cold last night?" whispered Albert, as though the subject in the sleeping bag could hear him. Early morning temperatures had dropped below freezing, in spite of the ocean influence.

Warden Albert realized he was going to need help. He couldn't be on both sides of the river at the same time. With the portable radio attached to his gun belt, he contacted Humboldt County Sheriff's dispatch and requested an immediate backup from Fish and Game Patrol Captain Brian Replogle. Nick knew that it would take Replogle at least forty-five minutes to respond. He also knew that his best chance of reaching the net was on the south side of the river. Albert turned around and backtracked downstream toward the bridge.

By the time Albert reached the bridge, there was plenty of sunlight, so he dropped behind a railing and directed his binoculars toward the gill net. He was just in time to see a man paddling across the river in the little orange boat. A few minutes later, the same man was freeing the gill net from the cement piling.

It's getting light, thought Nick. *It figures that this guy might be getting ready to leave. Should I wait for backup here by his truck or move in now, catch him in the act and make sure he doesn't get away?*

Twenty-four years and two promotions later, now retired Patrol Captain Nick Albert provided me with a little insight into the decisions he made that day. "Catching a gill-netter in the act was so difficult and rare that I was desperate not to let the violator escape. On the North Coast it was one of our major violations. I had hoped to catch him before he made it very far but that isn't what happened. Even though things worked out in the end, in hindsight I would have done it differently."

Without waiting for backup, the young, enthusiastic warden crossed the bridge and began a slow sprint up the south side of the river. Most of the south shoreline was exposed sandy beach with very few hiding places—Nick would have to stay out of sight the best he could and hope for the best. Fortunately, the original suspect and an adult female were busy pulling in the gill net as Albert approached.

Warden Albert stopped behind a pile of driftwood and watched the two gill netters remove a large salmon from the net. The woman was medium height, thin, and looked like she hadn't used a hairbrush in weeks. She wore a bright red, full-length coat. Albert watched her pick up the salmon by the gills and carry it across the beach toward a patch of high grass. The adult male suspect was about Albert's size, with short brown hair and a mustache. Both subjects appeared to be in their early to mid-thirties. The man continued to work on the net, removing debris and attempting to untangle a large steelhead.

I've seen enough, thought Albert. *It's time to end this thing.*

Stepping away from his cover, Warden Albert walked across the beach toward the violators. The woman, later identified as Marla Kay Vinuchi, spotted the warden first and dropped the salmon she was carrying. "State Fish and Game!" shouted Albert. "Stay right where you are." The male suspect, later identified as Ronald DeWayne Tucker, was preoccupied with trying to untangle the steelhead. When he finally saw the officer approaching, he jumped to his feet and stared, wild-eyed, back at him. Brandishing a large hunting knife, Tucker began walking toward Warden Albert.

"Drop the knife and stay right where you are," ordered Albert. Tucker ignored the command and kept coming. When he had reached a point Warden Albert considered his minimum danger zone, Albert drew his revolver. "I am not going to tell you again, drop the knife!" Tucker finally came to a standstill and tossed the knife aside. His eyes still had the crazed look of a trapped animal. Although no longer armed with a knife, Tucker was clearly weighing his options. Albert flashed back to the suspect's green pickup, which was missing both the front and back license plates; this scofflaw had little use for society's rules and regulations.

"Show me your ID," Warden Albert demanded, without lowering his gun.

"Gotta take off my chest waders first," Tucker said in a gruff yet whiny voice.

"Go ahead," Albert said, gesturing with the gun.

"That net ain't mine," said Tucker, as he took his time removing the chest waders. "Me and my girlfriend … we was just camping on the beach. We seen the net and thought we'd get it outta the river."

"I've been watching you for the last hour. You're both under arrest."

Upon being advised that he was under arrest, Tucker jumped to his feet, dove into the river and began swimming toward the other side. Vinuchi ran off in the opposite direction.

With the ambient air temperature in the thirties and the water not much warmer, Tucker's stunt took the young warden completely by surprise. Determined to prevent Tucker's escape, Warden Albert threw all caution aside, dropped his radio on the beach and dove in after him—in full uniform, including gun belt, boots, and jacket. He caught up with Tucker about a third of the way across the river. Already tiring, Tucker grabbed at Albert, trying to climb on his back. Warden Albert came to the wise conclusion that an arrest in ten feet of water could be extremely dangerous, particularly with a .357 Magnum revolver hanging from his waist, and the overwhelming weight of boots and a wet uniform pulling him down in the brutally cold water. He pushed Tucker away and swam back to the south shore.

Albert reached the shore and sloshed his way toward the orange rowboat.

Water gushed from the hole at the bottom of his holster and his soaked jacket weighed him down with every awkward step. Tucker had continued swimming across the river and was now crying out for help.

What a mess, thought Albert. *Now that crazy son of a bitch is about to drown.*

Albert picked up his portable radio, dragged the tiny row boat to the water's edge and jumped aboard. With a single oar to use as a paddle, he thrashed across the river, fighting the fatigue overtaking his frozen, water-soaked body. A few minutes earlier, Warden Albert's primary concern had been preventing the gill-netter from getting away. Now it was saving the man's life.

Meanwhile, Marla Vinuchi had made her way to a nearby road, where she tried to pay a couple fishermen to drive her into town. One of the fishermen happened to be the original informant. When he told her that he knew she was involved with the gill net and the game warden was after her, she ran back into the brush and disappeared.

Tucker continued to swim toward the north shore, all the while yelling for help. He managed to reach the shore just ahead of the rapidly paddling warden. In his stocking feet, Tucker climbed the steep riverbank and, for a few minutes, was out of Albert's sight. Warden Albert beached the boat and grabbed his radio.

"Outrun this," said Albert, gasping for breath and still soaked to the gills. "Humboldt Dispatch, Fish and Game 1313."

"Go ahead Fish and Game 1313."

"I would like to request a BOLO" (be on the lookout).

"Go ahead with your information."

"The adult male subject was last seen at 0845 hours, on the north bank of the Madd River, approximately one half mile downstream from Highway 101. He is running in the direction of Highway 101." Albert paused to catch his breath. "The subject is described as a white male, approximately thirty-five years old, five feet eight inches tall, with brown hair and a mustache. He was last seen wearing brown overalls and a blue jacket."

"Ten-four," said the dispatcher.

Water dripped from Warden Albert's clothing as he reached the top of the riverbank. He could see Tucker running across a pasture, in the direction of Highway 101.

"Humboldt Dispatch, Fish and Game 1313."

"Go ahead Fish and Game 1313."

"Be advised that the subject has removed his brown overalls and jacket. He is now wearing dark colored blue jeans, a white long-sleeved shirt and no shoes."

"Ten-four," said the dispatcher. "CHP has been advised of your BOLO and is responding."

Not to be deterred, Warden Albert continued his foot pursuit of Tucker. The desperate fish poacher had a hundred yard lead, but was slowed considerably by his lack of footwear and sore feet. He had climbed the rise leading to Highway 101 and was no doubt expecting to flag someone down and be halfway home before the exhausted warden reached the highway. What Tucker found, instead, was a black and white California Highway Patrol unit and two officers waiting to take him into custody.

When Warden Albert appeared on the scene a few minutes later, Tucker was already cuffed and sitting in the back of the CHP unit. Nick identified the suspect and established that Tucker and Vinuchi were from the nearby town of McKinleyville. He radioed Captain Replogle and advised him that the female accomplice was on foot and might be headed for McKinleyville. Vinuchi was described as thirty years old, five feet four inches tall, with dishwater blond hair. She was last seen wearing a red coat.

Replogle had just taken the Guintoli exit off Highway 101 and was headed toward the Hammond Trail Bridge. As he raced down Madd River Beach Road, a woman stepped out of the brush and flagged him down; she fit the description given by Albert and was wearing a red coat. When the woman realized that the green sedan was a Fish and Game patrol car, she did an about-face and began to walk away. Replogle managed to detain her long enough for Warden Albert to arrive in the CHP unit, along with Tucker. Albert identified Vinuchi as Tucker's accomplice and arrested her.

Captain Replogle transported Tucker and Vinuchi to the Humboldt County Jail, where they were booked for taking salmon and steelhead with a gill net and for resisting arrest. Tucker had been arrested before and knew enough to keep his mouth shut. Vinuchi, on the other hand, jabbered all the way to jail. "Ronnie just got fired and we needed money," she whined. "What are we supposed to do?"

"Shut up, Marla," said Tucker.

Warden Albert went back to the scene of the crime and began gathering evidence. He found the overalls that Tucker had stashed on the north side of the river; inside were keys to the green Ford pickup parked under the bridge. Also in the overalls were Tucker's California Driver's License, a California Fishing License, Tucker's Social Security Card, and two hundred and fifty-five dollars in cash. The cash had probably come from selling unlawfully taken salmon and steelhead. Albert seized and photographed a one-hundred-foot gill net, three large gill-netted salmon, and one large gill-netted steelhead, all lying on the south beach. The orange boat that Albert had left on the north side of the river was also eventually recovered and seized into evidence.

Later that morning, Warden Albert met Captain Replogle and a California Highway Patrol officer at the green Ford pickup that was parked under the bridge; the wheelbarrow was still lying upside-down in the bed. Fresh fish blood covered the wheelbarrow, which had obviously been used to transport the gill net and fish to and from fishing sites. Surprisingly, the doors to the pickup were unlocked. A fully loaded .22 caliber pistol was lying on the floorboard in front of the driver's seat.

Hindsight is always 20/20. Nick Albert says if he had to do it all over again, he would have ordered Tucker to leave his waders on and waited for Captain Replogle to arrive—a man isn't going to run or swim very far wearing chest waders. As it turned out, Tucker and Vinuchi both bailed out of jail before their trial date and fled to Louisiana. Warden Albert did some additional investigation and found out that just prior to the gill-netting incident, Tucker had been fired from a McKinleyville lumber mill for bringing a loaded pistol to work.

Warden Nick Albert went on to enjoy a long and productive career. He retired as a patrol captain in December of 2005. Federal statistics indicate that the two most dangerous law enforcement jobs in America are drug enforcement agent (DEA) and game warden. These criteria are based on the chance of being killed on duty. A very high percentage of the people that wildlife officers deal with are carrying firearms. More often than not, Fish and Game officers are working alone, miles from the closest backup.

Fortunately for Warden Albert, Ronald Tucker had left his loaded pistol on the floorboard of his pickup and did not have it hidden in his chest waders when Albert confronted him. Tucker's desperate actions, before, during and after this incident, clearly indicate that he was highly irrational and extremely dangerous. This case could have ended quite differently, but turned out to be just another adventure in the life of a California Fish and Game warden.

Outnumbered

M ost of the time large deer camps are occupied by friendly, law-abiding hunters, happy to have their deer validated and get a chance to ask the game warden a few questions. Every deer opener, however, we seemed to find at least one camp occupied by hunters with very little respect for game laws.

An experienced warden could detect a "dirty" camp within minutes of entering. The laughing and talking would end abruptly and people would drop out of sight. We would then discover all kinds of deer tag shenanigans: untagged, slick-tagged (tag not filled out), tagged with the wrong tag for that particular deer zone or tagged by people who hadn't killed the deer—many of whom had never fired a rifle in their lives. The law required a hunter to fill out his lawfully issued deer tag and place it on the buck's antlers immediately after the deer was killed. Once the tag was filled out and placed on the deer's antlers, it had to remain there until fifteen days after the close of deer season. The tag could not be used again and—unless this was a two-deer zone—the hunter had reached his season limit. He was done deer hunting in California until the following season.

Some "game hogs" would surreptitiously transport their deer home without filling their tag out and placing it on the deer's antlers; this meant they could illegally reuse their tag later and thereby exceed the season limit. Others would acquire the tags of friends or relatives, not using their own tag until the season was about to end—another unlawful means of exceeding the season limit. It was our job to expose these scams and take the appropriate enforcement action. Maintaining control of the situation was absolutely essential—a difficult task if the warden was significantly outnumbered.

II

On September 18, 1988, Warden Nick Albert and his reserve warden, Mel Thoreson, were patrolling the Pilot Hill area of Humboldt County. It was the second day of deer season and hunters were everywhere.

"Wow!" said Thoreson. "Did you see all the people in that camp? There must be ten pickups parked there."

"That bunch is camped in there every deer season," replied Albert. "We almost caught a couple of 'em spotlighting last year."

"They sure gave us the look when we went by," continued Thoreson.

"That's funny," said Albert. "Why would all those hunters be standing around the fire at 10:30 in the morning of the second day of deer season?"

"I was wondering the same thing," said Thoreson.

"We're going to turn around and drive by again," said Albert. "See what they do and try not to be too conspicuous."

Warden Albert drove his patrol truck past the suspicious camp and continued a half mile down the road. When they were clearly out of sight, he pulled over and turned off the motor. Albert told his reserve warden they were going to sneak back to the camp on foot and find out what those hunters were up to. There had to be a reason they were all in camp at this hour of the morning and not out in the woods deer hunting.

With careful, deliberate footsteps, Albert and Thoreson worked their way through the woods. They had reached a clearing about a hundred yards from the camp, when something caught their attention. A man at the far end of the clearing was bending over what appeared to be a small buck. With the aid of binoculars, Albert could see that the man was attaching a tag to the deer's antlers. Warden Albert recognized the man as Russ McCabe, a well-known violator who lived in Eureka.

McCabe was a husky, six-foot-two-inch borderline moron who gauged his success in life by the number of mounted deer heads hanging from the walls of his single-wide mobile home. He spent most of the money he earned at the tire shop paying taxidermists, drinking beer with his now thirty-year-old high school buddies, and buying hunting equipment. Still unaware of the officers, McCabe had begun dragging the deer toward camp. Every ten yards or so, he would stop and look around.

Before McCabe could reach his destination, Warden Albert walked up behind him and said, "What are you up to, Russ?"

McCabe's face turned bright red and his eyes grew wide with fright. Without a word, he let go of the deer's antlers and started heading toward the camp.

"I want you to stay right here until I take a look at your deer tag," ordered Albert.

McCabe reluctantly stood by while Warden Albert checked out the tag attached to his little forked horn buck's antlers. McCabe's deer was barely legal, having a tiny fork on one side and a spike on the other—spike bucks being protected in California.

This guy couldn't have known it was legal when he pulled the trigger, Albert thought.

McCabe's tag was not filled out, as required by law. His deer was cold and had obviously been dead for some time. Warden Albert suspected that McCabe had gotten spooked when he saw the Fish and Game truck drive by and rushed out to put a tag on his buck. After obtaining McCabe's identification, Albert instructed him to bring his deer and follow them into camp.

You could have heard a pine needle drop when Warden Albert and Reserve Warden Thoreson walked into the suspicious deer camp—Russ McCabe close behind, dragging his deer. Everyone stopped what he was doing and stared at the two uniformed officers. Albert spotted three bucks hanging near the edge of camp. Examining their tags, he found two in order, while one was not filled out. This "slick tag" was also the wrong one for that particular deer zone (B-1). The buck in question had been killed by a man named Kelly Dale Brooks.

When Warden Albert asked for Brooks's identification, all hell broke loose. It was as if the wardens had walked up to a hornet's nest and bashed it with a baseball bat—the entire camp started buzzing. Some of the hunters actually jumped into their pickups and attempted to leave. Based on the two illegally taken deer that Albert and Thoreson had already discovered, Warden Albert ordered everyone to remain in camp until his inspection was completed. The two officers were outnumbered fifteen-to-two, so maintaining control of the situation was not going to be easy.

Warden Albert knew that something was seriously wrong. Leaving Thoreson to keep an eye on the camp, he returned to the area where he had first seen McCabe with his illegal deer. Walking across the clearing, he noticed a pile of tree branches that had been intentionally stacked in place. Removing the branches, Albert found two forked horn bucks, both skinned, gutted and placed in white deer bags. Both were untagged. Things were getting more complicated all the time.

Warden Albert realized that he and his reserve warden needed help to keep track of fifteen hunters, all seemingly going in different directions.

Thoreson provided a set of eyes and ears, but he was only a reserve and had limited authority.

Patrol Lieutenant Steve Conger and Warden Jon Dunn were patrolling about ten miles away, so Albert radioed them and requested their immediate assistance.

"Let me have your attention," shouted Albert. We have some untagged deer here and I am ordering everyone to stay in camp until we get to the bottom of this."

Jake and Jarret Sugg, close friends of McCabe's, took Warden Albert's order as an invitation to scram. They turned and bolted into the woods.

All manner of chaos threatened to break loose when Kelly Brooks's sixty-two-year-old father—the owner of Brooks's Tire Shop—stepped forward and asked, "What's the problem, officer?"

"There are two untagged bucks unaccounted for," Warden Albert explained. "If no one claims them, I'll have to charge everyone in camp with joint possession of two unlawfully taken deer."

Brooks employed seven of the thirteen men still in camp. He called a meeting and within a few minutes, a man named Ronald Chaney stepped forward and said, in a quavery voice, "Those deer are mine."

Warden Albert wasn't buying it. Chaney only stood about five-six and weighed 130 pounds, soaking wet. Albert figured the smallest man in the group had been bullied into claiming the deer. He read Chaney his Miranda rights and after a series of questions was convinced that Chaney had killed at least one of the deer hidden under the branches. Chaney had apparently intended to kill even more deer, as evidenced by the two unused B-1 deer tags that Warden Albert found in his pocket. The tags were seized into evidence, along with the two untagged deer.

About that time, Lieutenant Conger and Warden Dunn arrived. When McCabe, Brooks, and Cheney had been properly identified and issued citations, Warden Albert asked if there were any more deer in camp or hidden outside. After a long pause, one of the hunters spoke up—a more senior member of the crowd with a weather-beaten face and bloodshot eyes. "No more dead deer, here!" the man said, gesturing broadly in every direction.

Based on his experience with this group, Albert seriously doubted the truthfulness of this man's answer. He advised everyone within hearing range that should they find any additional deer, the responsible parties would be charged with "failure to show on demand," in addition to any other violation.

Lieutenant Conger and Reserve Warden Thoreson walked outside the camp and began looking for additional deer. They found the two Sugg brothers—looking like two of your scarier extras in the cast of *Deliverance*—

hiding in some nearby brush. Jake and Jarred had fresh blood on their hands and wore defiant expressions.

With the likelihood of still more purloined deer stashed outside the camp, all four officers went to investigate. A few minutes into their search, Warden Albert asked who was keeping an eye on the hunters still in camp. Warden Dunn was closest to the camp so he sprinted in that direction. Dunn arrived just in time to catch Jake Sugg and a younger man, Scott Ryerson, dragging two more untagged forked horned bucks toward a waiting jeep. These deer had been hidden under some boards and a tarp at the edge of camp. Sugg and Ryerson were charged with possession of two unlawfully taken deer and failure to show on demand.

With four officers now present, they had enough authority to force everyone in camp to sit down in one location. Thoreson and Dunn were put in charge of supervising the hunters while Albert and Conger conducted a thorough search of the rest of the camp and the surrounding area. No other deer were found.

Six unlawfully taken deer were seized into evidence, all forked horned bucks. Charges were filed against Jake Sugg, Scott Ryerson, Ronald Chaney, Russell McCabe, and Kelly Brooks.

Although they had no way to prove it, the officers involved in the case suspected that all eight deer found in or near this camp had been shot illegally—after dark, with the aid of a spotlight. That would explain the group's better than average success rate and the fact that they were hanging around camp all morning.

No one had slept the night before.

Patrol to Fenders Ferry

One of the most enjoyable aspects of my job as a wildlife protection officer was patrolling. There was always the possibility of adventure as I drove through the countryside or skimmed across the water, looking for signs of illegal activity while enjoying nature in all its glory. I never knew what I was going to see or what type of violations I might encounter.

One of my favorite patrols was Fenders Ferry Road, north of Shasta Lake. Patrolling this long and winding dirt road over the mountains, through the woods and past four breathtakingly beautiful streams—the McCloud River, Squaw Creek, Potem Creek, and the Pit River—could take anywhere between four hours and an entire day, depending on what you ran into along the way.

Late one December afternoon, Warden Dave Szody and I were patrolling Gilman Road, north of Shasta Lake. We reached the McCloud River Bridge and stopped to admire this magnificent stretch of crystal clear, cerulean blue water. "That has to be the prettiest river in California," I said. "Too bad most people never get to see it."

Upstream from the bridge, much of the river was gated private property. An exclusive hunting club had closed the first few miles, a rich coffee heiress owned the property above that, and the Hearst Estate encompassed much of the rest. As Szody and I climbed out of the truck and scanned the river upstream from the bridge, I regaled him with a memory from my youth.

While working at the Mount Shasta State Fish Hatchery during the summer of 1966, I had learned an interesting story about the McCloud River and Dolly Varden trout. At that time, the McCloud River and its tributaries were the only streams in California where this rare species of trout still existed. As an enthusiastic seasonal hatchery employee about to enter college, I was fascinated by the three-foot-long Dolly Varden trout that swam around in the hatchery's display pond. "Where did that beautiful fish come from?" I asked.

Rube Davenport had worked at the hatchery since back in late twenties and was a walking encyclopedia of historic lore. He explained that a few years earlier, one of the caretakers at the nearby Hearst Estate had trapped several mice in one of the residences that had been closed up for the winter. Evidently the caretaker had swept one of the mice into the McCloud River, which flowed immediately below the building. Suddenly, a very large trout rose to the surface and swallowed the mouse. Amused by what he had seen, the caretaker swept another mouse off the footbridge and into the river. Again the trout rose and swallowed the mouse. The caretaker then grabbed a fishing rod and baited his hook with the remaining mouse. He tossed it off of the bridge and the next thing he knew he had a three foot long Dolly Varden on the end of his line. Some of the other employees at this Northern California Hearst Castle ran to the caretaker's aid. Upon landing the mammoth trout, they marveled at its unusual coloring—green with yellow spots.

The Castle's maintenance foreman telephoned the Mount Shasta Hatchery to see if they had any interest in saving the fish for display. A fish planting truck was immediately dispatched to Hearst Castle to pick up the fish and transport it back to the hatchery.

This rare and beautiful fish had been on display at the hatchery ever since and may have been one of the last, if not *the* last of its kind. Unfortunately, no Dolly Varden trout have been seen in the McCloud River or any of its tributaries for many years, and the original strain is believed to be extinct.

A couple of calls had come in the day before, complaining about people on Fenders Ferry Road shooting at squirrels out the window of a small, dark-colored foreign car. As we walked back to the patrol truck, Warden Szody and I discussed whether or not to make the long trip across to Fenders Ferry.

"It's three o'clock now," said Szody. "If we go all the way across to Fenders Ferry it will be at least seven before we arrive. Then it's another forty-five minutes out to the highway."

"If those guys are somewhere ahead of us, they should be coming out this way in the next couple hours," I replied. "Even if that group isn't up here, we might run into a couple of bear hunters. Let's do it."

It was one of those cold, dreary days, socked in with high clouds from the north. A few drops sprinkled the windshield but that was about it. Leaving the McCloud River behind, Szody stepped on the gas and accelerated up the hill. I pointed out that the lake was awfully low for that time of year and we needed rain badly. "There used to be a little resort and a camping area right down there," I said, pointing toward the river. "Our family came up here from Orland with my uncle and his family when I was a kid. Our dads went out in my uncle's boat and trolled for trout all day while the kids fished off a dock that's gone now. It rained so hard the day we left, we barely made it out in our old Oldsmobile."

The road to Fenders Ferry climbed for the first mile or so, then leveled out and traversed the mountainside for several more miles before dropping into a number of canyons. When Szody and I had traveled about five miles, we came across a small brown sedan. It was headed in the opposite direction and pulled to a stop near our patrol truck. We recognized the car and its three occupants as individuals we had contacted before.

"I remember these guys," said Szody, as we stepped out of the truck. Upon seeing us, the driver of the sedan turned off his motor, stepped out of the car, and handed Warden Szody his hunting license. I walked to the passenger side of the car. The man sitting in the front passenger seat handed me his hunting license through the open window. Without my asking, the man in back did the same.

"Mr. Saechao, how are you today?" I asked. "Do you guys have any game in the car?"

"Two squirrels," replied Saechao.

"Well let's have a look," I said.

The driver was already opening the trunk. These hunters must have been checked so many times that they knew the drill by heart. I reached inside the car and examined Saechao's shotgun for a possible live round in the chamber. Warden Szody did the same with the driver's shotgun and a .22 rifle in back. As Mr. Saechao had said, two gray squirrels lay in the trunk of the car. Neither Szody nor I sensed that anything was wrong, so we thanked the hunters for their time and sent them on their way.

Over the years, Warden Szody and I had checked thousands of hunters and fishermen—so many that we could usually sense a violation. Sometimes we were clued in by body language or nervousness; other times we detected a tiny feather on a car seat or a spot of blood on someone's boot. "Even these guys are having a hard time finding squirrels," said Szody, as we continued our patrol.

It was getting dark when we reached a wide spot in the road. An older model Plymouth sedan was parked at the canyon's edge: the kind of car Warden Szody and I referred to as a "tuna boat"—a long gas-guzzler with enough horsepower to run a small locomotive. "What do we have here?" I asked. "That car doesn't look familiar."

We climbed out of the patrol rig and quietly closed our doors. Szody felt the hood of the suspicious vehicle and whispered to me that it was cold— the occupants had been gone for some time. The car had Washington license plates. Through the windows, we could see a few scattered cassette tapes and a pair of small-sized sandals. I spotted a discarded .22 cartridge box on the floorboard, behind the driver's seat.

Just over the road bank was a frequently used foot trail leading into a heavily vegetated canyon. I suggested that we back off and wait for the hunters to come out. That late in the day, they could have anything—a couple of squirrels, a game bag full of mountain quail and song birds or possibly a closed-season deer. Szody and I formulated a plan: I would take my hand-held portable radio and watch from above the road while he drove the patrol truck back down the mountain and waited for my call.

Well-versed in this scenario, Warden Szody and I suspected that the hunters in the canyon would send up a scout if they had anything illegal in their possession. If the coast was clear and the scout thought that no game wardens were around, he would signal the others to come up.

With binoculars and radio in hand, I walked back down the road about forty yards, climbed up the bank and hid behind a patch of buckbrush. Warden Szody turned his patrol rig around and drove at a crawl back down the mountain. When he had gone a little less than half a mile, he reversed direction and positioned his rig to face the suspect vehicle. Once situated and far enough from the car to escape detection, Szody radioed the sheriff's dispatcher and ran a check on the Washington license plate. It came back registered to a man named Khamphouang Kahmphoukeo, out of Seattle, Washington.

While Szody waited for word from me, I remained perched on the bluff overlooking the road. It was almost dark when I noticed the silhouette of a male figure near the suspect vehicle. With the naked eye, it was difficult to tell if he was carrying anything. I focused my binoculars and whispered into the radio microphone, "There's somebody at the car and he's not carrying a gun." The man walked out into the middle of the road, glanced in one direction, then turned and looked in the other. "Now he's walking up the road away from me," I whispered. "This has to be their scout."

The scout walked up the hill until he faded into the darkness. "He's still somewhere up the road, probably looking to see if we're parked up around the bend." Szody keyed his microphone twice, to acknowledge that he had heard my transmission.

I did not hear the scout walking back down the road until he was directly below me. Although it was now too dark to see clearly, I could make out what appeared to be a small, dark-haired man, wearing what looked like an army field jacket. He continued down the road and out of sight. Not certain how far down the road the scout had gone, I discontinued radio traffic for fear of being overheard.

These guys are really being careful, I thought.

About five minutes later, the man walked by me again and headed back up the road, in the direction of the suspect vehicle.

Suddenly, I heard a male voice shouting into the canyon. Although I could not understand the foreign language he was speaking, I suspected that the man was telling his hunting partners, "Come on up, the coast is clear."

"He just called his buddies to come up," I whispered. Dave keyed his mic twice. As I watched the scout pop the trunk of the car, another man appeared on the scene, carrying two long guns and what looked like a backpack. "There's two of 'em standing next to the trunk of the car," I whispered. "They just put everything in the trunk, but they left the lid up. Let's make sure there isn't someone else still down there before you come up." I continued my surveillance as both men climbed into the front seat—the trunk still open. "They're just sitting in the car. It looks like they're still waiting for somebody."

With my radio volume turned down, I could barely hear two quick squelches, as Szody keyed his mic. About five minutes went by before a third subject appeared near the trunk of the car. Focusing my binoculars against the night sky, I was able to identify the silhouettes of another long gun and two more backpacks. The third man placed the backpacks and his gun inside the trunk and slammed the lid shut. He climbed into the backseat and I heard the motor start. "Come on up, they're getting ready to leave!" I said, no longer concerned about the suspects hearing me over the sound of their car engine.

The car was in the process of turning around when I heard the roar of another engine headed up the mountainside. Within seconds, Warden Szody was bearing down on the suspects with his red spotlight in full view. When he was ten yards from the vehicle, Szody turned on his overhead spotlight, lighting up everything within fifty feet. The Plymouth sedan was caught broadside, in the middle of the road, with its front end pointed toward the mountain and its rear end about five feet from the edge of the canyon.

"They're not going anywhere!" I blurted, as I sprinted toward the action.

All three men were staring into the spotlight when I arrived. "Turn off your motor and hand me the keys," I shouted. The surprised driver apparently understood what I was saying. He turned off the ignition, rolled his window down and placed the keys in my waiting hand.

We ordered the suspects to exit the car one at a time. All three men were recent immigrants from Southeast Asia. The driver and the man in the backseat had Washington Driver's Licenses, listing Seattle addresses. They also had California Resident Hunting Licenses, both with the same Redding address. The front seat passenger had a California Driver's License and a California Resident Hunting License, both with the same Redding address that was written on the other two hunting licenses. This was a pretty clear indication of license fraud, but we would sort that out later. Based on the suspects' suspicious activities over the last hour, we had more than enough probable cause to search the car for illegal game.

Szody kept an eye on everyone while I opened the trunk. Inside, I found three military-style green army backpacks, all stuffed with still-warm, boned out deer meat. The long guns, two .22 rifles, and one twelve gauge shotgun, were all unloaded. The California resident was allowed to drive the suspect vehicle back to Redding, where he lived. The two men with Washington IDs were booked into Shasta County Jail. All of the weapons were seized into evidence and later forfeited.

The next day criminal complaints were filed, charging all three subjects with unlawful possession of deer during closed season. Although Warden Szody and I suspected that the two Washington residents had not been residing in California for the required six months to obtain resident hunting licenses, we did not file charges for that violation.

Had we continued our patrol, we would have eventually crossed Squaw Creek, another achingly beautiful trout stream with a rare blue tint to its crystal clear water—I never could figure out what caused that unique color—and Potem Creek, locally known for its magnificent seventy-foot water fall.

The actual Fenders Ferry, which in days gone by had provided transportation across the Pit River, had been replaced with a bridge a hundred years back. No longer a premier salmon and steelhead spawning stream, the Pit River's once wild waters had been tamed by Shasta Dam and a series of smaller hydroelectric power dams further upstream.

The Unfortunate Tale of Lester Vail

Sometime during the summer of 1988, an anonymous caller gave the Redding Fish and Game office sketchy information about a man named Lester Vail, who had shot and killed a deer out of season. Vail lived at the bottom of a canyon, off the west end of Dog Creek Road, north of Shasta Lake.

When I walked into the regional office that morning, I was handed a small piece of notepaper providing nothing but the information above—no callback number. With little to go on, I asked Warden Merton Hatcher, who was in the office at the time, if he would like to take a ride—a long ride. Dog Creek Road was only twenty-five miles long, as the crow flies, but with countless side roads, steep canyons, and endless switchbacks. This dusty, dirt road required almost an entire day to cross.

We took Hatcher's patrol vehicle and headed north on Interstate 5 to the Dog Creek Road turnoff. During the summer months Dog Creek Road was exceptionally dusty, due to heavy logging-truck traffic. We had gone about five miles without seeing a truck, when I hollered "Stop! There's something in the road."

Hatcher stepped on the brakes just in time. I climbed out and walked to the front of the patrol vehicle. "Have you ever seen one of these?" I asked, as I reached down and picked up a two-foot long, multi-colored snake. "This is the first one I have ever come across in the wild." I held up the beautiful little creature for Hatcher to see. "It's a California mountain king snake."

Hatcher had never seen one, but was quite impressed with its brilliant red, white, and black coloring. "The herpers back in Southern California would give anything to get their hands on one of these little beauties," I said. "I'm going to get him off the road so he doesn't get run over by a logging truck." I carried the snake far into the woods and watched it slither under a decomposing log where it would be safe, at least for the moment, from passing cars and trucks.

Every year vehicles take a heavy toll on wildlife. Far more deer are killed by automobiles than by legal deer hunters and poachers combined. Many of those collisions could be avoided if drivers would simply slow down at the sight of an animal beside the road.

Warden Hatcher and I continued our patrol, with me pointing out all the new logging roads that had been punched into the mountainside since my last trip across. "Look at this," I complained, referring to a recent clear cut. "What a stinking mess. They trash the whole side of the mountain, rip out all the beneficial black oaks, and plant thousands of these little pine trees."

At the twelve-mile mark, we came to a side road leading south into a steep canyon. I pointed to a worn sheet of plywood nailed to a tree. Hand-painted on the plywood was the following barely literate warning:

PRIVAT PROPITY KEP OUT.

Neither Hatcher nor I had ever been down this segment of road. We climbed out of the patrol truck, walked to the road's edge, and peered over the side. The narrow switchback road disappeared into a forest of black oaks, Douglas-firs, and madrones. Somewhere in the distance we could hear the faint sound of a dog barking.

"Sounds like somebody's down there," said Hatcher, eyeing a gray colored wasp's nest that he had inadvertently parked under.

"Let's go before we get stung," I said.

Hatcher steered to the right and into the canyon. We traversed the canyon wall for two or three miles before reaching the bottom. Just beyond the last turn in the road we came to a sudden stop.

"What do we have here?" I said. "This guy must belong to somebody."

Hatcher whistled. "That's the biggest pig I've ever seen," he said. "It must weigh a thousand pounds."

Not wanting to alert the pig's owner, Warden Hatcher and I sat and watched for at least twenty minutes before the giant hog finally decided that a plant growing at the edge of the road might be good to eat. As I thanked our new friend for finally letting us pass, Warden Hatcher carefully maneuvered around the monstrous porker.

A quarter mile ahead was a small, gray, plaster-covered house—not really a house, by professional standards, but a shack slapped together with whatever building materials were available at the time. "Do you think this guy has a building permit?" I joked, as we stepped out of the truck.

Warden Hatcher and I tiptoed toward the front entrance. If this was the home of our deer poacher, we had no idea how he would react. Ever since the 1981 Claude Dallas incident in Idaho, when two game wardens were shot and killed, wildlife officers all over the United States had become extra careful when dealing with potentially dangerous individuals in isolated locations. The front door was wide open. Actually there was no door, just an entrance.

Hatcher and I were prepared to respond to any unusual movement but all we saw were three scrawny, mixed-breed dogs. Instead of barking at us, the uniformed intruders, the dogs seemed to be preoccupied with a pile of rib bones. "If I had to guess, I'd say those are deer ribs they're chewing on," said Hatcher. I picked up one of the bones and found easily identifiable deer hair and a small amount of fresh tissue still attached. I affirmed Warden Hatcher's assumption with a silent nod. Hatcher stuck his head in the doorway and shouted, "Is anybody home?" No one answered.

A beat-up old truck up on blocks with the tires missing was parked at the east side of the house. Coated with dust and swallowed in dense vegetation, it clearly hadn't been driven for some time. Lying on the hood was a fresh skull cap from a spike buck.

"Fresh blood," I said, swatting away the flies. "I bet this is part of the deer we're looking for."

Just then, we heard a vehicle coming down the road. An older model pickup rounded the bend and headed toward us. On full alert, Hatcher and I watched a slender but wiry little man climb out of the pickup. He sported a full gray beard and wore a dirt-stained, Massey Ferguson baseball cap. We caught a glimpse of a lever action rifle on the front seat as the pickup door closed behind him.

"What the hell do you guys want?"

"Are you Lester Vail?" I asked.

The little curmudgeon hesitated to answer, his brow knit in consternation. "Yeah, that's me. Whadda ya want?"

"We received a report that you killed a deer recently."

"Who told ya that?"

"Do you have any deer meat inside your house?"

"I ain't got no damned deer meat. You're welcome to look if you want."

As we were about to enter Vail's house, Hatcher and I heard snorting and noticed that the giant pig we had encountered earlier was walking down the road in our direction.

"Are there any other people living here, Mr. Vail?" I asked.

"Nope, just me and my pigs."

"How many pigs do you have?"

"I got a dozen or so runnin' around here."

There were no occupied pig pens, so all Vail's pigs apparently had free run of the adjacent woods. Hatcher and I stepped inside and began to look around. We easily found enough fresh deer hair and tissue in the kitchen area to put together a closed-season deer case against Vail. The fresh skull cap outside would make it a slam dunk. What puzzled us was Vail's serene countenance—he must have known we would find evidence of deer when he gave us verbal permission to search his house.

While I bagged up the evidence, Warden Hatcher peaked into the bathroom shower stall, where he discovered a freshly harvested crop of seven foot high marijuana plants. Forty or fifty of them were jammed into the stall.

"Mr. Vail, what's this?" asked Hatcher.

Without answering, the strange little man wrapped his arms around the marijuana plants and carried them outside. He proceeded to drop all of the plants on the ground in front of his giant pig. The humongous swine immediately began to scarf up the plants. Hatcher and I watched in disbelief as the pig munched away.

"Mr. Vail, this doesn't change anything," Hatcher said. "We have to report the marijuana to the sheriff's department, even if your pig eats most of the evidence." Hatcher photographed the plants then placed what was left in the back of his patrol vehicle.

Finally Vail began to show concern—his jaw was clenched and he paced back and forth nervously. Warden Hatcher asked for identification while I made sure Vail stayed away from his pickup and the rifle we had seen earlier. Vail produced a California Drivers License and Hatcher began copying the information.

"So what's going to happen?" asked Vail.

"I am going to give a report to the district attorney regarding your being in possession of a closed-season deer," replied Hatcher.

"What about the pot?" asked Vail.

"I will give the marijuana and a report to the sheriff's office. It will be up to them what they do with it," replied Hatcher.

"That's chickenshit!" shouted Vail. "I let you guys search for deer, not pot."

I got the impression that Vail had been busted for marijuana before and that he was worried about the possibility of going to prison. The misdemeanor Fish and Game violation didn't seem to bother him; it was clearly the marijuana he was worried about. Although we often ran across marijuana growers in the course of our patrols, I was more concerned about them poaching our deer and polluting our streams. It was our duty to report findings to the appropriate enforcement agencies, so we generally let the sheriff's office or the local drug task force decide how they wanted to deal with the situation.

In this case, Warden Hatcher turned the marijuana plants over to the sheriff's office and provided a written narrative of the circumstances. Neither Hatcher nor I were ever called upon to testify, so Vail paid a fine for the closed-season deer and that was probably the end of it.

Two or three years after this case was made, I read a disturbing story in the local newspaper. Lester Vail had heard a gunshot coming from the road above his house. Concerned that someone had harmed one of his pigs, he grabbed his rifle and ran up the hill. Reaching the upper road, Lester came face-to-face with his worst nightmare: a car parked in the road, with two men standing nearby. One of the men was holding a high powered rifle. Lying dead at the man's feet was Vail's prized pig. What happened next is debatable, but according to the only living witness, Lester went into a rage and pointed his rife at the pig shooter. The pig shooter reacted by pointing his rifle back at Vail. Both men fired at exactly the same time, each hitting his respective target. The pig shooter dropped dead and so did Lester Vail. So ends the unfortunate tale of Lester Vail.

Working the Tribs

I

As the Sacramento River flowed through Shasta County, it was fed by several tributary streams. Some were ephemeral, flowing only during the rainy season; others had reliable upstream water sources and flowed year-round. During wet years, we had salmon and Sacramento River rainbow trout spawning in almost all of the streams below Shasta Dam. Salt and Middle Creeks—two small tributaries just north of Redding—ran dry during the summer months, but hosted hundreds of three- to six-pound trophy Sacramento River rainbows during wet spawning seasons.

There were years when we had to almost stand guard on these streams to keep the poachers at bay. During drier years, spawning activity was restricted to the Sacramento River and larger tributaries like Battle Creek, Clear Creek, and South Cow Creek. From late September through December, wardens working in Shasta County generally had their hands full protecting these magnificent fish as they struggled against almost insurmountable odds to reach their spawning grounds and perpetuate the species.

II

The morning before Thanksgiving, 1990, Warden Dave Szody hopped in his patrol truck and headed out for a day of patrolling the Sacramento River tributaries. By late November, the only tributary streams that still hosted spawning Chinook salmon were Battle Creek and Clear Creek, so Dave concentrated his efforts there. The five-mile section of Battle Creek between Coleman National Fish Hatchery and the Sacramento River was closed to all fishing in an effort to protect the spawning salmon and steelhead. Ocean-run steelhead had become so scarce in the upper Sacramento River system that every spawner was critically important.

Szody drove into the County Line Bridge parking lot and noticed that it was empty. This usually meant there were no illegal fishermen on that stretch of Battle Creek, but sometimes people were dropped off. The only way to be sure was to get out of the truck and walk. Grabbing his binoculars, he followed a foot trail that began at the bridge and continued upstream for several miles.

Dead and dying spawned-out salmon lay all along the water's edge. *That's strange*, thought the warden, *the usual entourage of vultures, gulls, ravens, and bald eagles is conspicuously missing.* The absence of birds feeding on this stretch of stream could mean only one thing. Someone had recently passed through the area.

Alerted to the presence of possible violators ahead, Szody moved cautiously and kept out of sight as much as possible, using blackberry patches for cover. Just beyond the first bend in the stream, he discovered two men wading knee-deep in the water and casting into a shallow riffle. They followed each cast with a strong rearward jerking motion—a clear indication of snagging. Both men were braving the cold water in trousers and tennis shoes, standard attire for most salmon snaggers in their teens and early twenties.

Just a month earlier, thousands of salmon had worked their way up this classic spawning stream. Now Battle Creek's fall Chinook salmon run was largely over and the number of live salmon in the stream had thinned to a few hundred fish—a few of our invaluable steelhead among them.

In spite of their obvious efforts, neither of the two fishermen seemed to be having much success. Szody watched for a half hour or more until one of the anglers finally snagged a big hook-nosed buck (spawning male Chinook salmon) in the back. The young man was horsing the fifteen-pound salmon across the rocks and up on the bank when Warden Szody stepped from behind a patch of blackberries and instructed him to carefully release it. "Without breaking your lines, I want both of you to walk over here and set your fishing rods down on the ground," commanded Szody. "I repeat, do not break your lines." Both lines were tied to large treble hooks, weighted with wraparound pencil sinkers.

"Have you taken any other fish?" Szody asked.

They both shook their heads vigorously, and the taller of the two insisted, "No, no others."

Based on what he had seen and the fact that there were very few live salmon left in Battle Creek at the time, Szody was fairly certain that the two snaggers were telling the truth. He suspected that these men were after salmon row—egg skeins were ripped from the females and later used or illegally sold as trout and steelhead bait. There was no evidence of egg spillage on the bank and a cursory search of the area produced nothing suspicious.

"So how did you guys get here?" asked Szody.

"We're very sorry to have caused you this trouble, Officer Szody," said the shorter man, having read the name tag on Szody's shirt pocket. "My girl friend dropped us off."

Unlike most of the derelicts we caught snagging on Battle Creek, this young man seemed respectful. When Szody asked for identification, he learned that the shorter man was actually on leave from the U.S. Army. Being a former air policeman in Viet Nam, Szody knew that the kid would have hell to pay if his CO found out about him being busted. Because both men had valid fishing licenses and hadn't killed anything, the soft-hearted warden gave them a stern warning and advised them not to come back.

During the walk back to the parking lot, Warden Szody noticed that some of the birds had returned, including an immature bald eagle. With long, graceful wing beats, the startled raptor flew to the top of an old cottonwood tree and waited for the three intruders to pass. During the fall and winter months, when salmon were present, as many as forty bald eagles haunted the lower stretches of Battle Creek. Most of the salmon had died, but their decaying carcasses would provide essential food for a dozen bird species, otters, raccoons, mink, invertebrates, and thousands of hatchling salmon and steelhead.

It was mid-afternoon when Warden Szody made his way across the valley. Since he was the only enforcement unit working in Shasta County that day, Szody decided to venture out of his own district and patrol lower Clear Creek. Clear Creek still had a fairly substantial salmon run and some of the local outlaws knew it. Beginning at the mouth, where Clear Creek entered the Sacramento River, Szody's patrol would proceed several miles upstream to one of the more heavily poached sections of water in the area.

The weather that afternoon was cold and overcast. By the time Szody had worked his way to the end, it was approaching 4:00 p.m. and the sun was already going down. He pulled off Clear Creek Road, onto a well-traveled dirt road that dead-ended about one hundred yards from the stream. There he saw an obvious red flag: a Chevy pickup surreptitiously parked behind a manzanita thicket. He turned off his engine and walked over to the suspicious vehicle. The hood was cold, which didn't mean much, considering the forty-eight degree ambient temperature. Inside the cab was a pack of cigarettes and a dark blue jacket. The registration sticker on the rear plate was, to Szody's amazement, surprisingly current.

Binoculars in hand, Warden Szody locked his truck and started out on foot patrol. As he approached Clear Creek, the sound of spawning salmon splashing in the shallows caught his attention. He was encouraged by the healthy number of fish and the many redds—depressions in the gravel created by spawning salmon. Unlike many of the Sacramento River tributaries, Clear Creek maintained a constant flow of cold water year-round. This water originated from the depths of Whiskeytown Reservoir, several miles to the west.

If anyone is poaching salmon, they will be down at the bend, thought Szody.

Over the years, area wardens had made dozens of salmon poaching cases at the "bend." Every fish had to swim through a narrow, very shallow riffle and negotiate a small waterfall. If the fish made it past the riffle, they generally stacked up below the falls—vulnerable to snag hooks, spears, nets, rocks, and even shotguns. (Yes, we had even made a few cases involving people shooting salmon with shotguns.)

Szody quietly made his way downstream. He was still fifty yards from the bend, when he heard male voices laughing and calling to each other.

"You missed, here comes another one," one voice shouted.

"Let me have the spear; there's one right there," said another.

Ducking behind a large rock outcropping, Szody directed his binoculars toward the commotion. He immediately spotted four men chasing fish up and down the stream—all of them tolerating the cold water in trousers and tennis shoes, a clear indication that they were young and stupid.

Taking turns with two long metal spears, the young men were stabbing at the half exposed salmon as the frightened fish tried to swim the gauntlet through the shallow riffle. Thrusting back and forth with all of the energy left in their exhausted bodies, these determined marvels of nature became easy targets for the excited poachers.

Disgusted by what he saw, Szody's first inclination was to confront the violators immediately. Being an experienced professional, however, he knew that blundering in and hoping for the best was not the way to go. By being patient and keeping watch for a while, he could determine the extent of the crime and come away with a far stronger case. Besides, these idiots were wet up to their asses—the cold water and forty degree air temperature would soon dampen their enthusiasm.

A mere fifteen minutes later the four salmon poachers started complaining about the cold and finally ended their carnage. Peering through his binoculars, Szody wondered what they were doing down by the water's edge, behind a patch of alders. He had seen the men successfully spear one salmon and miss a dozen more, but the patient warden had no idea how many fish these men had killed before he arrived.

Warden Szody would later say that the sight of the four men and their illegal booty reminded him of the old African game-beaters photographs in *National Geographic*: the culprits had threaded each salmon's gills through the ends of the two metal spears. One spear contained nine eight-to-ten-pound salmon, with a man on each end. The other spear contained eight salmon, also with a man on each end. As the four men clumsily staggered up the trail, laughing and joking as they went, Szody slipped in behind them. Each time they stopped to rest, he stepped off the trail to find cover. More than once, the plundered fish almost ended up on the ground.

"We made it," said the first man to reach the pickup.

"Not quite," said Warden Szody, as he lit them up with his flashlight. "Who's the driver of this pickup?"

"I am," responded a tall young man with an expression on his pleasant-looking face that instantly shifted from ultimate exhilaration to serious melancholy. The others looked as if someone had just thrown a bucket of cold water in their faces.

"Hand me your keys," said Szody. "Now I need to see identification from all four of you."

The driver kept repeating the same thing over and over, "My dad's gonna kill me." He was a twenty-year-old college student, home for the Thanksgiving holiday. The others were a cousin and two friends from high school, attending the local community college.

Driver's licenses in hand, Warden Szody radioed Shasta County Sheriff's dispatch and asked if any of the four subjects had outstanding warrants; they all came back clear. After checking for weapons, Szody instructed the men to load all of the fish and the two spears into the bed of his patrol truck. With no outstanding warrants and good identification, all four men were issued citations. They were charged with unlawful take and possession of seventeen salmon in closed waters and with unlawful method of take—spears.

The Clear Creek salmon appeared to be in much better condition than those found in Battle Creek, so Warden Szody took evidence photographs and delivered the fish to the local rescue mission. While unloading the pickup, he noticed that the spears had been made out of TV antenna poles, smashed at one end. "No end to American ingenuity," he said, shaking his head.

A month or so later, the four salmon poachers were each fined over $1500 and placed on one year's summary probation—a small price to pay for the potential harm they had inflicted on future Clear Creek salmon runs. These were less numerous and significantly more valuable wild fish—not fish that had been artificially propagated in a hatchery.

The Fall River Elk Killings

I

Approximately sixty-five miles from Redding, in the northeast corner of Shasta County, is a place called Fall River Valley. At thirty-four hundred feet above sea level, this large expanse of agricultural lands, marshes, lakes, streams, and crystal clear springs is watched over by Mount Shasta on the north and Mount Lassen on the south. Fall River, from which this beautiful region gets its name, is a world-renowned fly fishing stream that meanders through farmlands and creates habitat not only for trophy-sized trout, but also thousands of waterfowl and other wildlife.

During its journey across the valley, Fall River intersects with the Tule, Little Tule, and Pit Rivers. Near the confluence of Fall River and the Pit River is the little town of Fall River Mills, with a population of about six hundred and fifty. Five minutes up the highway is another little town called McArthur, with a population of about three hundred and fifty. The valley contains a few other tiny hamlets with names like Dana, Glenburn, and Pittville, but for all practical purposes, the entire valley functions as one community, where everybody knows everybody and nothing happens that the entire population doesn't hear about.

Almost a century ago, fifty Rocky Mountain elk (*Cervus canadensis nelsoni*) were transplanted from Yellowstone National Park to northeastern Shasta County. California Department of Fish and Game biologists estimate that today between four hundred and five hundred elk are scattered across the mountains and foothills of Shasta, Siskiyou, Modoc, and Lassen Counties.

Whether or not they all originated from the Yellowstone contingent is very much in question. Slightly larger Roosevelt elk (*Cervus canadensis roosevelti*) are suspected to have migrated south from Oregon into northern California, and the two subspecies may well have interbred.

People living in the intermountain areas of Burney and Fall River Valley enjoy seeing small herds of these majestic animals from time to time, particularly during the winter months. That is the time of year when elk migrate to lower elevations and congregate where most of the forage is available. Other than a few elk that were killed legally by hunters who had won public drawings and been issued individual hunting permits, these giant grazers have enjoyed protection for over ninety years. Harm one and you not only break the law, you incur the wrath of an entire community.

II

No one knows exactly what happened on December 8, 1991, except the defendants themselves. The following account is based on statements made by the defendants, physical evidence, knowledge of the area, and information gathered by the investigating officers.

Early on the morning of December 8, 1991, Jesse Lee Brewer drove his Ford Bronco through the quiet streets of McArthur. He was twenty-three years old at the time, just under six feet tall and about thirty pounds overweight. Lying on the front seat next to Brewer was his 7mm Remington Magnum, high-powered rifle. Jesse's first stop that morning was the home of Beau Hammond. Hammond and Brewer had attended school in the valley and like many of the local boys, hung around after graduation and never managed to leave. Beau was twenty-five years old, a few inches shorter than his hunting buddy and noticeably thinner.

Hammond started the day with a half-full box of 30-06 ammunition sticking out of the pocket of his hunting jacket. Reaching the Bronco, he laid his rifle across the backseat and climbed in. It was cold, dreary, and slightly overcast as the two would-be bear hunters pulled onto the highway and headed west toward Fall River Mills.

Every house in Fall River Mills had a wood stove going. Some still contained the smoldering log from last night's fire while others were re-stoked and ready for the new day. With no recent wind or rain, chimney smoke hung over the town like a dark gray blanket. Fall River Mills was like so many other small mountain towns: its citizens had depended on the lumber industry for their livelihoods and were now either permanently or temporarily unemployed. Some were associated with agriculture, some were retired and a few relied on government assistance to make it through the long, cold winter months. Half of the homes in Fall River seemed to be well-cared-for and the other half, not so much. It was not unusual to see derelict cars and old pickups sitting in driveways and alongside houses, jacked up with the tires missing.

Brewer's Bronco pulled up in front of an older, two-story house with a Toyota pickup parked in front. As Brewer and Hammond climbed out of the Bronco, they were met by Robert "Bob" Stokes and his twenty-five-year-old son, Robbie (Robert Stokes, Jr.). Bob was forty-four at the time, stood five feet eight inches tall and weighed about one hundred and eighty pounds. Robbie was a slimmer version of his old man, about the same height. They loaded two more rifles, a backpack full of hunting equipment, some groceries, and an ice chest full of Keystone beer into the Bronco. Off they went, across the valley, on what Beau Hammond later described as a day of bear hunting.

The Bronco headed north, past Glenburn, past Eastman Lake, past Ahjumawi Lava Springs State Park, and into the Shasta National Forest. From there they continued north about ten miles, all the way to Wiley Ranch. Sometime late that afternoon the hunting party drove through Adobe Flat, a meadow scattered with buckbrush and Ponderosa pines. There they came across a small contingent of the elk herd that spent the winter months in that area. According to wildlife biologists, this little herd consisted of eighteen animals, but they occasionally dispersed into smaller groups.

It is not clear how many elk were present. We do know there were at least five—two cows, a six month old calf, a spike bull, and a mature six-point bull. Brewer hit the brakes a short distance from the grazing animals. The elk paid little or no attention and continued to munch on the limited grass that was available. A mature bull raised his head, exposing a good-sized set of antlers, but that was about the extent of the herd's reaction.

Beau Hammond would later tell Shasta County Sheriff's Sergeant Ron Bushey that Robbie Stokes, Bob Stokes, and Jesse Brewer jumped out of the Bronco and started shooting. Twenty or more shots were fired in succession, all with high powered rifles. Based on Hammond's questionable account of the incident, he did not participate in the initial onslaught. "It wasn't even hunting," said Hammond. "It was like shooting cows in a pasture." Four of the elk dropped dead on the spot. One crippled cow tried to get away but was chased down and finished off by Jesse Brewer.

The small elk herd had become so habituated to humans that they displayed no fear of man. Instead of cameras, they were facing high-powered rifles. Sadly, these beautiful giants of the deer family just stood there and allowed themselves to be slaughtered.

Over the next several hours, the men worked frantically to recover as much meat as possible from four full-grown elk and one calf. The cows weighed over five hundred pounds, the spike probably weighed seven hundred pounds and the mature bull may have weighed as much as a thousand pounds. Hams, back straps, ribs, and as much other meat as could be cut away from the carcasses was removed from the five dead animals. The haul was substantial. one mature bull elk can easily fill the bed of a full-sized pickup.

Sometime after dark, the elk poachers slipped into town with truckloads of elk meat, antlers and assorted body parts. Beside an isolated road in Adobe Flat they had left gut piles, forelegs, heads, carcasses, and empty beer cans. Hammond would later tell Sergeant Bushey that he and his partners worked in his garage until daylight deboning elk meat. Robbie Stokes would later state that it took them five days to complete the task, continuing to process elk meat behind his grandfather's house.

III

On any list of the most beautiful birds in North America, the golden eagle would have to be right there near the top. Bald eagles are magnificent, but nothing can match a mature golden eagle for elegant grace and beauty. Anyone lucky enough to get a close-up look at the brilliant gold reflection from the back of a golden eagle's neck while it is perched in full sunlight will never forget it.

By coincidence, as I wrote about this incident from twenty years back, I received a related email from my old friend and working partner, Dave Szody. Dave had just returned home from a trip to Colorado with his wife and had this to say:

> I saw a lot of really impressive wildlife, including a golden eagle feeding on a dead elk along I-70 in Utah. You would have gone nuts. I passed it at rather high speed but he had the classic adult head with the huge eyes and was absolutely majestic.

So what does this have to do with the elk poaching case? If not for a golden eagle, the case never would have been made. In 1991 a bird watcher by the name of Herb Watters lived in McArthur. On Thursday, December 12, 1991, Watters happened to be bird-watching out around Adobe Flat. From a distance, he noticed a group of ravens feeding on something. Amongst the ravens was another bird, several times their size. Watters focused his binoculars on the large bird and immediately identified it as a golden eagle. Wanting to get a closer look, he made his way toward the feeding birds. Rather than a dead cow or possibly a deer, the object of the avian feeding frenzy turned out to be the fresh head and gut pile of a cow elk.

As a longtime resident of Fall River Valley, Watters knew all about the small herd of elk that lived in the area. He had seen them many times and was furious about what he had just discovered. Watters immediately drove back to McArthur and contacted the local Fish and Game warden, Lloyd Friesen. Watters and Friesen made plans to drive out to the site of the dead elk the following day.

On Friday, December 13, Herb Watters and Warden Friesen arrived at Adobe Flat in Friesen's patrol vehicle. In searching the area, they discovered far more than one poached elk. What they found amounted to a small-scale massacre. Five elk had been killed and butchered: two cows, a calf, and two bulls. Both of the bulls' heads had been cut off and were missing. Scattered amongst the carnage were exactly twenty sawed-off elk legs and several beer cans displaying the Keystone label.

Warden Friesen was overwhelmed by the immensity of the crime and immediately contacted his Lieutenant, Al Mathews, who lived an hour north of Fall River. Upon receiving Warden Friesen's request for assistance, Mathews telephoned his captain in Yreka. Within twenty-four hours, the story hit the newspapers and was broadcast on the TV news. The tiny town of Fall River was suddenly on the map.

Word spread throughout the inter-mountain area. People were outraged that someone had wiped out a quarter of Fall River Valley's prized elk herd. Herb Watters was interviewed by the area newspaper and quoted as saying, "These are sacred cows up here." Friesen's captain offered a reward of up to one thousand dollars for any information about the elk killings.

Speculation was running rampant. "I'd estimate that between fifteen hundred and two thousand pounds of meat could have been harvested from these five elk," commented Warden Friesen, speaking to newspaper reporters. "Considering the massive scale of this crime, it could have been committed by professionals." By mentioning professionals, Friesen was referring to a possible commercial poaching ring. Lieutenant Mathews was asked to chime in. On the record, Mathews went along with Warden Friesen's assumptions. Off the record, he was mulling over a completely different theory: the sloppy mess had been left by amateurs from right there in the valley. Professionals wouldn't have left carcasses out in the open for somebody to find. There were beer cans and shell casings all over the ground and what about that fresh set of tire tracks?

Lieutenant Mathews didn't know how right he was. While the wardens were gathering evidence, four of those amateurs were scampering around Fall River Mills and McArthur, filling freezers with packaged elk meat.

Don Jacobs was Lloyd Friesen's neighboring warden. Lean and six feet tall, this forty-five-year-old, prematurely gray warden had cracked more important cases during his twelve years in the Burney Patrol District than most wardens did in a career. Burney's law-abiding citizens loved him, while the serious violators cringed at the mere mention of his name. Many a night, Warden Jacobs received threatening phone calls from local outlaws, too cowardly to identify themselves.

The Burney Patrol District encompassed the higher elevations immediately west of Fall River Valley. It also included the lower reaches of the Pit River and two classic trout streams—Hat Creek and the Rising River. During the week of the elk killings, Warden Jacobs had been on a trip with his family and missed the initial excitement. Like Friesen, Jacobs was supervised by Lieutenant Al Mathews and the Yreka patrol captain. The captain knew that bringing the perpetrators of this heinous wildlife crime to justice was going to take a lot of work and some superior investigative skills. With that in mind, Jacobs was assigned to assist Warden Friesen with the case.

By the time Warden Jacobs became involved with the Fall River elk case, the incident had received almost daily media coverage. With significant rewards offered for information leading to the arrest and conviction of those responsible, Jacobs was confident that the phone lines would soon be ringing at CalTip, the California Department of Fish and Game hotline, or Secret Witness, Shasta County's hotline. Two thousand pounds of elk meat couldn't just vanish and secrets were difficult to keep in a small community like Fall River Valley.

Warden Friesen had already collected a certain amount of physical evidence and taken several rolls of photographs at Adobe Flat. Samples of blood, hair, and tissue were taken from the elk remains for possible future comparisons. During the time of this investigation, the California Department of Fish and Game employed James Banks, possibly the best wildlife forensic pathologist in the western United States. Banks and his extensive laboratory were three hours away in Sacramento. Also nearby was the U.S. Fish and Wildlife Laboratory in Ashland, Oregon. Although no useable fingerprints were lifted from the Keystone beer cans found at the crime scene, the fact that the culprits drank that particular brand was surely a clue. One suspicious vehicle track was pronounced enough to make a plaster cast.

Everyone in the intermountain area was talking about the elk killings. Right from the start, Warden Jacobs had a feeling that the culprits were nearby. Eventually one of them would brag about his diabolical accomplishment in front of the wrong person.

Jacobs's assumptions soon proved to be correct. A little over a week after the five dead elk were found, an informant by the name of Matt Parsons came forward with information the investigators had been waiting for.

Parsons had recently eaten dinner over at Beau Hammond's house. The main course was fresh elk steaks. Sneaking a peak in Hammond's freezer, Parsons saw that it was stuffed with packaged meat. After Beau Hammond saw Parsons looking in the freezer, he began bragging about all the "illegal elk meat" he had. Parsons also noticed hair and blood stains all over Hammond's cement garage floor.

Warden Jacobs recorded the information provided by Parsons and asked if he had anything else to add. Parsons, a longtime acquaintance of the four eventual suspects, proved to be a wealth of information. He went on to say that he had been at Jesse Brewer's house a few days earlier when Bob and Robbie Stokes had shown up. "Bob and Robbie started bragging about shooting ducks," said Parsons, "but I don't think they were talking about 'ducks' at all. Robbie said he jumped out and knocked three down. Bob chimed in and said he killed two." Bob Stokes had described how Jesse Brewer tracked down one of Robbie's wounded ones and finished it off.

The story Bob and Robbie Stokes recounted to Matt Parsons obviously had nothing to do with ducks. Jacobs recalled that one of the poached elk had actually been wounded and was found a short distance from the other four. That was undoubtedly the animal Jesse Brewer had tracked down and finished off.

Parsons even knew what kind of beer the suspected elk poachers liked to drink—Keystone. Having hunted with the four suspects on previous occasions, Matt Parsons was able to describe the caliber of rifles that Bob Stokes and Jesse Brewer generally carried: Bob Stokes used a .270 or a .243 and Jesse Brewer shot a 7mm.

As for where all that meat might have ended up, Parsons said word on the street was that Bob Stokes's father, Jasper Stokes—a former butcher and general store operator—kept a big freezer out behind his house. "Chances are the boys also used Jasper's butchering tools to process the elk meat," he said. "Jesse Brewer's sister and husband keep a giant freezer out behind their mobile home. Jesse made a heck of a lot of trips back and forth to his sister's."

Wardens Jacobs and Friesen were able to corroborate the information that Parsons had given them with physical evidence found at the crime scene. Shell casings were of the same caliber, the beer can labels had read Keystone, and the tire tracks matched up with Jesse Brewer's Ford Bronco.

Parsons had an excellent motive for coming forward. He had known the four suspects for years and even considered them friends, but this time they had gone too far. His conscience would simply not let him stand by and do nothing.

Believing they had accumulated enough probable cause to obtain search warrants, Wardens Jacobs and Friesen contacted Deputy District Attorney

Larry Allen at the Shasta County District Attorney's Office. Larry Allen was not only a highly skilled prosecutor, he was also genuinely concerned for California's wildlife and eager to help Fish and Game with important cases. Due to the daily media attention and incredible public interest, the case was given top level priority by the Shasta County District Attorney's Office.

Public sentiment was running high for bringing the poachers to justice. Search warrants were prepared for five Fall River Valley residences. The first would be the home of Robert Stokes, his wife Cynthia and their son Robbie. Along with the house, they'd be searching a Toyota pickup belonging to Robert "Bob" Stokes. The residence of Jasper Stokes, Bob's father and former town butcher, was number two on the list—Jasper's garage was reportedly the site of much of the processing. Number three was the mobile home of Fred and Esther Hutchins—Esther was Jesse Brewer's sister. She and her husband owned a large freezer that Brewer might be using to store elk meat. Jesse Brewer's residence and his Ford Bronco were number four, and the home of Beau Hammond was named in the fifth search warrant.

On Saturday morning, December 21, 1991, five separate teams—each made up of Fish and Game officers and Shasta County deputy sheriffs— knocked on the doors of the five houses simultaneously. Deputy District Attorney Larry Allen participated in the search of Fred and Esther Hutchins's mobile home. "Is that elk meat I smell?" commented Allen, as he entered the Hutchins residence. Much to the searching officers' disappointment, it turned out to be venison steaks in the frying pan and not elk. The Hutchins's freezer, located in a rear outbuilding, was plugged in and running, but it appeared to have been recently emptied. A frost line near the top indicated how high the meat packages had been stacked, but the freezer contained nothing at all.

No packaged elk meat was found at Hammond's or Brewer's residences. In spite of what Parsons had seen a few days earlier, their freezers were also empty. Jasper Stokes's freezer was empty, just like the others. Bob Stokes's large standup freezer was plugged in and operating, but also seemed to have been cleaned out recently. There were imprints on the walls of the freezer, indicating that packages had been stacked inside. Stokes and his accomplices had also divested themselves of the rifles used to kill the elk. None was found by the searching parties.

As the searches progressed, it became abundantly clear that someone had tipped off the suspects. Finding all of the freezers completely empty, one officer commented, "They must have been so panicked that they threw out everything. The woods are probably littered with TV dinners, pot pies, and frozen peas."

Our suspects might have gotten away with their blatant violation of the law, had it not been for one thing—they failed to clean up their mess. Jesse

Brewer's Bronco turned out to be a virtual storehouse of evidence. Liberal amounts of elk blood and hair were found inside the vehicle, along with a number of empty Keystone beer cans. Tire tracks on Brewer's Bronco matched up perfectly with a plaster cast made at the scene of the crime. Brewer's Bronco was seized into evidence and taken to the Redding Fish and Game office. Elk blood covered a pair of black Levis found on Brewer's porch.

Although no packaged meat was found at Beau Hammond's residence, his garage floor remained just as it had been the night of the killing spree—splattered with elk blood, hair, and tissue. No one had even attempted to clean it up.

Bob Stokes must have felt he had dodged the proverbial bullet until the search team found blood, hair, and tissue in the bed of his Toyota pickup. Hidden in that same truck was a meat tenderizer that no one had bothered to clean; it was also covered with blood, hair, and tissue. Lab tests confirmed that all of the animal evidence found inside Bob Stokes's pickup came from elk. Stokes's Toyota pickup was seized into evidence and transported to the Fish and Game office in Redding.

Getting rid of two thousand pounds of elk meat isn't easy, as the four suspects would soon find out. Over the next few days, Fish and Game initiated an all-out search. Jesse Brewer eased the officers' task by shooting off his mouth one night in a local bar. "The cat fishing is going to be very good in the Pit River," Brewer was overheard saying.

Warden Jacobs heard what Brewer had said and began searching along the Pit River. He found out just how panicked the poachers must have been when he easily located the first batch of evidence. It was submerged in a few feet of water, directly under the nearby Pit River Bridge. In addition to packaged elk meat, Warden Jacobs found a neck roast that pathologist Jim Banks matched up with an elk head found at the scene of the crime.

Two members of the Department's exclusive and highly skilled scuba diving team were brought in to search the deeper water. On any given day, Larry Bruckenstein and Jauquin Mariante could be diving for gunny sacks of illegal abalone off the shark-infested Marin Coast or, in this case, packages of elk meat from a Northern California trout stream. While scouring the river bottom, our divers found shell casings, elk ribs, elk antlers, and a cardboard box filled with packaged elk meat. For weeks, wardens and private citizens ran across discarded meat and elk parts all over Fall River Valley. A ride in the California Highway Patrol helicopter allowed Warden Jacobs to get a bird's eye view of areas where evidence might have been dumped. Sure enough, he and the pilot spotted meat packages that had been thrown off a cliff near Pit River Falls.

Although none of the rifles used in the crime were found, several incriminating statements had been made and numerous evidential pieces could be matched up and connected, directly or indirectly, to the four suspects: the tire tracks from Brewer's Bronco; elk hair, blood, and tissue all over Brewer's and Stokes's vehicles and the meat tenderizer found in Stokes's pickup, elk blood and hair on the suspects' clothing; elk blood, hair and tissue on a tarp and on garage floors; Keystone beer cans; incriminating statements by neighbors who had been given elk meat; and most importantly, statements by Matt Parsons.

Deputy District Attorney Larry Allen charged Robert Stokes, Robert Stokes Junior (Robbie), Jesse Lee Brewer, and Beau Hammond with felony conspiracy as well as unlawful take and possession of elk. There was also a substantial case of "wanton waste of game," involving literally hundreds of pounds of elk meat discarded all over the valley. Twenty-five thousand dollar felony arrest warrants were immediately issued for Beau Hammond, Jesse Brewer, Robert Stokes, and Robert Stokes, Jr.

Cuffs were slapped on Beau Hammond, as Sheriff's Sergeant Ron Bushey read him his Miranda rights. Although Bushey worked for the Shasta County Sheriff's Department, he was as familiar with wildlife law enforcement as any veteran Fish and Game warden. Ron's father had been the Burney Fish and Game warden many years earlier and Ron's brother was currently a warden with the Department of Fish and Game.

In Hammond's account, he'd had nothing to do with the initial attack. "When they saw all them elk, they just went nuts!" he said. "They just jumped out of the Bronco and begun blasting away. No one gave it a second thought. I knew it couldn't lead to nothin' good. After that we had no choice but to see it out. We had to butcher all that meat as fast as we could. So we hauled it to my garage, and that's where we stayed all night.

"After I heard about those search warrants," Hammond went on, "I just panicked. I tossed a bunch o' the bones and hides in the river. The packages were harder ta get rid of, so I stashed 'em in the basement of that old, boarded-up farmhouse out on Ashby Road."

Sergeant Bushey checked out Hammond's story and found 170 pounds of packaged elk meat left to rot in the old farmhouse.

Jesse Brewer and Robert Stokes didn't have much to say when they were arrested. On the evening after the search, Robert Stokes telephoned one of the Fish and Game wardens he had known for many years.

"We screwed up big time," said Stokes. "I just want to get this damn thing over with, even if it includes jail."

Like the others, Robbie Stokes had a twenty-five thousand dollar warrant out for his arrest. He was skiing at Lake Tahoe on the day the search warrants were served and had missed all the excitement. Instead of coming home after the ski trip, Robbie stayed at his girlfriend's house in Burney. Robbie's mother kept him apprised of developments by phone. The younger Stokes and one of his friends had already purchased plane tickets to Alaska, where they hoped to find work. So Robbie fled to Alaska instead of going home and facing the music.

A bit of investigative work by Warden Jacobs produced Robbie Stokes' Anchorage address. Alaska State Troopers easily located the fugitive and tossed him in the local jail. Because Stokes was wanted on a felony arrest warrant, he was thrown in with the hardened criminals—murderers, thieves, and drug dealers—who wanted to know what this skinny kid from California was in for. Stokes would have been better off telling them he had robbed a bank. When he told this group he was being extradited to California for poaching elk, Robbie might as well have written the word "snitch" across his forehead. Nobody believed him. The young man from Fall River Mills spent a few sleepless nights before Warden Jacobs showed up to transport him back to California. When Jacobs did arrive, Stokes greeted him like a long-lost friend. He would later say that he was never so glad to see a game warden in his entire life.

Warden Jacobs picked up Robbie Stokes in Anchorage at 6:00 a.m. on March 1, 1992. Both men were in for a long day. Because of a limited flight schedule and several layovers, they would be together until 8:00 p.m. that night. During the fourteen-hour trip back to California, Robbie Stokes was eager to talk about the elk case and his involvement.

"Just remember that you already invoked your Miranda rights in Alaska," Jacobs warned. "You can talk all you want, but I can't ask any questions related to the case."

After spending time in jail with hardened criminals, Robbie Stokes realized he had bitten off way more than he could chew. Jacobs would say later that Robbie reminded him of an excited dog greeting his owner after a long absence—he wouldn't sit still and chattered about the elk case all the way home. "I wanted to close my eyes and snooze a few times," said Jacobs. "Just when I was drifting off, Stokes would start up again."

Warden Jacobs had a tape recorder in his shirt pocket and recorded much of what was said.

"Don, I'm guilty of killing a few elk," said Robbie, "but I can't tell ya how many until I talk to my attorney back home. I just want to do my time and pay my fine—whatever I have to do so I can go back to Alaska."

Robbie said he had been in frequent phone contact with his mother, his father, and Jesse Brewer. He said he was aware of what had been going on at home in Fall River. Jacobs was completely surprised by what he heard next.

"Do you know why you didn't find the meat?" asked Robbie.

"No," answered Jacobs. "We figured you were tipped off by someone."

"You bet," replied Stokes. "It was Margie McBride who tipped us off." Robbie described how a local female bartender had spilled the beans about the forthcoming search warrants to Jesse Brewer. "Jesse then called my dad and told him. I think they also told Beau. Jesse told me this himself and I believe it. They moved all the meat the day before you guys showed up with the warrants. I don't have no idea where they hid the meat, but I'm sure it's wasted."

"Beau hid his share in that old house on Ashby Road," said Jacobs.

"If Margie hadn't told Jesse," Stokes said, "then you guys would have gotten everything—the meat, the guns, everything."

This gave Jacobs pause. "We thought Matt Parsons was the one who tipped you guys off," he said.

"No, it was Margie," insisted Stokes. "All Matt told Jesse was that he had turned us in."

During the remainder of the plane ride back to Redding, Robbie Stokes continued to blab on and on about the elk case.

"I got no idea where my dad hid the rifles," said Robbie. "He and Jessie both said I didn't need to know."

"I heard the guns and the meat were destroyed before the search," said Jacobs.

"All I was told is they're somewhere safe and I'm not supposed to worry about it," said Robbie. "Since I had nothin' to do with gettin' ridda that meat, I shouldn't be charged with the 'wanton waste violation,' right? Just for killin' the elk. But I ain't sayin' how many until I talk ta my lawyer."

Warden Jacobs was about to nod off, when Stokes thought of something else that was bothering him.

"Is grandpa gonna get charged?" he asked. "I know they found some blood and stuff at his place, but grandpa wasn't involved at all. We packaged the meat below his house but he never came down and he had no idea what we was doin'."

Warden Jacobs listened intently. If Stokes began to talk about something relevant to the case, Jacobs would turn on his pocket tape recorder. This last recorded statement by Robbie Stokes summed up his version of the elk killings:

> It was just the four of us. We went bear hunting for the day and we cut across Wiley Ranch to Adobe Flat. It was toward evening when we saw the elk. At this point things just really went crazy. After all the shooting, we realized we'd screwed up. It was total chaos at this point.

We had all those elk down and a really sickening feeling came over me but it was done. And, you know, it took us five days to take care of all that meat. It was a hard job, and I hear Beau said he didn't shoot. If you got his .30-06 rifle and any shell casings, your tests may show something different.

Jesse Brewer pled guilty to one count of felony conspiracy and possession of unlawfully taken elk—a misdemeanor. He was sentenced to sixty days in jail, fined five thousand dollars, and placed on formal probation for five years. Beau Hammond pled guilty to one count of felony conspiracy and was sentenced to forty-five days in jail. Robbie Stokes pled guilty to one count of felony conspiracy and was ordered to do one thousand hours of community service. Ironically, Robbie—the most prolific elk-killer of them all—received the most lenient sentence: his community service consisted of helping out at a local fish hatchery. Robert "Bob" Stokes was the last to have his day in court. He pled guilty to one count of felony conspiracy and five misdemeanor counts of unlawful take of elk. Bob was sentenced to 270 days in jail, ordered to pay a $5,000 fine, and placed on five years formal probation.

IV

The notion that these men set out to go bear hunting on December 8, 1991, is very hard to swallow. Without hounds, they would have had a better chance of winning the lottery than finding and killing a bear. I suspect the bear hunting story was made up to explain all the high-powered rifles and butchering equipment in the suspects' possession when they came across the elk. Bear season was the only big game season still open at the time of the elk killings.

These men must have had a whole butcher shop full of equipment with them when they came across the elk. Included was at least one meat saw, used to cut off twenty legs and the heads of the two bull elk. Would the suspects have taken all that equipment with them if they had planned on only killing a bear? Without all of that equipment, they could never have finished the job out at Adobe Flat before daylight.

It is more likely that these four supposed bear hunters set out in two vehicles rather than one—Bob and Robbie in Bob's Toyota pickup and Jesse and Beau in Jesse's Bronco. Significant evidence was later found in both vehicles. There is no way they could have transported the meat and body parts from five elk in the back of Brewer's Bronco. I'm guessing that the suspects left town with the specific intent of finding that known elk herd and coming back with enough elk meat to fill their own freezers as well as the freezers of several friends and relatives.

This may well have been this group's annual ritual. Their chances of being caught were remote. If it hadn't been for that golden eagle, Watters might never have found the elk remains. Given a few more days, the carcasses and body parts would have been eaten, completely decomposed, or dragged off by scavengers.

I don't believe that any of these elk poachers regretted what they had done. Beau Hammond bragged to Matt Parsons about all the "illegal elk meat" he had in his freezer, yet he claimed not to have taken part in the shooting. Robbie Stokes told Warden Jacobs that "a really sickening feeling" came over him after seeing what they had done. Stokes didn't seem conscience-stricken when he bragged to Matt Parsons about "knocking three down."

Two words keep popping up in my head—"freezer paper." An incredible amount of freezer paper would be required to wrap two thousand pounds of elk meat. If the suspects wrapped all night and for the next five days, where had they gotten all that butcher paper? Purchasing it from the local market would surely draw unwanted attention. I suspect our four elk poachers had access to a large commercial roll of butcher paper, such as those used in grocery stores and butcher shops. Who, besides a former grocery store operator and butcher, might have such a roll and enough professional butchering equipment to process five elk? The trail leads straight to Jasper Stokes.

I have to believe that Jasper Stokes, Bob's father, was somehow involved in this adventure gone wrong. Significant amounts of elk blood, hair, and tissue were found on a tarp inside his garage. Robbie Stokes admitted to processing meat for five days behind Jasper's house. The big freezer out behind Jasper's house was conspicuously empty on the day the search warrants were served. No reasonable person would believe that this man—still in his sixties—an avid hunter himself, with no apparent mental or physical handicaps—was unaware that four men had been using his equipment to butcher elk behind his house for five days.

How did Margie McBride know that the search warrants were about to be served? That question, which haunted me the entire time I was writing this story, remains unanswered.

Sentinel of the North Coast

I

At the far northwest corner of California, in Del Norte and northern Humboldt Counties, lies a landscape of breathtaking scenery and unrivaled grandeur. This is a magical place where the Pacific Ocean crashes against tiny offshore islands and exposed rocks, occupied by barking sea lions, harbor seals, and thousands of sea birds of every shape and color. Moisture from the ocean blankets the land and is lapped up by centuries-old forests of coast redwoods—*Sequoia sempervirens*—the tallest trees on earth.

Although ninety percent of the original redwood forests are gone, what remains has been preserved in state and national parks stretching from the Oregon border sixty-five miles south to the small ocean-side community of Trinidad. Thanks to the Save the Redwoods League, concerned citizens and some farsighted elected officials, future generations can enjoy not only these magnificent trees, but all of the natural resources they support—world famous salmon and steelhead streams like the Smith and Klamath Rivers, dozens of smaller anadromous streams and hundreds of bird and mammal species, including deer, bear, and herds of majestic Roosevelt elk.

The Klamath Fish and Game Warden's Patrol District covers much of this region. With all its natural resources, this highly active patrol district has always had its problems. The Klamath River is a virtual quagmire of federal fishing regulations, designed around ancestral Native American fishing rights. Salmon have been gill-netted for decades, and it has been the daunting task of the current Fish and Game warden to determine who is doing it legitimately, for ceremonial purposes, and who is violating state law by transporting gill-netted fish off of the reservation and selling them for personal profit.

Outlaws living in the backwoods and small communities of Humboldt and Del Norte Counties have been poaching salmon, steelhead, sturgeon, deer, bear, and particularly elk since they were old enough to operate a gill net, cast a snag hook or shoot a rifle. These people have no respect for the law or any of the officers who enforce it.

In 1987 a new sheriff came to town. A six-foot-two inch, twenty-nine-year-old graduate of Humboldt State University's Wildlife Management Program became the Klamath Fish and Game warden. His name was Rick Banko and he had no tolerance for salmon snaggers, outlaw gill netters, or big game poachers. Banko accepted this assignment knowing that it was one of the most dangerous districts in California for a rookie Fish and Game warden to begin his career. He knew that he would frequently be called out in the middle of the night to deal with spotlighters and salmon poachers. Most of those outlaws would be armed and many of them would be under the influence of alcohol or drugs. With the next warden an hour or more away, Banko would learn to rely on his own law enforcement skills, common sense and courage to solve his new district's problems. He cared deeply about the resources he was sworn to protect and intended to make a difference. Rick Banko became a highly skilled investigator and developed a number of reliable information sources. It took him the first five years, but this new sheriff in town put a significant dent in the North Coast's unlawful hunting and fishing activities.

II

On October 5, 1992, Fish and Game Warden Rick Banko heard from one of his reliable informants that a well known outlaw, Cliff Rhodes, had recently killed three elk and obtained transportation tags from the Bureau of Indian Affairs to transport them to his home in Crescent City.

Rhodes looked like a typical Caucasian—light skin and short brown hair—but apparently had enough Native American blood flowing through his veins to qualify for the Yurok Tribal Rolls. As a member of the Yurok Tribe, Rhodes could legally hunt and kill deer and elk on the reservation, despite statewide hunting regulations.

Warden Banko had a degree in wildlife management and kept a pretty close eye on his district's elk herds. He knew where these majestic animals generally hung out, and it wasn't on the local Indian reservation. Most of the elk herds stayed on private land holdings or within the safe confines of the state and national parks. Rick had received this type of information about Cliff Rhodes before. With no witnesses or physical evidence, he would be unable to prove that the three elk had not been killed on the reservation.

Late on the afternoon of October 7, Warden Banko got the break he had been hoping for: Simpson Timber Company employees had discovered fresh elk remains on the Simpson Timber Company's S-300 road, over two miles from the Reservation.

The following morning Banko went to investigate, accompanied by Simpson Timber Company Patrolman Gene Fuller. Banko discovered three separate gut piles, each with large quantities of dried blood, rumen contents, and elk hair. The culprits had been so confident no one would come by that they had taken the time to field-dress and section the animals on the spot—an indication that the elk may have been spotlighted late at night or during the early morning hours.

"You go one way and I'll go the other," said Banko. Let me know if you find anything suspicious."

Warden Banko began walking the dirt road and the immediate area around the gut piles, looking for clues. After about seventy yards he noticed the sun reflecting off a small, brass-colored object lying at the north edge of the road. So as not to alter any fingerprints, Banko used a pen from his shirt pocket to reach down and pick up a high powered rifle casing. Stamped into the base were the symbols 7mm REM MAG (7 millimeter Remington Magnum). Within eighteen inches of the first casing were two more high-powered rifle casings, also 7mm Remington Magnum. "Three dead elk, three casings," said Banko. This vantage point looked very much like the one from which the three elk had been shot.

After documenting his find, Warden Banko walked back to the three gut piles. Gene Fuller pointed out a .22 caliber rim-fire casing lying on the ground next to what Banko had identified as gut pile number one. On the ground next to gut pile number three were two more .22 caliber rim-fire casings. Banko contemplated the three gut piles and the .22 casings, imagining what might have taken place.

"It looks like they knocked the three elk down with a seven millimeter and finished 'em off with a .22," said Banko, thinking aloud.

Fuller added, "These elk had to be either standing in the road or crossing it when they were shot."

"How far would you say we are from the boundary of the reservation?" asked Banko.

"This is definitely Timber Company property," Fuller said. "I'd say we're at least two miles from the reservation. I'll get an exact figure for you."

Warden Banko strongly suspected that these were the same three elk that

Cliff Rhodes had killed a few days earlier. After photographing the crime scene and collecting a significant amount of physical evidence, he drove to the Bureau of Indian Affairs office in Klamath. Warden Banko was greeted by BIA Investigator Bruce Carney, who confirmed that Rhodes had brought three elk into the office three days earlier. He gave Banko a copy of the transportation permit Rhodes had been issued on October 4, for two cow elk and one spike bull.

"He came in about 9:30 in the morning with two cows and a bull in the bed of his pickup," said Carney.

"Was anybody with him?" asked Banko.

"No, he was by himself. He said he killed 'em up off the S-10 Road, inside the reservation. All that information and his address are on the copy of the permit I gave you."

Warden Banko thanked Carney, went back to his headquarters and began working on a probable cause statement for the search warrant affidavit he would prepare during the next few days. Banko would need to make the case in his affidavit that any reasonable person, based on the totality of circumstances, would conclude that the elk remains found two miles from the reservation came from the three elk that Cliff Rhodes killed on October 4th. Rhodes would likely have in his possession a seven millimeter rifle used to take the elk, a .22 caliber weapon used to administer the final kills, and meat from the three unlawfully taken elk.

On October 10, 1992, at 2:30 p.m., armed with a search warrant, the following officers arrived at the Crescent City home of Clifford Rhodes: Warden Rick Banko, Warden Nick Albert, Warden Paul Weldon, Captain Steve Conger, and Del Norte County Sheriff's Sergeant Larry Graben. Warden Banko's search warrant authorized the officers to search the residence, vehicle, and person of Clifford Charles Rhodes.

When the officers arrived, thirty-nine-year-old Rhodes was outside doing bench presses. Muscle-bound and covered with tattoos, the five-foot-eight-inch, one-hundred-ninety-pound weight lifter had weights, bars, and dumbbells spread all over the carport.

"What's this all about?" said an angry Rhodes, as the officers walked up.

"We have a search warrant for your residence, vehicle, and person," said Banko. "Is anyone else here?"

"Susan," shouted Rhodes.

"Whaddaya want?" came a raspy female voice from inside the house.

"Get your ass out here," shouted Rhodes. "We got company."

A painfully thin, five-foot-two-inch woman with a cigarette in her mouth came storming out the side door of the house in her bare feet. She had blondish hair, with dark-colored roots, and a small tattoo on the side of her neck.

"Is this your wife?" asked Banko.

"No I ain't," announced the woman. "None o' your damn business who I am."

Warden Banko handed a smug Rhodes a copy of the search warrant and began asking a series of questions. The other officers secured the area and kept a close eye on the woman, identified as Susan Frank, Rhodes's live-in girlfriend.

"Mr. Rhodes, you obtained elk transportation tags on October 4, for three elk. Did you shoot and kill all three of those elk?"

"Yeah, I shot 'em," mumbled Rhodes.

"Where did you kill the three elk?"

"Up off the S-10 Road."

"Were the elk in the road when you shot them?"

"No, we were way up on the hill. We gutted 'em up there, then we dragged 'em back to my truck."

"Who was with you?"

"Scotty Pringle."

"Were you inside the reservation when you shot the elk?"

"Yes."

"Where are the three elk now?"

"Most of it is right here in the carport."

Based on Rhodes's statement, the first place the search team looked was the carport. They found two elk hindquarters and a front half hanging inside a burlap sack. Two ice chests, also located in the carport, yielded boned-out elk meat. More boned-out elk meat was found inside the kitchen refrigerator. All of the elk meat discovered during the search was seized into evidence.

When Warden Banko entered the dining room, he immediately spotted what he had been looking for: leaning against the wall was a Remington Model 700, 7mm Magnum, bolt action rife, with a Simmons scope attached. After documenting the rifle's serial number and describing the weapon on the evidence log, the rifle and scope were seized into evidence. Banko knew that Rhodes spent much of his time hunting and was likely to have a stock pile of ammunition somewhere in the house. It wasn't until the search team reached the master bedroom closet that Banko's suspicions were proven correct. The closet contained five boxes of 7mm Remington Magnum ammunition and several boxes of .22 rimfire cartridges. The search team also found and seized into evidence a Browning .22 semi-automatic rifle and a Sterling .22 semi-automatic pistol. One of those weapons had no doubt been used to finish off the three elk that Rhodes and Pringle had taken.

Cliff Rhodes's Ford pickup turned out to be a jackpot of incriminating evidence. In fact, it seemed to be Rhodes's primary place of business. Inside the cab, the search team found sixteen 7mm Remington Magnum cartridges, two elk bugles, several .22 rimfire cartridges, two hunting knives covered with blood, a Simpson Timber Company S-10 road key, two game transportation tags, and three spotlights. Two of the spotlights were behind the seat and one was sitting on the front seat—as if it had recently been used. The transportation tags—for one cow elk and one bull elk—had been issued on October 4, 1992, by BIA Investigator Bruce Carney. The third tag was conspicuously missing. All of the items discovered inside the cab of Rhodes's pickup were seized into evidence. As expected, the bed of the pickup was splattered with dried blood and hair. The search team gathered samples of each.

Halfway through the search of Rhodes's residence, one of the officers discovered a cache of illegal drugs. Sergeant Graben arrested Rhodes and his girlfriend. They were immediately transported to the Del Norte County Jail.

Based upon the extensive amount of evidence found at Rhodes's residence—particularly the three spotlights in his truck—investigators suspected that Rhodes had been killing deer and elk for commercial purposes and not simply for his own consumption. A considerable amount of meat seemed to be missing, along with one of the transportation tags that Bruce Carney had issued on October 4.

"This guy is bad news," commented one of the wardens, as Banko signed the evidence receipt and placed it on Rhodes's dining room table.

"We have a lot more work to do before this investigation is over," replied Banko.

On October 12, 1992, at 12:10 p.m., Fish and Game Wardens Rick Banko and Paul Weldon contacted Cliff Rhodes's hunting companion, Scott Pringle, at Pringle's mobile home in Crescent City. Pringle was on parole at the time. Tall and thin, with pockmarks all over his face, thirty-five-year-old Pringle was pleasant enough to talk to, but lacked self confidence and common sense. While most people avoided trouble, he seemed to welcome it at every turn.

"We're here to investigate the three elk killed by Cliff Rhodes on October 4," said Banko. "Cliff said you were with him when it happened?"

It was obvious that Pringle knew Fish and Game would be calling and had rehearsed his statement. "I was fishing on the Klamath River, near Cliff's father's cabin," said Pringle. "Cliff came by to check out his boat. He was giving me a ride to Crescent City when we saw three elk standing in the road. Cliff stopped the pickup and shot all three of 'em. They dropped dead right in the road."

Banko found it curious that Pringle had made a point of saying that all three elk had "dropped dead in the road." He asked Pringle about the weapons inside Rhodes's pickup at the time of the elk killings. Pringle said the only weapons he saw were a bolt action, high powered rifle and a shotgun. He admitted to helping Rhodes field dress and section the elk.

"I asked Cliff if we were on the reservation," said Pringle, jittery and well aware of his predicament. "He told me they were legal kills."

"So the elk were in the road when he shot them?" asked Banko.

"Yeah, they were standing in the middle of the road. I helped Cliff load the elk into the pickup and we drove directly to the BIA office, where Cliff got the transportation tags."

"Then whaddya do?" asked Banko.

"Then we drove to Cliff's house."

Pringle's account of the elk falling dead on the road did not match up with the .22 caliber casings found near the gut piles. It was also unlikely that three elk had just stood there while Rhodes took careful aim from seventy yards away and shot them dead. More likely, Rhodes took three quick shots—probably gut shots—and wounded each of the animals enough so they couldn't run away.

By making a point of saying that the elk had fallen dead, Pringle had actually drawn attention to himself. As a parolee, Pringle could not be in possession of a firearm.

Why would Pringle be so concerned about this issue, thought Banko, *unless it was he who had administered the coup de grâce with the .22?*

Pringle had also lied about the number of weapons in Rhodes's truck and about being with Rhodes at the BIA office in Klamath. BIA Investigator Carney, who had inspected the elk in the bed of Rhodes's pickup, said Rhodes had been by himself. Warden Banko suspected that the elk might have been spotlighted during the hours of darkness, but since there was no way to prove it, he did not press Pringle on that issue.

Anticipating a visit from Fish and Game, Scott Pringle was smart enough not to have disposed of the elk meat Rhodes had given him. He gave Banko and Weldon permission to search his place and told them they would find two cut-up front shoulders inside his kitchen refrigerator. In addition to the meat, which was seized into evidence, Warden Banko found two elk teeth sitting on the kitchen counter.

Later that week, Banko again dropped by Pringle's residence. Pringle stepped outside to meet him.

"I have something I want you to look at," said Banko. "Do you recognize this rifle?" Warden Banko held up the 7mm rifle seized from Rhodes's residence.

"Yeah, that's Cliff's rifle, the one he used to kill the elk."

"Are you sure?"

"Positive."

It was an established fact that three elk had been unlawfully killed on the S-300 road, two miles off the Yurok Indian Reservation. Three gut piles, three 7mm Remington Magnum casings, and three .22 rimfire casings had been found at the kill site. It was also a fact that Clifford Rhodes and Scott Pringle had killed and possessed three elk within two days of the three gut piles being discovered. Scott Pringle had identified the rifle that Rhodes used to kill the three elk as a 7mm Remington Magnum. He also stated that the three elk were standing in the road when Rhodes shot them and not up the hill, as Rhodes had said.

Any reasonable person would put two and two together and conclude that Rhodes and Pringle had unlawfully taken three elk off the reservation. Nevertheless, before the district attorney would approve criminal complaints against Rhodes and Pringle, Warden Banko would need to further connect the dots—tying the evidence found at the kill site with evidence found at Rhodes and Pringle's residences.

On October 15, 1992, Warden Banko hand-delivered blood samples from the elk kill sites on the S-300 road, blood samples from the bed of Clifford Rhodes's pickup, and meat samples from Rhodes's and Pringle's residences to pathologist Jim Banks, at the California Department of Fish and Game Wildlife Forensics Laboratory in Sacramento.

On October 16, 1992, Banko hand-delivered all of the weapons seized at Clifford Rhodes's residence and all of the empty shell casings found at the kill sites to the California Department of Justice Ballistics Laboratory in Eureka.

Jim Banks identified the blood and tissue samples taken from the kill site as elk, but that's all he could do; it would be another year before Banks's laboratory was fully qualified to analyze DNA. The U.S. Fish and Wildlife Laboratory in Ashland, Oregon, performed DNA analysis and clearly matched blood samples taken from the kill site with elk seized at Clifford Rhodes's residence.

The Department of Justice (DOJ) Laboratory in Eureka matched the three 7mm casings found near the kill site with Clifford Rhodes's 7mm rifle. They also matched the three .22 casings found at the kill site with Clifford Rhodes's .22 caliber Sterling Arms pistol.

Clifford Rhodes and Scott Pringle were prosecuted and eventually found guilty of unlawful take and possession of elk. Rhodes was ordered to pay a fine of $2,000 and serve thirty days in the Del Norte County Jail. Pringle had violated the conditions of his parole and was sent back to prison.

Twenty-five years later, now-retired North Coast Patrol Captain Nick Albert told me, "Rick Banko has undoubtedly made more elk poaching cases than any warden in the history of the Department of Fish and Game."

Banko has remained in Del Norte County throughout his successful career, eventually promoting to patrol lieutenant and more recently to patrol captain. For twenty-five years, he has been a constant thorn in the side of area poachers and has earned the title respectfully bestowed upon him by fellow Fish and Game officers—Sentinel of the North Coast.

Banko's Bait Pile

I

Nothing motivates a California black bear like food. Being an omnivore, a bear's limited natural menu includes insects, rodents, fish, frogs, nuts, berries, grass, honey, and carrion. Unnatural sources, on the other hand, are virtually limitless: meat, bones, vegetables, fruit, pastries, wheat, cereals, bread, flour, milk products, chocolate, beer, and soda—anything that is or has ever been edible. What better place to find these voracious eating machines than a garbage dump? Like giant open-air buffets, garbage dumps have attracted bears for centuries. Today, California law prohibits the take or pursuit of any bear within a four hundred yard radius of a garbage dump. Hunters are also prohibited from placing any food, bait, or attractant in a feeding area for the purpose of taking or pursuing bears.

Law-abiding California bear hunters send their hounds out into the woods to locate a fresh scent; then they begin the pursuit. There is no limit on the number of dogs, as long as bear season is open and the general deer season is closed. During deer season, no more than one dog may be used. Unfortunately, a few bear hunters opt for the easy way; they cheat. They bring garbage—decaying meat and other food items—into the woods and hide it in secluded places where the local game warden can't find it. The garbage attracts bears, and the outlaws pursue the bears directly off these "bait piles" or indirectly off of the fresh tracks (scent) the recently fed animals leave behind.

II

Sometime during the week of October 24, 1994, Loretta Chappell pulled up to the loading dock behind a well known Crescent City butcher shop.

Loretta was a stocky, average-height woman in her early forties—garrulous and strong enough to make her living as a lumberjack. She clearly had no use for womanly wiles. Her features were plain and unadorned by cosmetics. Her clothes might have been purchased in the Menswear department at Peterson's Feed and Grain. She was driving a beige-colored Toyota pickup, with a dog box mounted in the bed.

"Where do you want this?" asked the shop attendant.

"Just throw it in back, behind the dog box," replied Loretta.

With that, the attendant lifted a large feed bag, filled with cow bones, skulls, fat, and meat scraps into the bed of Chappell's pickup.

"Thanks," said Loretta, as she drove away, "I'll see you again next week."

Harley and Loretta Chappell had convinced the butcher shop operators that the weekly bag of tallow they were picking up was being used to feed the Chappells' hungry hound dogs. That wasn't entirely true. A few bones may have been thrown to the dogs, but most of those butchered cattle and pig remains were being driven twenty miles down Highway 101 to a secluded location on Simpson Timber Company property—a large tract of private land south of Redwoods National Park. Hunters were given written permission to pursue game inside this private landholding as long as they respected the area and adhered to state hunting regulations.

On October 29, 1994, Fish and Game Warden Rick Banko received information that someone had unlawfully placed a bait pile on Simpson Timber Company property. The informant couldn't provide an exact location, saying only that the bait pile was somewhere off the H-200 logging road. That afternoon, Warden Banko headed north on Highway 101, from Klamath. He turned east, near Wilson Creek, onto Simpson Timber Company property. This was rugged country, heavily vegetated with second growth timber. Reaching the H-200 Road, Banko scanned the area for any sign of recent human or bear activity.

Warden Banko had driven a few miles down the H-200 road when he noticed a heavily used bear trail, leading uphill. "Wow!" exclaimed Rick, as he stepped out of his patrol truck. "That's not hot biscuits I smell." He recognized the unpleasant, pungent odor of rotting flesh. It was 2:00 p.m. when Banko began following the bear trail up the hill. He hadn't gone fifteen yards, when he came upon a three-foot-high pile of skulls, bones, meat, and scraps. The pile was so white that it might have been mistaken for a patch of snow at a distance.

Dodging the swarming yellow jackets, Banko took a close look at the huge pile of tallow. Some of it had been there for several days, but on top there was a significant amount of fresh cattle remains, possibly dumped that morning. Not wanting to be seen at the site, Banko quickly returned to his truck and grabbed his camera. After taking several photographs of the scene, he covered his footprints and drove away.

Gene Fuller was the Simpson Timber Company security officer. A sixty-year-old retired LA cop, Fuller had come to the North Coast on a fishing trip five years earlier and decided to make his home in the area. He and Banko had a good working relationship and kept each other advised of anything suspicious happening on the Simpson property. Warden Banko drove to Fuller's office on the afternoon of October 29th and told him what he had found. Together, they returned to the bait pile and set up a hidden surveillance camera to monitor the baiting station. The timber company did not allow violations of state law on the property and was particularly intolerant of anyone disposing of garbage there.

During the week that followed, Banko and Fuller returned each day to check the camera. Each time they turned on the playback mechanism, nothing happened. Convinced that the battery had gone dead, Warden Banko removed the camera from its casing and prepared to replace the battery.

Suddenly the playback function began to work. It showed a beige-colored Toyota pickup with a dog box mounted in the bed—hounds milling about excitedly atop the box. The pickup was parked on the H-200 road, next to the trail leading to the bait pile. Warden Banko was surprised to learn that the camera had also recorded the vehicle's license plate. Although already familiar with Harley Chappell's hound rig, Warden Banko confirmed his suspicions with a record check of the plate. As if that were not enough, the camera had also recorded Loretta Chappell walking up the bear trail to the bait pile. The date on the screen was Sunday, October 30, at 7:30 a.m. Based on what the camera had recorded and knowledge of Harley Chappell's normal work schedule (weekends off), Warden Banko surmised that the next bear hunt would probably take place on Saturday, November 5.

Before daylight on November 5, Warden Rick Banko and Simpson Timber Company Patrolman Gene Fuller began a stakeout of the bait pile. Hiding Banko's patrol vehicle some distance away, they had climbed to a location on a ridge, overlooking the H-200 Road. With the aid of binoculars, Banko and Fuller could clearly see the bait pile and the road.

It was exactly 6:44 a.m. when things began to get interesting. "We've got company," whispered Banko, focusing his binoculars on an exceptionally large, black-colored bear slowly lumbering up the road. "He's a pretty one," commented Banko, noticing an almost blue sheen reflecting off of the bear's jet-black coat. California black bears come in a variety of colors, including several shades of brown. Seeing a robust, black individual was not unusual, but it didn't happen every day. The curious bear stopped and sniffed the air several times before finally sauntering up the hill to the bait pile.

At 7:30 a.m., the entire canyon erupted with the echoing sound of baying hounds. As quiet and peaceful as the canyon had been a few minutes earlier, it was now in chaos. The terrified bear bolted into the woods. Banko and Fuller could hear branches shattering as the four hundred pound bruin crashed its way down the canyon. Two pickups appeared on the H-200 Road, headed in the direction of the bait station. The first was a beige Toyota—hounds standing on the dog box. Warden Banko did not recognize the second pickup, a light green Chevy, with a dog box mounted in the bed.

Both pickups came to a stop below the hidden officers. Loretta Chappell climbed out of the beige Toyota and walked up the bear trail to the bait pile. A burly, middle-aged man exited the driver's side, wearing light brown, suspendered overalls. Warden Banko immediately recognized him as Harley Chappell, a well known houndsman. Like male and female bookends, Harley and Loretta had the same, moderately rotund body shape and each stood about five-feet-seven inches tall.

Two adult males stepped out of the Chevy pickup. The driver was later identified as Harley Chappell's twenty-three-year-old nephew, Cletis Chappell. There was a slight family resemblance, although Cletis was several inches taller than his uncle, much thinner and still had a healthy crop of hair. Melvin Chappell, Harley's seventy-year-old father, was an older version of his son, also bald and wearing faded, blue denim overalls.

"Something's been here!" echoed a high-pitched, ear-piercing shriek from the bait pile. "Let 'em loose!"

Loretta came thundering down the hill toward the Toyota pickup. Warden Banko watched as she released the hounds from the top of the dog box. Harley and Cletis did the same with the hounds from the Chevy's dog box. Free to roam, all of the baying hounds dashed up the hill toward the bait pile before running off in the direction of the bear that had recently fled.

Warden Banko and Patrolman Fuller had seen enough and began making their way down the ridge, toward the action. They approached the H-200 Road just as both pickups started up. The vehicles headed north for a short distance before turning around. When the beige Toyota had reached a point adjacent to the bait pile, Banko stepped out into the road and stopped it. Harley Chappell was driving and Loretta was sitting in the passenger seat. Both of them had slack-jawed expressions of shock on their faces. The green

Chevy pulled up behind the Toyota, with Cletis driving and Melvin sitting in the passenger seat.

"What are you guys up to?" asked Banko.

"We're just h-huntin'," replied Harley, stammering slightly and avoiding Banko's eyes.

"Harley, I'd like you to step out of the truck and walk up the hill with me," said Banko, pointing in the direction of the bait pile.

Both men were hiking up the bear trail when Chappell stopped.

"We don't need to go any farther," said Chappell. "There's no sense in lying to you. I have bait up there and we just released our dogs after a bear."

Chappell admitted to releasing three hounds from his truck and three more from Cletis's truck. Up to that point, his account had been fairly truthful. When Warden Banko asked him how long they had been baiting, Chappell replied that they had just started that day.

"I found bait here last week," countered Banko.

"I meant that I added more bait today," replied Chappell.

"Do you have more bait in your truck?"

"Yeah, there's another sack in there," admitted Chappell, reluctantly.

Warden Banko inspected the bed of Chappell's pickup and found a feed sack filled with fifty pounds of butchered meat scraps and animal fat.

Banko began checking all the subjects' hunting licenses and bear tags. Everyone had a valid California Hunting License and everyone except Loretta, who had already killed a bear that season and tagged it, had a valid bear tag. Banko suspected that Loretta's bear had been illegally taken off the same bait pile, but knew that without proof, pursuing the issue would just lead to an unwinnable argument.

Sitting on the front seat of the Toyota pickup was a .30-30 lever action rifle, belonging to Harley Chappell. There were five live rounds in the magazine— none in the chamber. Another .30-30 lever action rifle, belonging to Cletis Chappell, was sitting on the front seat of the Chevy pickup. There were six live rounds in its magazine—none in the chamber.

"I'm responsible for the bait pile," Harley proclaimed loudly, before anyone else could speak. "None of the others had anything to do with it."

Banko shook his head before countering, "Gene and I just watched Loretta walk up to the bait pile and yell out instructions to release the dogs. We also saw Cletis help you release the dogs from his pickup." Warden Banko did not want to reveal the existence of the hidden camera, so he did not mention their filming Loretta replenishing the bait pile a few days earlier.

All four subjects were issued citations for unlawfully "using bait for the purpose of taking or pursuing bear." Both rifles and the bag of bait found in Chappell's truck were seized into evidence.

As Harley Chappell was about to leave, Gene Fuller spoke up. "One more thing," he said. "As far as hunting on Simpson Timber Company property, you're done."

Later that week, Warden Banko contacted all the Crescent City butcher shops, in an effort to find out where the Chappells had been getting their bait. He found one shop that said Loretta Chappell had been coming in once a week to pick up tallow—claiming it was to feed their dogs.

III

Nearly a year later, on the afternoon of October 19, 1995, Wardens Rick Banko and Don Kelly were sitting in an unmarked boat near the mouth of the Klamath River. Although the river remained open to the take of silver (Coho) salmon, it was closed to the take of king (Chinook) salmon. Fresh out of the ocean, it's difficult to tell the two species apart, except for the fact that kings average over ten pounds—some are much larger—and silvers usually weigh six or eight pounds. There is one surefire way to tell the difference and it was up to every fishermen to be aware of it: the inside of a king salmon's mouth is completely dark, while silver salmon have white or "silver" gums surrounding their teeth.

Banko and Kelly were dressed in civilian clothes, pretending to be fishermen, all the while watching others who were fishing from boats or along the shoreline. It was about 3:15 p.m. when Warden Kelly trained his binoculars on a bank fisherman who had just hooked a fish. Based on the way this man's fishing rod was bent over, it was a fairly large one. "This guy's got a good sized fish on," said Kelly.

Warden Banko directed his binoculars in the same direction and began watching, as the heavyset man, who looked to be in his mid-forties, continued to play the fish. "That guy looks familiar," said Banko, in a low voice.

The fisherman finally landed a ten or twelve pound salmon. Banko and Kelly suspected that it was a king. "Let's see what he does with it," said Banko. As the wardens continued to watch, the fisherman walked over to some calm water and began cleaning the fish. By this time, Warden Banko recognized the fisherman.

"Ya know who that is," whispered Banko. "That's ol' Harley Chappell!"

When he had finished cleaning his fish, Harley Chappell walked eastward for about a hundred yards and met with another man Warden Banko recognized as Chappell's nephew, Cletis. Cletis was carrying a feed bag with two salmon inside. Harley removed a smaller salmon from the bag and replaced it with the salmon he had just caught. He then returned to his fishing spot, carrying the salmon that he had just removed from the bag.

Warden Banko radioed Captain Steve Conger, who was nearby in a patrol unit, and asked him to intercept Cletis Chappell and inspect the bag he was carrying. Conger had actually checked Cletis and his two legal silver salmon earlier in the day. Apparently believing that Cletis would not be checked again, Harley had decided to make the switch.

Banko and Kelly drove the boat across the river and contacted Harley Chappell. Although Chappell scowled at the sight of Warden Banko, he was happy enough to show off the silver salmon he claimed to have just caught. Leaving Harley with his "fresh catch," Banko and Kelly walked up the beach to where Captain Conger had just contacted Cletis Chappell. Inside Cletis's bag was a silver salmon and a considerably larger king salmon.

"Is this king salmon the one that your Uncle Harley just caught?" asked Banko.

Realizing that their little game was over, Cletis answered, "Honestly, yes."

Warden Kelly walked to the river and asked Harley Chappell to return to the area where his nephew and the other officers were waiting. When Kelley and Harley Chappell reached the others, Kelly advised Harley that he and Warden Banko had seen him switch the king salmon with the silver salmon in Cletis's bag. Kelly said that Cletis had confirmed the switch.

"Cletis, you know that ain't true," Harley said, putting his fists on his hips and jutting his head forward to give the younger man the evil eye. "Admit it, now. That king salmon is yours." Harley had reason to be concerned that the judge would throw the book at him: he was still on probation for the bear bait pile conviction, eleven months earlier. When Cletis refused to change his story, the furious Harley Chappell turned to Warden Kelly and said, "Just write the damned ticket!"

Warden Kelly issued Harley Chappell a much-deserved citation for unlawful take and possession of a king salmon during the Klamath River king salmon closure. As Wardens Banko and Kelley climbed back in their boat and pulled away from shore, they heard Harley Chappell cry out, "Banko, I hate your guts!"

Not in My Stream

I

One of the most important duties of a California Fish and Game warden is keeping pollutants out of state waters. Some wardens avoided these types of cases because they were generally complicated and required a considerable amount of sample taking, investigation, and report writing. The good wardens saw that pursuing these cases was not only their duty but also a very important part of protecting the resource.

During my years in the Redding area, I organized a task force of city, county, and state investigators (Water Quality Control Board, County Health Department, and City Sewage Treatment) to contact local businesses that were disposing of pollutants incorrectly and in some cases, illegally. These businesses were encouraged to clean up their acts or be prosecuted.

Radiator shops were a classic example. One shop, located in downtown Redding, had been in business for over fifty years and had been dumping their toxic waste on the ground behind the shop the entire time. The fear was that harmful chemicals would eventually end up in the ground water or travel down one of the city storm drains and into the Sacramento River. Although it was more interesting catching individual poachers, we probably saved a thousand times more fish by performing these more prosaic duties and keeping pollutants out of the Sacramento River and its many tributaries.

II

Summer was the slowest time of year for Redding area Fish and Game wardens. Temperatures soared into the triple digits and it was sometimes difficult to find anything of consequence going on. Warden Dave Szody referred to this as "the time of year when you have to kick over rocks to find a good case."

One hot July morning in the 1990s, Szody was patrolling a series of logging roads near the tiny foothill community of Manton. A set of fresh tire tracks led him down an unnamed road to a pristine little trout stream. This was one of those streams that was too small and too isolated for the Department of Fish and Game to stock with trout, but it supported a healthy population of native, six-inch, beautifully parr-marked rainbows.

Though no vehicles were present, Szody decided to check out the stream. At the water's edge he noticed an impression in the sand where someone had recently parked. Next to the impression and ten feet from the water's edge was a cardboard box.

"Unbelievable," muttered Szody. "Somebody changed his oil here." Inside the box were a used oil filter, four empty quart size oil cans, a plastic bucket filled with used oil and two empty beer cans.

To say that Warden Szody was outraged would be a gross understatement. He had seen this same scenario so many times before and could envision the ultimate outcome—*The first time it rains, the bucket will overflow and the box will decompose. All the oil and trash will be washed into the stream.* Warden Szody diligently began searching the area for any clue as to who might have done this. He walked back and forth through the high grass until he spotted a small piece of white paper lying about ten feet from the cardboard box.

I have always believed in Karma. Don't get me wrong; not everyone who commits a crime against nature gets the punishment he deserves. Every day, people pollute the air, poison our waters, destroy wetlands, harpoon whales, remove mountain tops, and pass environmentally damaging legislation without the slightest consequence. Occasionally, however, Mother Nature gets in the last punch.

This was one of those instances.

The tiny piece of paper that Warden Szody found was a receipt—a receipt for the purchase of four quarts of oil, an oil filter, and a twelve pack of cheap beer. "I got ya!" Szody said, pumping his fist into the air. The receipt was dated the previous day and had been issued by a convenience store in Cottonwood. Cottonwood is a small town on Interstate 5, located about thirty miles west of the scene of the crime. Now confident that he would make the case, Warden

Szody meticulously photographed the entire scene, secured the bucket full of oil so it wouldn't spill, and loaded the evidence into his truck.

It was mid-afternoon when Warden Szody reached Cottonwood. He drove to the convenience store and questioned a clerk behind the counter.

"Were you working here yesterday?" he asked.

"Yes I was," replied the clerk.

"Do you remember this transaction?" asked Szody, handing the receipt to the clerk.

"Yeah, I remember that," replied the clerk. "The guy was driving a little orange pickup."

"By any chance do you know this guy's name?"

"Not his last name, but I think his first name is Wes."

"Do you know where Wes lives?"

"Not quite sure … I think he lives on a dirt road, out past Gas Point Road."

Warden Szody appreciated the information that the clerk had given him, but got the impression that he was holding back a little.

I bet old Wes buys a lot of beer in that store, thought Szody, as he drove away. *He's probably one of its best customers.*

Like a bloodhound on a scent trail, Szody spent the next two hours driving up and down several dirt roads that intersected with Gas Point Road. He had no luck finding the little orange truck, so he resolved to try again the next day.

That night, Dave had difficulty sleeping. He cherished the beautiful trout streams that flowed through his patrol district and took a dim view of anyone who threatened to harm them. This investigation would not end until he had located and prosecuted the person responsible for that careless and irresponsible act.

The next day began much like the previous day had ended—with Szody driving up and down every dirt road that intersected with Gas Point. Luck was on his side. Warden Szody spotted the orange truck in only forty-five minutes. The old, beat-up Isuzu was parked in front of a single-wide mobile home. Before pulling into the long, unpaved driveway, Szody grabbed his binoculars and focused on the suspect vehicle's license plate. He ran the plate through dispatch and learned that the tiny truck was registered to a Wesley Charles McPherson, at that same Cottonwood address.

No Cottonwood area contact would be complete without running the gauntlet of a pack of barking dogs. They were all there to greet him as he pulled up in front of the residence—two black and white border collies and some kind of white, mixed-breed pit bull. A little apprehensive about the yapping dogs at his feet, Szody knocked at the front door. Lying next to the porch were several empty beer cans, all the same cheap brand that Szody had found in the cardboard box left beside the stream. His knock set off another barrage of barking inside the house.

This ought to be fun, thought Szody. *Odds are this guy is going to have an attitude or he wouldn't have done what he did in the first place.*

The door opened slightly and the bald head of a middle-aged, unshaven man appeared in the opening. A waft of cigarette smoke met Szody's nostrils, blown by the noisy swamp cooler inside.

"I'm Warden Szody, with the Department of Fish and Game. May I speak with you?"

"What? Max, shut the hell up. Just a minute while I get my cigarettes."

The door closed briefly. When it reopened, the man stepped out on the porch wearing nothing but a pair of boxer shorts and a dirty white T-shirt. He quickly closed the door behind him as Max continued to bark inside.

"Are you Wesley McPherson?"

"Yeah, waddaya want?"

"Were you up near Forward Mill Road the day before yesterday?"

"Why?"

There's my answer, thought Szody. *Otherwise, he would have said no.* After three or four minutes of playing cat and mouse, McPherson admitted that he had been in the area and did change the oil in his truck.

"What did you do with the oil cans and the waste oil?" asked Szody.

"I took it all with me," replied McPherson.

McPherson was obviously lying, but Szody knew he would eventually pin him into a corner that he couldn't get out of.

"Are you sure about that?" asked Szody.

"Positive," replied McPherson.

"What did you do with it after that?"

McPherson had to think of a good answer for that question. It took him a minute or two. "I think I threw it all in a dumpster, downtown."

"How about you showing me where you changed your oil?"

The suspect was hesitant, but after a few more minutes of verbal sparring, he agreed to show Szody where he had changed his oil. Warden Szody followed McPherson out to Manton and up the mountain to the exact location where the discarded box of material was found. Szody pulled the Fish and Game truck in behind the orange Isuzu and walked over to where McPherson was standing.

"See, I told you I took everything with me," said McPherson, sounding smug.

"Well, Mr. McPherson, I appreciate you showing me where you changed your oil, but I have something to tell you. The box isn't here because I picked it up yesterday. I will be filing a report with the district attorney and sometime soon, you will receive a notice to appear in court."

Wesley McPherson stood next to the beautiful little trout stream with a perplexed look on his face. He wanted to stand there and argue with Warden Szody, but the experienced wildlife protection officer had proven his case and was already walking back to his patrol truck.

A few months later, McPherson was fined $2,500 in Shasta County Superior Court, for litter and placing oil products where they could pass into the waters of the state.

Chalk up one small victory for Mother Nature.

Bears and Bad Guys

I

For several years during the mid-nineties, California Fish and Game officers working in and around Shasta County kept hearing rumors about illegal bear hunting activities. The lucrative black market for bear parts had turned the local sport of bear hunting into the dirty business of killing California black bears for their gallbladders.

The practice of killing bears for their gallbladders has been going on for thousands of years. Ever since the early days of recorded Chinese history, there has been a belief that bear bile contained medicinal powers and could be used to treat certain ailments. Present-day laboratory tests have proved that the principal ingredients in bear bile can be duplicated synthetically, but that fact has not put an end to the quest to obtain the real thing. The inhumane business of killing bears for their gallbladders has spread from China to Korea and other Asian countries, contributing to the depletion of Asian bear populations in the wild. As Asian species have declined, other species throughout the world have become targets—among them the California black bear.

The "sport" of hunting wildlife with hound dogs has a long tradition in America. It spread from England during colonial times, when some rich dandy arrived in the colonies with the first pack of hounds. Many of today's hound strains are said to have originated from those dogs. Setting the hounds on bears, raccoons, fox, and other wildlife was particularly popular in the South. Generation after generation has chased hounds through the woods.

Just north of Redding, California, lies Shasta Dam. This massive cement structure at the north end of the Great Central Valley was constructed between 1938 and 1945. People were unemployed at the time and came from all over the country to work on this seven-year project. Many came from Southern States and settled down in Northern California to raise families and establish communities like Central Valley and Project City. With them, they brought a culture that centered on hunting wildlife with dogs—hound dogs, that is—Walker Coonhounds, Redbones, English Coonhounds, and Blueticks. Nothing made a transplanted Southerner feel more like he was back home than chasing a pack of floppy-eared, howling mutts through the Northern California woods.

Word got back to friends and families that the weather was good out here and the bear hunting was even better. More Southerners arrived and for the next twenty-five years they were happy to run their dogs and hunt bears for the "sport" of it. Some became licensed guides and profited modestly by guiding other hunters during the two- or three-month California bear season. That all changed sometime in the 1970s when word got out about a lucrative market for bear parts. Bear gallbladders were being sold in Korea, China, and other Asian countries for thousands of dollars. With very large Korean and Chinese populations living in California, a market was also growing here in the United States.

Instead of discarding all the entrails as they had done in the past, unscrupulous houndsmen began carefully removing the gallbladders and tying them off with string to prevent any of the valuable bile from escaping. They collected these organs in plastic baggies and secretly sold them to a middleman (usually another houndsman) or directly to a black marketeer. Word eventually spread that California's black bears were being chased down and killed simply for their gallbladders. With big money at stake, it didn't seem to matter if the season was open or closed.

II

Captain Jack Weaver was in charge of Redding area Fish and Game wardens during the late seventies. Reports were coming into the Fish and Game office about bears being killed illegally for their parts. Although gallbladders were the primary target, paws and claws were also prized.

Local houndsmen had discovered an easier way to find bears than driving mountain roads all day in search of a fresh scent trail. They collected leftover food and garbage from butcher shops, restaurants, and markets. Barrels of this stuff would be transported into the woods and piled in secluded areas.

There were even reports of deer being shot and thrown on the pile. The combined stench of garbage and rotting animal flesh would attract hungry bears from miles away. Hunters could kill bears at the bait pile or run their dogs off of the scent trails that bears had left behind. This practice was quite illegal but finding the bait piles and catching these cagey woodsmen in the act was difficult, if not impossible to do. Not to be deterred, Weaver brought in an undercover warden from Southern California.

Although the local hound community was reluctant to trust an outsider, this particular undercover officer seemed to infiltrate their ranks fairly easily. A Caucasian of average height and weight, he could do a convincing good ol' boy impersonation. In a surprisingly short time, Weaver's man managed to convince the local houndsmen that he was one of them. For three months, he hunted with them, ate with them, and played the role of a Northern California houndsman to the hilt.

By the time the detail came to an end, the undercover warden had documented several violations, the majority of which involved hunting off of bait piles. These cases were difficult to prove in court. Defendants claimed they didn't know the bait piles were there. Most of the charges were eventually dismissed due to sketchy evidence and various technicalities. It was a good effort but the local hound community became warier than ever of outsiders. Fifteen years would go by before another attempt was made to crack this carefully-guarded secret.

III

In November of 1995, Fish and Game Warden Dave Szody and I opened an investigation into a number of bear-related violation reports in and around Shasta County. We followed up on any leads, regardless of how small or ambiguous they might be. Between us, Szody and I had over forty years of experience catching and prosecuting wildlife violators. None of those violators, however, were as secretive, crafty, and hard to catch as outlaw houndsmen. Arrogance and disrespect for game regulations permeated the local hound community.

Although the sale or possession for sale of bear parts was now a California felony, there was big money to be made and violations were reportedly rampant. A rumor was floating around about a Korean businessman who periodically came up from Los Angeles to buy gallbladders from the local houndsmen. It was not much to start with, but it was all we had.

During the course of a routine investigation, Warden Szody and I came across a man named Dan Searcy. Searcy had grown up in Central Valley (currently Shasta Lake City), lived there all of his life and had a pretty good handle on everything that went on there. With absolutely no prompting from us, Searcy expressed his concern about all of the wildlife violations taking place.

"You wouldn't believe all of the stuff I hear about," said Searcy. "They're killing bears just for their gallbladders. I used to join in," Searcy admitted, "but I feel bad about it now."

Szody and I were trying to gauge if Searcy was just trying to impress us or if he really knew something. With the mention of gallbladders, we began to pay close attention. "I've seen bear cubs killed and their remains fed to the dogs," continued Searcy. "They bait the bears in with piles of garbage; then they kill 'em."

I asked Searcy if he could provide any names. The first name out of this man's mouth was Buck Millsap. According to our new informant, Millsap had been buying and selling bear gallbladders for years. Szody and I recognized the name. Millsap had been the subject of an undercover bear investigation back in the late seventies. His name popped up whenever bear violations were mentioned.

I asked how Searcy knew that Millsap bought and sold gallbladders. "Because I've seen him do it," replied Searcy. "One year I sold him seventeen myself. He paid me fifty dollars apiece."

Searcy said he had become disgusted with it all some time ago and sold his dogs. I asked how well he knew Buck Millsap. "I've known him for years," replied Searcy. "I heard some Korean guy is supposed to come up around Thanksgiving to meet with him."

Warden Szody and I were pretty good at recognizing the difference between a load of bull and the truth. We both had the feeling that Searcy was sincere. I asked if Searcy would be willing to introduce an undercover officer to Buck Millsap. After carefully considering the proposition, he replied, "Sure I would."

Szody and I drove back to Redding discussing our new informant and the possibility of bringing in an undercover officer. "Now what do we do?" Szody asked. "We can't use anybody from around here; the houndoggers will recognize him."

"The guy would have to fit the part," I said, "someone who looks and talks like a real houndsman." One man came to mind. This Fish and Game warden worked far enough out of the area that no one would recognize him. He was a big, six-foot-four-inch cowboy who talked like he just got off the bus from San Antonio.

"Big Al McDermott!" blurted Szody.

"I was just thinking the same thing."

That night I telephoned Al McDermott and asked if he would be willing to come down periodically and play the role of Dan Searcy's visiting uncle from Montana. Without hesitation, Al said he would be glad to do it.

The next morning, Warden Szody and I found ourselves sitting in front of the regional patrol chief's desk. I explained the situation and made our case for bringing in an undercover warden from outside the area. "Warden Al McDermott is our first choice," I said.

The chief was skeptical. He didn't believe the new informant was trustworthy and he was particularly leery of using Al McDermott as the undercover operative. The chief and McDermott had a history. Years earlier the chief had been McDermott's lieutenant. Although the chief reluctantly approved our undercover investigation, Szody and I couldn't help thinking that he believed McDermott was bound to fail and make a fool of himself.

Dan Searcy didn't disappoint. He got in touch with some of his houndsmen acquaintances and arranged to join them, along with his Uncle Jack, on a hunting trip. Al McDermott would play the role of Searcy's Uncle Jack Russell, a ranch manager from Montana who was in town looking for cattle to buy. We provided McDermott with ID, business cards, a phone number, and a Montana license plate for his unmarked truck.

On December 9, 1995, at 4:30 a.m., Dan Searcy and Warden Al McDermott—aka Jack Russell—joined a group of local houndsmen on a bear hunt in the mountains of western Shasta County. They met at a mini-mart on the outskirts of Redding. Buck Millsap was already there when Searcy and McDermott arrived. He was driving a three-quarter-ton pickup with a dog box in the bed. Soon after Searcy and McDermott arrived, several more pickups started pulling into the parking lot. Searcy identified two of the other hunters as Stan Harder and Larry Cogle. Harder and Cogle were two tobacco-chewing rednecks out of central casting. Similar in height and coloring and almost as jowly as their dogs, they could have passed for middle-aged brothers. Each man drove his own pickup. Harder's pickup contained a dog box, filled with hounds belonging to Buck Millsap.

As was usually the case during organized bear hunts, three or four others showed up and tagged along. Searcy introduced Jack Russell (McDermott) to Millsap and Harder. Millsap was in his late fifties at the time, but his tendency to hunch over, along with his weather-beaten face, made him look at least ten years older. With good posture he would have stood about six feet tall.

"Are you the guy they named that little dog after?" said Millsap.

McDermott laughed. "That's me!" he said. Seeing the joke as an opening, he made an extra effort to get acquainted. With his ten-gallon cowboy hat and slow Southern drawl, the six-foot-four-inch McDermott fit right in without drawing too much attention to himself.

When everyone had arrived, McDermott and Searcy followed the caravan in McDermott's pickup. The actual hunt began on an unpaved U.S. Forest Service road near Jerusalem Creek. Suddenly the two lead pickups, driven by Millsap and Harder, came to a stop. Buck Millsap removed his "strike" dog from the wooden box in the bed of his pickup. When the excited hound had finished relieving itself, Millsap lifted it onto a wooden platform mounted on the hood of his truck. As a rule, the "strike" dog had the best nose in the pack and was used to sniff out the first bear scent. Once the hound was tethered to the hood, the caravan proceeded down the road.

After about forty-five minutes, the "strike" dog picked up a scent, and the chase was on. Most of the other dogs from both trucks were turned loose. Within an hour they had treed a bear. Everyone walked to the tree, with the exception of Buck Millsap. Millsap would hang back if there was any walking to do, McDermott observed. Harder led the way, followed by Cogle and the others.

McDermott was still some distance behind when a shot rang out. Seconds later, he heard the hounds resume the chase. Apparently the bear had been wounded. A second shot was fired within a few minutes of the first. Again, the dogs took up the chase. McDermott arrived just in time to see the bear turn and face the oncoming dogs. When the dogs had come within striking distance, it swatted at them with its right paw and gave off a low-pitched moan. One of the men McDermott didn't recognize lifted a rifle to his shoulder and fired the killing shot.

Although Warden McDermott was not sure who had fired the first shot, the bear was eventually tagged by a large, heavyset man in striped overalls named Orville Samples. A big snaggle-toothed grin crossed Samples's face as he pulled the tag from his pocket and began to fill it out.

Harder, who always seemed angry for some reason, transported the bear to the road, where Millsap was waiting. McDermott watched carefully as Larry Cogle field-dressed the bear. Cogle removed the gallbladder, tied it off with a string and handed it to Buck Millsap. Millsap placed the gallbladder inside a utility box mounted behind the cab of his pickup.

Some questionable things happened during Warden McDermott's first undercover bear hunt, but none of them were specific violations. McDermott did, however, establish himself with the group and manage to confirm that Buck Millsap was collecting gallbladders.

I was fiercely passionate about the natural resources that we were sworn to protect and believed that anyone who worked for a state or federal resource agency shared that same view. It didn't matter if that person enforced the law, managed a wildlife refuge, drove a tractor, raised trout, mopped floors, or sat at a desk, he or she was expected to be above reproach when it came to fish and wildlife laws. I soon learned that not everyone felt that way.

On December 16, 1995, Warden Al McDermott, working in his undercover capacity, went on a bear hunt in eastern Shasta County. Sometime before 11:00 a.m., Buck Millsap released his hounds on a small set of bear tracks near Tamarack Road. The hounds pursued the little bear for over an hour before it crawled into a cave at the edge of a rock cliff.

As was usually the case when a walk of any distance was required, Millsap stayed near his truck and sent his tagalongs after the bear. One of those tagalongs was a forty-year-old man with a butch haircut and a big handlebar mustache named Fred Belcher. The self-appointed leader of the hunt, Belcher asked who in the group had a bear tag and wanted to shoot the bear.

"How big is it?" said another of Millsap's tagalongs.

"It ain't very big," said Belcher, spitting a wad of tobacco onto the dry ground.

They were all hemming and hawing, shifting from foot to foot outside the cave, when Bruce Vanosek, a middle-aged, average-height man with a thick, salt-and-pepper beard, spoke up. "I have a bear tag, but my son is going to shoot the bear," said Vanosek.

Vanosek's twenty-two-year-old son, Darrel, was about the same size as his dad, without the beard and the pot belly.

With no apparent reservations, Darrel Vanosek stepped forward and walked toward the cave entrance. He was carrying a large caliber rifle; McDermott thought it was a 30-06. Bruce Vanosek maneuvered into position so he could photograph his son shooting the bear.

"How we gonna get the bear outta that cave?" asked one of the tagalongs.

"I got somethin' in my truck that'll do the trick," replied Larry Cogle.

On that particular day, there were ten people in the hunting party, including somebody's wife. They waited outside the cave entrance as Cogle walked back to his truck. While everyone stood around, Warden McDermott overheard someone say, "Is that Fish and Game guy's kid gonna shoot the bear?"

When Warden McDermott heard these words, the hair stood up on the back of his neck. *Are they talking about me?* After listening for a while longer, McDermott learned that Bruce Vanosek worked at a state fish hatchery.

What a mess this is turning out to be, thought McDermott. *The older Vanosek is going to illegally tag the cub bear that his kid shoots and his kid doesn't even have a bear tag.*

Larry Cogle returned to the cave carrying a handful of road flares. "Pull the dogs back," shouted Belcher, as Cogle lit a flare and tossed it into the cave. For a minute or two, the hounds stopped barking and people standing around could hear a faint huffing sound coming from inside the cave. Houndsmen in the crowd recognized it as an expression of fear or agitation, sometimes made by treed or cornered bears.

Cogle tossed a second flare into the cave. "It's comin' out!" shouted one of the tagalongs. A small, cinnamon-colored bear slowly exited the cave, one careful step at a time. Members of the party fell back, allowing room for the younger Vanosek to shoot. Had this been an average-sized adult bear, the crowd would have scattered like a covey of quail. Since the frightened animal was no bigger than a good-sized cub, they showed no fear and stood their ground.

If this little guy weighs more than fifty pounds it won't be by much, thought McDermott. California hunting regulations prohibit the take of cub bears at any time—a cub being a bear weighing fifty pounds or less.

With no tree to climb, the petrified little bear had nowhere to go. It started to run back into the cave but stopped when it saw the smoke. A sharp report from Darrel Vanosek's rifle echoed across the hillside. At a range of fifteen feet, he couldn't miss. Vanosek's bullet hit with such force that it knocked the bear backwards, killing it instantly. Warden McDermott felt a mighty urge to walk over and arrest both Vanoseks on the spot, but for the time being he had bigger fish to fry.

Bruce Vanosek was busy photographing his son's ill-gotten trophy when the only woman in the crowd bent over the dead cub and said, "He shot Winnie the Pooh!" Everyone in the crowd laughed, except the Vanoseks.

Warden McDermott put on a good acting job and laughed along with the rest of the demented group. Inside, he was fuming.

One of the tagalongs picked up the small bear and carried it back to the pickups where Buck Millsap was waiting. Stan Harder found a hunting knife and began gutting the bear as the elder Vanosek reached for his bear tag and started filling it out. Since he had not killed the bear himself, every hand-written entry on the tag would be considered a false statement, constituting license fraud.

"Do ya want the goodies?" asked Harder, as he carefully removed a small green gallbladder and held it up for the older Vanosek to see.

Bruce Vanosek's cheeks flushed as he shook his head side to side in refusal. He did, however, hand Harder a plastic bag to put it in.

That's interesting, thought McDermott. *It looks like Vanosek might have done this before.* Harder tied the gallbladder off with a string and placed it inside his dog box. When Harder had finished gutting the bear, Darrel Vanosek picked it up by the scruff of the neck and lifted it into the back of his father's pickup. *If this guy can pick up the bear that easily, it can't weigh over fifty pounds*, thought McDermott.

The hunting party began to disperse. Warden McDermott managed to hang back, claiming to have stepped in something left by one of the hounds. "You guys go ahead," said McDermott, "I gotta clean off my boot." Warden McDermott walked around, pretending to look for a stick until the last cloud of dust had disappeared over the horizon. When the others had gone, he walked over and began picking up bits and pieces of hair and tissue from the unlawfully killed cub bear. He carefully bagged the evidence, walked back to his truck and sat in the driver's seat, thoroughly disgusted by what he had just witnessed.

Two days before Christmas, the boys were at it again. Although Buck Millsap was never that friendly, he seemed to tolerate Al McDermott being around. Al happened to be standing near him when one of the tagalongs approached.

"Buck, I hear ya killed a cat this week."

"Yep," said Millsap.

"How big was it?"

Millsap indicated that it was about seven feet long.

They could only *be talking about a mountain lion*, McDermott thought. McDermott began pumping Millsap for clues. "Are you going to have it mounted?" he asked, knowing full well that mountain lions were protected in California and could not be possessed. Millsap answered that he had left the lion in the woods.

Now that the cat was literally out of the bag and the new guy had overheard the conversation, Millsap apparently felt that he needed to cover his tracks. This was also a sign to Warden McDermott that Millsap did not completely trust him. "I killed it under one o' them depredation permits," declared Millsap.

Later that day, McDermott told me what Millsap had said. I checked all the depredation permits that had been issued during the previous two months. Only a couple had been issued and none of them had anything to do with Buck Millsap. We preferred not to issue depredation permits, but they were sometimes unavoidable when a mountain lion killed livestock.

A week later, Warden Al McDermott and Dan Searcy joined a group of hunters on Jackass Springs Road, in Trinity County. Stan Harder released one of Millsap's hounds on a fresh scent. A few minutes later, Fred Belcher followed suit and released another of Millsap's dogs. Millsap had gone on ahead with two suspected clients and was not in the area at the time. The two hounds immediately started baying, having picked up a fresh scent. They released the rest of the dogs and within minutes, they had treed an animal.

Harder, Cogle, Belcher, and Samples ran up to the tree, with Harder yelling, "Go get my .22 rifle." Belcher and Samples returned to the trucks, where Belcher grabbed his own .22 caliber rifle. McDermott and Searcy followed Belcher back to the tree. Belcher was about to hand the rifle to his wife when Harder shouted, "No, I'll do it!"

McDermott looked through the tree branches and saw an adult mountain lion peering down at the crowd. He was able to take a quick photograph of the terrified cat, approximately fifteen yards away.

At exactly 12:45 p.m., Warden Al McDermott and Dan Searcy watched Stan Harder aim a .22 caliber pump action rifle at the mountain lion and fire. The bullet hit the lion in the lower head region, causing tissue and bone matter to fly off in all directions. Instead of falling to the ground, the wounded mountain lion climbed down from the tree and ran off.

"I shoulda used my own rifle," complained Harder. "Those round-nosed bullets ain't powerful enough."

Within minutes, the dogs had treed the same lion again. McDermott could see blood dripping from its head, just below the right eye. "Let Larry have the first shot this time," shouted a member of the group, his voice barely audible over the constant barking of the hounds.

It was as if they were all taking part in some kind of recreational turkey shoot, and it was now Larry Cogle's turn to have a go. Cogle aimed his .30-.30 rifle and fired at the mountain lion, hitting the already wounded cat in the neck. Once again, the lion jumped to the ground and fled. Several members of the group attempted to locate the seriously injured mountain lion, with no success.

What a tragedy, lamented McDermott. *As badly as that cat was wounded, it will surely crawl off and die somewhere.*

McDermott took some consolation in knowing that Stan Harder and Larry Cogle would eventually pay for their crimes.

The next day Warden Al McDermott, Warden Dave Szody, U.S Forest Service Special Agent Frank Packwood and I returned to the scene of the crime. Concerned about blowing Warden McDermott's cover, we traveled in an undercover vehicle and kept him out of sight. Though we searched for several hours, we never found the wounded mountain lion.

The 1995 bear season eventually ended but Warden Szody and I instructed Warden McDermott to continue his friendly relationship with Buck Millsap. McDermott was able to convince Millsap of this cover story—that he was making periodic trips out to California from Montana to buy cattle for the ranch he managed. During the first few months of 1996, Big Al stopped by occasionally to see his new hunting buddy. With little else in common, they usually got around to the subject of bear hunting and gallbladders.

Although Millsap remained cautious, he eventually opened up to

McDermott and began telling him about his involvement in the gallbladder business. According to Millsap, a man would come up from Southern California to buy gallbladders from him. "Ya need ta have at least ten before he'll show," said Millsap. The houndsman went on to say that he had to be extra careful because of the new law. He described a newspaper article that he had read recently, explaining California Fish and Game Code Section 12012 (effective January 1, 1996), which provided for a maximum $30,000 fine and one year in jail "for selling bear parts or taking wildlife for commercial purposes ...."

"I was charged with a bunch a bear crimes by this undercover game warden back around 1980," said Millsap. "The guy didn't know what the hell he was doin' or they coulda hung my ass."

"That undercover game warden was wearin' a wire," said Millsap's wife, listening in. She was a bit younger than him and had long gray hair pulled into a tight ponytail. With her aggrieved scowl and puffy eyes, it was hard to imagine the young woman she had been. "It cost us ten thousand dollars to get out of it."

Warden McDermott jokingly said that he wasn't wearing a wire and offered to show Millsap and his wife. Fortunately the Millsaps declined his offer, because McDermott was, in fact, wearing a wire at the time.

"Be careful Al," I cautioned. "Don't give these people any ideas."

Of course McDermott couldn't hear me—Warden Szody and I were sitting in the dark, a few blocks away, eavesdropping on the conversation.

By now it was clear to Szody and me that our suspect was heavily involved in the buying and selling of bear gallbladders. Warden McDermott had provided us with a series of incriminating tape-recorded conversations. Now it was time to bait the hook. We had accumulated a supply of bear gallbladders from road kills, depredation bears, and the Sacramento Fish and Game Evidence Lab.

"Each time you visit Millsap," I instructed McDermott, "bring him a couple gallbladders and see how much he offers to pay you for them. Tell him you're getting them from a friend who doesn't want his name mentioned."

Over the next three months, Warden McDermott would arrive at Buck Millsap's residence with a small number of gallbladders. Each time McDermott dropped by, Millsap offered to take the gallbladders off his hands for one hundred dollars apiece, payable when his buyer came up from Southern California and paid him. Buck Millsap also provided McDermott with another important piece of information. His buyer was Korean.

We thanked Warden McDermott for the outstanding job he had done. With no previous undercover experience, Al had given an Academy Award winning performance and played a critical role in our ongoing investigation.

Now he could go back to his own district until it was time to testify in court.

Warden Szody and I had a lot of new information to sift through and we were absolutely determined to reveal the identity of our mysterious Korean gallbladder buyer. We researched all recent Department of Fish and Game records related to bear hunting. For several weeks, Szody and I waded through stacks of hunting guide applications, guide logs and bear tag returns.

Like a complicated thousand-piece puzzle, a picture of our suspect slowly came into focus. We were a little embarrassed to find that this man had been right under our noses the entire time. He was not only a licensed guide, but he was also a Fish and Game certified hunter education instructor.

"Now that we know who this guy is," I said to Szody, "we have to catch him."

IV

Jason Lee was his name. At least that's what he called himself. Lee held a California Guide's License and had been arranging guided bear hunts for some time. Based on the guide logs that Szody and I examined, all of Lee's clients were of Korean descent and most of them lived in the Los Angeles area. Jason Lee's real name was Chung-Hee Lee. He'd picked out the name Jason to make it easier on his American business associates.

According to informants, Lee didn't actually own hound dogs. He would provide the clients and transport them to the Redding area where they would meet up with local houndsmen. A few of the local houndsmen were also licensed guides. The locals would provide the dogs, vehicles, and expertise, while Lee played big shot and acted like he was part of the process. They'd split the profits at the end of each hunt.

Experience told us that the odds of catching Jason Lee in the act of buying gallbladders were slim to none. The only way to get a foot in the door was by going undercover, just as we had with Millsap and others. Lee would smell a rat if we approached him with a Caucasian client, so the search was on for an Asian officer who could play the part.

We had no success at the Department of Fish and Game. We contacted our friends with the U.S. Fish and Wildlife Service, also with no success. Dave and I decided to try Frank Packwood and Pat Anjola, two Redding area U.S. Forest Service special agents we sometimes worked with. Most of the illegal bear hunts were being conducted on national forest lands, so our investigation would fall well within their jurisdiction. Packwood and Anjola had spent their careers investigating serious crimes on national forest lands and were two of the most skilled and resourceful law enforcement officers Szody and I would ever work with.

Mother Nature must have been smiling on us, because Frank and Pat knew of a special agent who just might fit the bill. According to Agent Anjola, this young special agent was from another region, experienced as an undercover agent, and smart as a whip. Around five-foot-seven, he was slightly built and could easily pass for a college student. Most importantly, this young man was Asian.

"We'll take him," I said. "If this kid is as smart as you say he is, he'll work out perfectly."

Arrangements were made for the four of us to meet with Special Agent Don Hoang in September of 1996. After the initial meeting, we all agreed that Hoang was perfect for the part. Within a few weeks, Agent Hoang's undercover assignment was approved by the U.S. Forest Service and the joint California Department of Fish and Game/U.S. Forest Service undercover investigation had begun.

"He's just what we wanted," I said to Warden Szody, "someone who is smart enough to pull it off but not intimidating enough to make Jason Lee uncomfortable."

Hoang appeared a little timid and soft spoken, but there was an air of confidence about him that Szody and I noticed immediately.

With Szody, Packwood, and Anjola present, I explained our carefully thought-out plan to Agent Hoang. "Until additional players are needed, the only people who will know anything about this undercover investigation will be two environmental prosecutors, our immediate supervisors and those of us in this room."

Agent Hoang's undercover name would be Quan Vanh. He would introduce himself as a graduate student who also worked for his parents part-time. We provided Hoang with a set of business cards that identified Quan Vanh as the North American representative of a Thailand-based import-export business owned by his parents. Hoang was also given necessary identification, a California hunting license and a 1996 California bear tag. Warden Szody and I briefed him on everything we knew about Jason Lee and several local houndsmen Hoang might contact. Of particular concern was a houndsman named Jimmy Westerby, known to be heavily into drugs, borderline crazy, and extremely dangerous. Agent Hoang was instructed to contact Jason Lee at his Los Angeles office and arrange a guided bear hunt.

On October 28, 1996, Special Agent Don Hoang telephoned Jason Lee.
"Hello," said Lee, answering the phone in English.
"Is this Jason Lee?" Hoang asked, in a tentative voice.

"Yes, this is Jason Lee," he said, although his tone suggested suspicion.

"My name is Quan Vanh. I am interested in going on a bear hunt."

There was an uncomfortable thirty second pause before Lee responded. "Who referred you to my business?"

"One of my friends had your business card," replied Hoang. "I heard you had a good reputation and guaranteed a successful hunt."

Again, Lee hesitated before continuing the conversation. "What nationality are you?" Lee inquired. "You're not Korean." It sounded like an accusation.

"Vietnamese," Hoang replied.

"What do you do for a living?" Lee asked.

"I'm a grad student from Fresno," Hoang explained. "I work for my parents part-time."

"Why do you want to go bear hunting? Have you ever hunted before?" asked Lee.

"No, I've never hunted," Hoang confessed, "but I've always wanted to kill a bear. My parents agreed to help pay the fee."

More at ease now, Lee described what others were charging for guided bear hunts. He told Agent Hoang how much the hunt would cost, depending on the size of the bear killed. According to Lee, a "monster-sized bear" would cost between $2,600 and $3,200. Hoang made an audible gasp into the phone as Lee explained that an average-sized bear would cost about $1,500. Lee finally relented and offered Hoang a flat rate of $1,500, no matter what size bear was killed; this rate would include housing, food, dressing the bear, and any other odds and ends. He went on to say that the hunt would last one or two days.

"Do you have a hunting license and bear tag?" asked Lee.

"Yes," said Hoang.

"You need a rifle? I can get you one."

"No," Hoang said, "I have a 30-06 rifle with a scope."

Apparently Jason Lee had accepted Hoang, because the next question he asked was, "When do you want to go?"

Lee had several hunts already scheduled in the Redding area and offered to pick Hoang up on the way. Hoang said he was not ready to go that soon and scheduled a face-to-face meeting with Lee for November 5th at Lee's Los Angeles office. They would plan the hunt then.

Special Agent Don Hoang walked into Jason Lee's Los Angeles office on November 5, 1996. Special Agent Pat Anjola was parked nearby in case anything should go wrong. As Hoang entered the office, which was arranged like a classroom, he noticed several mounted animals. Framed photographs of Asian men with dead bears covered the walls. Two middle-aged Asian men were standing at the other end of the room, deep in conversation. The larger man was toying with a high-powered rifle as they talked. Although both men noticed Hoang standing there, they continued their discussion.

Finally, the smaller of the two men crossed the room toward Agent Hoang. He was slightly taller than Hoang and couldn't have weighed more than 140 pounds. A cigarette pinched between the tips of his right thumb and forefinger, the neatly dressed man wore slacks and a long-sleeved dress shirt. "This is where I teach hunter safety. I am also a licensed hunter education instructor," said the man.

That's strange, thought Hoang. *Isn't he going to introduce himself?*

"I am Quan Vanh," said Hoang, as he held out his hand.

Instead of returning the gesture and extending his own hand, the stranger just stood there with a curious look on his face. After what had to be the longest minute Agent Hoang had ever experienced, the man stuck the cigarette in his mouth, reached out and lightly gripped Hoang's hand. Again removing the cigarette, he said, "I am Jason Lee." Within minutes of their first meeting, Agent Hoang learned that Jason Lee was all business. This self-made entrepreneur apparently had no use for small talk or friendly chitchat. "Why do you want to go bear hunting?" Lee asked.

Hoang remembered that Lee had already asked that question over the telephone. It was, however, the opening he needed. "My parents are in the import-export business in Thailand. They sell herbal medicines," explained Hoang, as he handed Lee one of his business cards.

The card read: *Vanh Enterprises, Silom Road, Bangkok, Thailand*. It listed Quan Vanh as the *North American representative*.

Lee appeared more interested, but still cautious. After another long pause, he asked Hoang what part of the bear he was interested in. "It's okay, you can feel free to tell me," he added.

"The head, hide, paws, and the gallbladder," responded Hoang.

"All my clients hunt bear for the gallbladder," said Lee.

Lee laid it on thick, claiming that bear galls had medicinal powers while touting his expertise on the subject. According to Lee, the Chinese also used the heart, liver and bones in their traditional herbal medicines. Agent Hoang felt it was the right moment to interrupt. "I will have to check back with my parents on what parts of the bear they want."

Jason Lee started to let down his guard as the conversation continued. He began bragging about what a good guide he was and guaranteed Hoang that he would get him a bear. "I hire three or four Redding area men to help with the hunt," Lee explained. "One of them is also a guide."

Hoang already knew that Lee was just the money man and most of the hunting expertise would be provided by the area hunters.

"Did you say that you have a license and bear tag?" Lee asked. Hoang said that he did. "That's lucky," Lee said, "because the tag quota has been reached. There are no more bear tags available this year."

"You know me and my helpers always obey Fish and Game laws," insisted Lee, in an obvious effort to impress the prospective client. "I will tell you how a typical bear hunt works. There are two methods. One is by using a striker dog and the other is by running the dogs. With the striker dog, they drive their trucks through an area with the dog running down the road in front. When the dog starts barking, the men go out and try to find the bear's tracks. If tracks are found the other hounds are released. Sometimes they just release all of the hounds at the start. The houndsmen track them by listening for their barks and using radio collars. The dogs eventually tree the bear; then we come shoot it."

While listening to Lee, Agent Hoang flashed back to the conversation he and I had about hunting with hounds. I had told him that hounds sometimes chase a bear for hours before the bear finally climbs up a tree. Mother bears teach their cubs to run up a tree to avoid danger. It is that parental training that often leads to the pursuer's success and the bear's demise.

"You know the size of the gallbladder is not determined by the size of the bear," said Lee, as he brought out a photograph album. The album was full of Korean clients with their trophies. Some of the photos showed clients and Lee holding up multiple gallbladders. "If we come across other animals while we are bear hunting, we kill them, too," added Lee. In addition to dead bears, there were photographs of clients with deer, pigs, squirrels, and bobcats.

Agent Hoang said he had to leave but he would meet Lee in Redding that coming weekend. Lee gave Hoang directions to an Anderson gas station where they would meet. "We will stay at the house of one of my associates," said Lee. "I will need a two hundred dollar deposit before you leave."

Hoang paid Lee the two hundred dollars, with a balance of thirteen hundred dollars to be paid when a bear was killed.

Just as Agent Hoang was about to walk out the door, Lee called him back. He had one more question to ask. "Are you an undercover agent for the Department of Fish and Game?" Surprised that Lee would ask such a question, Hoang held back a reactive chuckle.

"No, I just want to go bear hunting," Hoang replied.

"That's good," said Lee.

U.S. Forest Service Special Agent Don Hoang, acting in an undercover capacity for the California Department of Fish and Game, drove his black Ford Mustang into the Anderson, California, Shell Station on November 8, 1996. The time was 5:45 p.m. Hoang had agreed to meet Jason Lee at 6:00

p.m., in preparation for a guided bear hunt. As Agent Hoang filled his gas tank, a brown-colored Ford Bronco, with Jason Lee at the wheel, drove in behind him. A few seconds after Lee arrived, a newer model silver van pulled into the adjacent gas lane.

Lee and another Korean man got out of the Bronco and walked over to Hoang. "This is Mr. Park," said Lee. Hoang recognized Park as the mysterious man he had seen playing with a rifle at Lee's LA office.

About that time, a group of people began to climb out of the silver van. One of them approached while the others stood back. "This is Mr. Hu (pronounced Hoo) and his family," said Lee. "Mr. Hu is also a client."

Agent Hoang marveled at how many people Mr. Hu had brought with him. They were later introduced as Hu's wife, his mother, his son, his brother-in-law, his sister, and his daughter. Mr. Hu, himself, appeared to be in his early forties. He was about the same height and weight as Jason Lee and had a friendly grin on his face. Hu didn't speak much English, so he just smiled when anyone spoke to him. His twenty-year-old son, who was three or four inches taller, spoke fluent English and acted as an interpreter when Jason Lee wasn't around.

Once all three cars were filled with gas, Jason Lee led Hoang and the others to the home of local houndsman and licensed guide, Henry Jessup.

Jessup lived on a country road, a few miles from Redding. When they pulled into the unpaved parking area next to Jessup's house, Henry was standing outside. Dogs from a kennel in back began barking. Agent Hoang, who was the last one to pull in, hesitated for a few minutes before climbing out of his Mustang. He needed the extra time to survey the scene, but more importantly to slow his heart rate, relax, and assume the role of Quan Vanh, novice bear hunter. Jason Lee and Jessup were walking toward his car, so he stepped out to meet them. Henry Jessup walked with a bit of a limp; he was an inch or two taller than Hoang, with twice his girth. Jessup had a ruddy complexion and a full gray beard.

"Mr. Vanh, this is Henry Jessup, my helper," said Lee. Hoang shook hands with Jessup and recognized a Southern accent in his speech.

Jessup invited everyone to join him in his living room. The house was fairly small, but had three bedrooms. Seeing no feminine touches, Hoang assumed that Jessup wasn't married. Hu's family remained in the living room, watching TV, while Lee, Park, and Jessup led Agent Hoang and Mr. Hu into the kitchen. Seated at the kitchen table, they began discussing the next day's hunt. A few minutes into the conversation, a green Ford pickup pulled into the yard. A man named Hal Neeley got out, knocked on the back door, and entered the kitchen. Neeley was bent over slightly and stiff from a long drive. About six feet tall, he wore gray overalls, a long-sleeved cotton shirt and work boots. A week's worth of gray stubble covered the lower half of his fifty-year-old face.

"This is Hal Neely," explained Jessup. "He's an old huntin' buddy of mine from Oregon. Hal's gonna hunt with us tomorrow."

It was about 8:00 p.m. when Henry Jessup called Agent Hoang over to the kitchen counter and asked to see his bear tag. Hoang pulled the tag out of his fanny pack. Jessup took the tag and began filling out a guide log. Soon after, Jessup and Jason Lee walked down the hall, went into Jessup's bedroom and closed the door. Hoang thought that was a little strange. It seemed even more unusual when they did it again after everyone had gone to bed.

Bedtime as at nine p.m., so sleeping territories were staked out. Mr. Hu and his wife took one of the bedrooms. Hu's sister and her husband took the other one. Everyone else just found someplace to throw down a sleeping bag. Jessup offered Hoang the couch, since he was a client, and Hoang gladly accepted.

The next morning, at exactly 4:30 a.m., Agent Hoang woke to find Henry Jessup and Hal Neeley in the kitchen. A few minutes later they left the house and drove away, each in a separate pickup. At 5:30 a.m., Lee, Hoang, Park, Hu, Hu's brother-in-law, and Hu's son all crammed into Jason Lee's Bronco and left the house. Unbeknownst to Lee and the others, an unmarked enforcement vehicle, driven by Agent Pat Anjola, was in position to watch them as they headed west on Highway 36, in the direction of Platina.

About 6:30 a.m., Henry Jessup came over the CB radio and said they had treed a bear. "We're at the same place we killed that bear the other day," announced Jessup. Lee drove the Bronco to the intersection of two Forest Service roads, with Hoang making a mental note of the location.

"When ya get to the intersection, wait there," said Jessup. "Art will meet ya."

Who is Art? wondered Hoang, squashed in the front seat between Lee and Park. *How many more people are going to join us?*

As if sensing Hoang's question, Lee said, "Art is Henry's son. He is also a licensed guide."

Who isn't? thought Hoang.

It was almost 7:00 a.m. when Art Jessup pulled up next to Lee's Bronco in a cloud of dust. He was driving a beige Toyota pickup with a dog box mounted in the bed. A young kid—an awkward sixteen- or seventeen-year-old boy with acne covered cheeks—was in the passenger seat.

"Follow me," said Art.

Lee headed up the road behind Art's pickup. As dust billowed into the Bronco, Lee and Park rolled up their windows. Hoang continued to act interested, all the while wondering why anyone would actually pay money to endure such torture. Fifteen or twenty minutes down the road, they caught up with Art, who had rendezvoused with two other pickups.

"This is where the bear is," said Lee. "Everyone must stay with me at all times."

Jason Lee and his entire entourage followed Art down a fairly steep embankment for a hundred yards or so until they came to a large pine tree. Henry Jessup, Hal Neeley, and two other men were standing at the base of the tree, next to a pack of baying hounds.

This was a new experience for Agent Hoang and the dogs' incessant barking added to his stress. With everyone watching, Hoang peered into the tree's upper limbs and saw a small, brownish-colored bear staring down at them. "That bear is too small," shouted Hoang, barely audible over the background noise. "I'd rather not shoot it."

Lee appeared disappointed that Hoang didn't want to shoot the bear, but agreed that it was too small. "Yes, it is too small. We will let it go."

Agent Hoang was carrying a 30-06 rifle and noticed that Henry Jessup and Jason Lee were also packing rifles. One of the other men, later identified as Red—a red-haired hollow-cheeked tagalong—was holding a .44 caliber handgun. It was obvious to Hoang that the so-called helpers were displeased. They had gone to all that trouble and one of their clients wasn't going to kill the bear. The bear was little more than a cub but they surely would have killed it had he not objected.

They set the hounds loose again a few miles down the road. Agent Hoang became concerned about the way some of the dogs were being treated. He saw Henry Jessup pick up one of his dogs by the collar and the tail. In a fit of anger, Jessup threw the yelping dog off the side of the road. That dog must have been sore or injured, because it didn't want to hunt. Jessup threw it back in the dog box and took out another. Hoang couldn't help but feel that Henry was taking out his anger over not killing that little bear on the dogs. Some of Neeley's dogs wouldn't stop barking, so Neeley used his stun gun on them.

These are swell people, thought Hoang.

After an hour or so, another bear was treed. Just as Agent Hoang was about to follow the group up the mountainside to the treed bear, he was cornered by Jason Lee and Henry Jessup.

"This bear is wild and unpredictable," said Lee. "You will need to do exactly as I say." Hoang wondered what this was really all about. Lee provided a little insight: "If you are not ready to shoot and the bear is going to get away, would it be all right if I shoot it?"

What is this? thought Hoang. *I was under the impression that the guy with the bear tag was supposed to shoot the bear, not the guide.*

It didn't take Agent Hoang long to figure out that these people had no interest in the sport of hunting; every bear represented a significant amount of money—the sooner it was killed and processed, the sooner they could go on to the next one. Not wanting to draw attention to himself, Hoang responded, "You're the guide."

The treed bear was on a steep slope, uphill from the road. Henry Jessup was already there, holding several barking hounds on a leash. Lee stood directly under the tree, holding a rifle. Agent Hoang was still downslope, positioning himself for a clear shot at the bear. The last thing he wanted to do was take a risky shot and wound the animal.

Agent Hoang continued to mill about, trying to see the bear through the thick branches.

"Come on, hurry up!" yelled Lee, angrily.

A shot rang out, originating from Lee's rifle. "It was coming down," he shouted.

"Sure it was," mumbled Hoang, sarcastically.

Fortunately Hoang's spontaneous slip of the tongue was drowned out by the hounds' monotonous, non-stop barking. Agent Hoang could see the bear well enough to know that it had no intention of coming down. Lee's first shot had missed the bear but caused it to change positions.

Art Jessup was standing next to Hoang as Lee fired a second shot. This time the bear was clearly hit. A medium-sized brown-colored bear crashed through the branches and fell to the ground. Landing on its back, the wounded animal climbed to its feet and lumbered down the hill.

"One of my dogs is loose!" shouted Henry Jessup. He grabbed Lee's rifle and chased after the wounded bear. Lee followed Jessup. Just as Lee was out of sight, two more shots rang out. Jessup had obviously killed the bear, but by the time Hoang got there, Lee was again holding the rifle. Agent Hoang never did see the alleged loose dog that Henry Jessup seemed so concerned about.

"This bear weighs about two hundred and fifty pounds," said Lee. "Shoot it here." Hoang noticed that Lee was pointing at the bear's neck.

"Isn't it already dead?" asked Hoang.

"Just shoot it!" ordered Lee, obviously irritated.

Knowing that the bear was already dead but not wanting to antagonize Lee any further, Agent Hoang fired a shot into the bear's neck. Photographs were taken of Hoang and the others with the dead bear.

"Where's your bear tag?" asked Henry Jessup.

Hoang handed Jessup the tag. Jessup fiddled with the tag and placed it inside the bear's right ear. He finished by taking a strip of duct tape and taping the ear closed, around the tag.

Henry and Art Jessup rolled the bear down the hillside to the road, where more photographs were taken. Henry Jessup and Jason Lee gutted the bear.

Hoang paid close attention to where the bear's gallbladder ended up. Lee removed it and tied it off with a string. He then placed it inside a plastic baggie and handed it to Hoang. The bear was eventually loaded into Art Jessup's pickup.

Everyone went back to the original Forest Service road intersection. Without taking a break, Jason Lee, Art Jessup, Hu, and several others headed out again, in pursuit of a bear for Hu.

Agent Hoang, Henry Jessup, Park, and a few others broke for lunch. "Me and Hal are gunna go look for a lost dog," said Henry Jessup. "Park is gunna take the rest o' ya down to Jimmy's camp."

Agent Hoang agreed to go wherever they wanted to take him. Jimmy and his group were camped down the road a few miles. On the way, Hoang reflected on the briefing that Warden Szody and I had given him on a houndsman named Jimmy. Hoang could not remember Jimmy's last name, but figured it had to be the same guy.

Sometime around 1:00 p.m., Agent Hoang and the group arrived at Jimmy Westerby's camp. Judging from the setup, Westerby spent a lot of time there. There were couches, chairs, tables, a water tank, and a sink with running water—all in the middle of the woods. Several camp trailers were set up around a central fire pit—a regular modern-day wagon train.

Jimmy Westerby saw Hoang arrive and walked over to greet him. Westerby was tall and lean, over six feet and all muscle. He had greasy, reddish-blond hair and his face was dotted with freckles. What struck Hoang first about Westerby was the exceptionally large hunting knife dangling from his belt.

As the man approached, Hoang recalled our warning. Westerby had a reputation for being unpredictable, irrational, and dangerous.

"This is quite a camp," said Hoang.

"Yeah, this is where I make my livin' from September through December," replied Westerby.

While Agent Hoang and Westerby got acquainted, Hoang realized that this was the base camp for a fairly significant bear guiding operation. Later that afternoon, Jason Lee's assistant, Mr. Park, walked outside the camp carrying a shotgun. Park, whom Hoang had first seen in Lee's LA office, was a husky five-foot-nine, with short dark hair. He always wore camouflage clothing. Agent Hoang watched Park draw down on a perched Steller's jay and shoot it out of a tree. Appalled by what he had seen, Hoang grabbed his camera and offered to photograph Park, along with his kill and the Browning gold-engraved shotgun he was carrying. Park had no idea that the photograph would later be used as evidence against him.

Henry Jessup returned to camp after supposedly looking for a lost dog. He walked over to Hoang's bear and began removing the duct tape from its ear.

Jessup had never really filled out the tag, as required by law.

"Hey Quan, come over here," said Jessup. "I need ya to bring me more hunters."

Agent Hoang thought for a second before responding, "Well, I have quite a few friends and acquaintances who might like to go bear hunting."

"How much is Lee chargin' ya for the hunt?" asked Jessup.

"Fifteen hundred dollars," replied Hoang.

"Me and Art can guide ya for a thousand," responded Jessup. "Us guides are gettin' tired of Lee." The conversation caught Agent Hoang by surprise. He knew there was no honor among thieves, but this was awfully sudden. "Here's my business card. Don't say anything to Jason about this," said Jessup.

It was after dark when Jason Lee and the rest of the party returned to camp. They had killed another bear. This one had already been skinned and the carcass was cut into sections. Of particular interest to Hoang were the bear's ears. There was no bear tag attached to either one. Hoang walked over to Jason Lee and asked, "How big is Mr. Hu's bear?"

Lee and Henry Jessup were reluctant to discuss this particular bear, but Lee answered, "It's a three hundred pound male."

While the bear was lying in the bed of Jessup's pickup, Jessup rolled up some cellophane and stuck it in the bear's ear. Lee then held the ear while Jessup taped it closed over the cellophane. Without drawing attention to himself, Hoang could not get close enough to see if there was actually a tag inside the bear's ear.

The following morning, back at Henry Jessup's residence, Agent Hoang noticed that the garage door was open and Hu's bear hide was lying on a bench inside. Hoang entered the garage and managed a close look at the bear's ear. As the observant agent suspected, the inside of the bear's ear contained nothing but cellophane. Jessup and Lee had failed to tag the bear. Agent Hoang also noticed that the bear had been shot in the head. He doubted very much that Hu had actually killed the bear. More likely it was Jason Lee or Art Jessup who had fired the fatal shot. Hoang walked outside the garage just as Henry Jessup was coming out of his house.

"I got some questions for ya," said Jessup.

"I'll do my best," replied Hoang.

"What do you guys use the bear galls for?"

"The bear gallbladder, in Asian culture, is revered as a cure-all for many ailments."

"What kind a prices do ya sell 'em for and how is that determined?"

"That depends on the size of the gallbladder and the market demand."

Although Agent Hoang had answered Jessup's questions off the top of his head, Jessup was apparently convinced of Hoang's legitimacy. Jessup's next question was the one Agent Hoang had been waiting for: "Are ya interested in some bear galls?"

Agent Hoang did not want to answer too quickly, for fear of appearing over-anxious. He waited a beat or two, then replied, "I might be."

Jessup asked for Hoang's phone number, and Hoang obliged. He told Jessup that he frequently traveled to Asia and would not always be available; however, Jessup could leave a message.

"When I run into some gallbladders I would like to be able to call ya and see if you're interested," said Jessup.

Again Hoang waited to answer. "Yes," he said, finally. "If you come into some bear gallbladders, I will gladly do business with you."

A fleeting smile crossed Henry Jessup's face. "Let's keep this between the two of us," he said. "Don't mention it to Jason."

Everyone was preparing for breakfast at Henry Jessup's house on the morning they were scheduled to leave for home. Henry tapped Agent Hoang on the shoulder and asked if he would like to have breakfast in town with him and Neeley. Hoang glanced over at Jason Lee. It was clear from the look on Lee's face that he was not pleased about Jessup's offer and did not want Hoang to accept. Hoang hesitated for a few minutes before telling Henry that he would like to go.

On the way into town, Jessup and Neeley began asking questions about the average price of bear gallbladders. Hoang stuck to his story: it all depended on the size of the gallbladders and the demand at the time.

"I have to ask ya something," said Jessup. "Are you working for Fish and Game?"

"No," replied Hoang, narrowing his eyes at the men as though the question was an insult.

"Are ya willing to work out a deal on the gallbladders?" asked Jessup, reaching out and shaking Hoang's hand.

"Yes," replied Hoang. "I will contact my parents and see what kind of price we are willing to pay."

"That's great," said Jessup. "Gimme a call when you're ready."

"I've got some gallbladders in Oregon right now," said Neeley. "I'll bring 'em down when you guys get ready to do business."

During breakfast, Henry Jessup left the table for a few minutes. While Jessup was away, Agent Hoang asked Hal Neeley what Jason Lee was currently paying them for bear galls. Neeley said he would tell him, but Hoang was not to breathe a word of it to Henry or anyone else. According to Neeley, Jason Lee was paying between two hundred fifty and three hundred dollars each, depending on the size. A few minutes later, Jessup came back to the table.

"Henry, what is the going rate for bear galls around here?" asked Hoang.

"Two hundred fifty to three hundred dollars," replied Jessup.

Henry Jessup's off the cuff answer came as no surprise. Agent Hoang was not a real businessman, but it didn't take a financial genius to figure out that Jessup and Neeley were squeezing him to offer more than Lee was paying. That became very clear on the ride back to Jessup's house.

"Ya know, Quan, you're going to have to make it worth my while for me to do business with ya. I don't want to go to jail for a few hundred dollars," said Jessup. Hoang nodded. As the three men climbed out of the pickup at Jessup's house, Henry repeated himself. "Remember, Quan, we'll only do business if it's worth the risk."

Jason Lee was busy cleaning bear carcasses when Agent Hoang returned to Jessup's house. Lee appeared a little miffed at Hoang, but asked him what part of his bear he wanted to take home. Hoang said he wanted the head, hide, paws, gall, and some of the meat. Agent Hoang told Lee that he was going to run into town to get some ice for the trip home. He did pick up ice, but Hoang also telephoned his enforcement contacts and advised us of his current status.

When Agent Hoang returned to Jessup's house, Henry Jessup and Hal Neeley were out in the back by Jessup's horses. Hoang walked back to thank them and say goodbye. As he was about to walk away, Henry said, "Gimme a call when you're ready to play ball. When ya call, don't mention gallbladders over the phone. Refer to the gallbladders as baseball cards and just say you're ready to play ball."

It was abundantly clear to Agent Hoang that Jessup and Neeley knew the seriousness of the conspiracy they were engaging in and the possible consequences if they got caught. They might talk like they just fell off the turnip truck, but these two were shrewd characters.

Hoang's first clue was the little shell game they were playing—stuffing cellophane into the bears' ears instead of the required, properly filled-out bear tags.

Where are the actual tags going? Hoang wondered. *Are they being used to kill additional bears? How many bears are really being taken by the tag holders, as the law requires? My tag was attached to a bear I didn't shoot and it's doubtful that Hu shot that three-hundred-pound male bear. Lee seems to have an unending supply of Korean clients from Southern California. Maybe paying for a bear hunt is the client's way of assuring that the product they're paying for is authentic.*

Finally responding to Henry Jessup's parting words, Agent Hoang said, "I'll call you in a week or two."

Before leaving Jessup's house, Agent Hoang approached Jason Lee and paid him the remainder of the money owed for the guided bear hunt. He also asked Lee about any contacts he might have who could supply gallbladders. "I know a lot of people who deal in gallbladders," said Lee, "but I am still uncertain about you. I need to get to know you better before I introduce you to anybody." Hoang told Lee he didn't blame him for being careful. Lee responded by inviting Hoang to call if he is in the LA area—they could get together. Hoang said he would and drove away.

V

Agent Hoang telephoned Henry Jessup on November 19, 1996 and began the conversation just as Jessup had instructed.

"Henry, I'm interested in playing ball. Do you have any baseball cards to sell?"

"Yeah, I know a guy with some cards he wants to sell but he's holding off. He wants a better price than what this regular guy is offering. Call me next time you're up here. I would like to meet with ya."

"I definitely will," responded Hoang

"When do ya think that might be?" asked Jessup.

"I'll be coming through Redding on December third or fourth, on my way back from Washington."

"Well, gimme a call and we'll get together."

It was about 3:00 p.m., on December 3, 1996, when Agent Hoang returned to Redding and held a short meeting with Anjola, Packwood, Szody, and me. I provided Agent Hoang with funds for the gallbladder transaction. Hoang telephoned Henry Jessup from our meeting site.

"I'm in Redding," said Hoang.

"Oh, you are?" replied Jessup, sounding surprised. Jessup was obviously preoccupied with something and seemed to be uncomfortable talking on the phone. He finally explained to Hoang that Jason Lee was there and it was not a good time for him to talk. Jessup asked Hoang how long he was going to be in Redding. Hoang said he would be there until the following evening.

"Okay, call me tomorrow afternoon after Lee and his group leave," said Jessup.

Agent Hoang telephoned Henry Jessup at 1:00 p.m. the following afternoon. Jessup asked Hoang if he could come by the house. When Hoang arrived, Jessup said he had been trying to get in touch with a guy that he knew had gallbladders. So far he had not been able to reach him by phone. Jessup said he thought the guy with the gallbladders was home, but might be outside.

He said he would go to the man's house and it would probably take about an hour and a half. "I know a lot of people in Siskiyou County and in Oregon who also have gallbladders," said Jessup. "I just have to go up and get 'em. Bear season is over, but for them it's not, if ya know what I mean. Call me about three o'clock. I should be back by then."

Agent Hoang telephoned Henry Jessup at 3:00 p.m. "What did you come up with?" Hoang asked.

"Come on over. I got somethin' for ya," said Jessup.

When Hoang arrived, Jessup led him to a refrigerator in his garage. Jessup reached inside and pulled out a large plastic bag containing nine bear gallbladders. "How much are ya willin' ta pay for these?" Jessup prodded. Hoang carefully examined the gallbladders, pointing out that some were bigger than others. He provided Jessup with a ballpark price range. Jessup walked over to a second refrigerator and pulled out another plastic bag, containing four more gallbladders. The four gallbladders in this bag were two or three times larger than those in the first bag. Hoang did not want to appear too anxious, so he bartered with Jessup for a few minutes and said he wasn't prepared to buy all of them at that time.

"Could you keep a few of them here for me? I'll pay you for them next time," Hoang proposed.

"I don't like keepin' 'em here at the house and neither does the other guy," replied Jessup.

Henry Jessup was obviously well aware of the fact that possession of more than one bear gallbladder legally meant they were for sale, and the sale or possession for sale of bear parts was a felony. After a little more bartering, Jessup agreed to sell all thirteen gallbladders for $3,150 in cash. Although inexperienced in the art of buying and selling bear gallbladders, Agent Hoang convinced Jessup that he knew exactly what he was doing. He individually priced each gallbladder, ranging from one hundred and fifty dollars for the smaller ones, to four hundred dollars for the larger ones. After a few minutes of small talk, Agent Hoang left Jessup's house. It was 3:40 p.m.

Agent Hoang telephoned Henry Jessup again on December 20th. "Henry, my father was very pleased with the quality of the product."

"That's good," replied Jessup. "Are ya gonna be up this way in the next couple weeks?"

"I don't know. What do you have going?"

"We're gonna do some bobcat huntin' in January. If ya can make it, you're welcome to stay here at the house."

Hoang and Jessup eventually settled on a date for the hunt. Hoang was to show up on January 23 and possibly stay until the next day. Since Agent

Hoang and Henry Jessup were now business partners, Hoang was allowed to go straight to Jessup's house instead of meeting at the gas station or some other neutral ground.

Henry Jessup was full of new information when Agent Hoang arrived on January 23. He seemed particularly concerned about another houndsman named Ricky Nettles. "Nettles is goin' around buying a lot a gallbladders," said Jessup. "He's a real bad guy. I heard that Fish and Game was after him." Hoang asked Jessup what else he knew about Nettles. "I just know he's someone ya don't want to deal with," said Jessup.

While Hoang and Jessup were talking, Jimmy Westerby called on the telephone. When Jessup hung up the phone, he said that Westerby had a bear gall to sell. Hoang said he would look at it after the next day's hunt.

The next morning, Henry Jessup and Agent Hoang were on their way to meet Jimmy Westerby at the Bowman Store, near Cottonwood. It was about 8:00 a.m. when they arrived. Westerby had an older man with him.

"Who's the old codger with Jimmy?" asked Hoang.

"That's DeWayne, one of Jimmy's buddies," said Jessup. "He likes to tag along sometimes. Don't worry, he's okay."

Rather than get out of his truck, Westerby motioned for Jessup to follow. He and Hoang drove behind Westerby's Toyota pickup out Highway 36 toward Platina, eventually setting out on a group of unpaved Forest Service roads. At that point Jessup and Hoang headed one way and Westerby and DeWayne went another.

Several miles into the woods, Jessup got Westerby on the CB and said his dogs had not picked up on anything. "Head over this way," replied Westerby. "My dogs are on a scent right now."

Jessup and Hoang caught up with Westerby and followed his pickup down the mountainside. The hunters drove the switchback Forest Service roads and the hounds traveled cross-country. They all eventually came to a gate with a PRIVATE PROPERTY-*NO* HUNTING OR TRESPASSING sign posted on it. The dogs couldn't read, so they kept on going. Jessup said that Westerby had permission to hunt on the posted property.

Interesting, thought Hoang. *If Westerby has permission to hunt the property, why doesn't he have a key to the gate?*

After parking the pickups, all four hunters walked past the gate and down the narrow dirt road to a location where the hounds had treed an animal. At the base of the tree, Westerby handed Hoang his .22 magnum rifle with a scope attached and asked, "How'd ya like ta shoot a cougar?"

Hoang's agile mind started racing. *How am I going to get out of this one?* The last thing Agent Hoang wanted to do was shoot a mountain lion, especially with a .22 rifle, and end up wounding it.

"Is that what the dogs have treed?" asked Hoang.

When the hunters finally located the animal, high in the branches of a large pine tree, Agent Hoang sighed inwardly. *Thank goodness that's not a mountain lion.*

"That's a fisher," said Jessup.

"I run in ta five or six o' those things durin' bear season and killed 'em all," bragged Westerby.

Hoang was aware that fishers—weasel-like creatures—were protected in California. He thought to himself, *Westerby is exactly the kind of lowlife the Fish and Game guys said he was.*

"Ya know, fishers are some kinda protected species," continued Westerby. "It's against the law ta kill 'em."

Hoang and Jessup continued to watch the fisher, high up in the tree. DeWayne, whose last name turned out to be Autrey, started walking back toward the trucks. "I got leg problems," said DeWayne. "I need ta get off my feet." Hoang was photographing the fisher when Westerby asked him if he would like to shoot it.

"No, that's a waste," said Hoang. "I'd rather just take a picture of it."

"I'll give ya a close up," replied Westerby, as he fired two quick shots with his .22 rifle. The fisher bounced off several branches before falling to the ground, dead. Westerby picked up the fisher and threw it to his dogs, which proceeded to chew it up like it was a play toy. "Whatever my dogs tree, I kill," said Westerby. "Don't matter what it is."

Agent Hoang managed to snap another photograph of the fisher before they walked away. He relished the idea of prosecuting Westerby sometime in the future.

Within twenty minutes of treeing the fisher, two of Westerby's dogs set out on another scent. Agent Hoang climbed into Westerby's truck and rode with him to catch up with the dogs. Jessup and Autrey lagged behind. As expected, Westerby starting quizzing Quan about his business.

"We buy a lot of things." said Hoang. "Whatever we can sell to make a profit."

"How 'bout marijuana?" asked Westerby.

"That depends," answered Hoang.

"I'm kinda like you," said Westerby. "I push marijuana and other drugs—whatever I can get my hands on to make a livin'."

As a U.S. Forest Service Special Agent, Don Hoang was very familiar with marijuana. Forest Service lands all over the United States were being used to grow this popular and illegal plant.

"Green dope around here is runnin' about five thousand a pound and Mexican marijuana is runnin' eight-fifty," said Westerby.

"I understand you have something for me," said Hoang, changing the subject.

"Yeah," Westerby said. "It's at my buddy's house."

When all the dogs had been rounded up and put back in their boxes, Westerby led the others to Dale Riggens's ranch. Jessup and Autrey waited at the front gate while Westerby and Hoang drove on in. Westerby introduced Hoang to Riggens and his wife, Brenda. Hoang recognized Brenda as the attractive woman who had directed them to Westerby's camp during the recent bear hunt. No longer wearing Levi jeans and a dirty sweatshirt, thirty-six-year-old Brenda was decked out in a flowered dress and high-heeled shoes. Her husband, Dale, seemed unusually clean-cut and well-groomed for the crowd he ran with. Smelling of aftershave cologne, the five-foot-ten-inch rancher looked like he had just stepped out of a band box—Wrangler jeans, spit-shined cowboy boots, and white Stetson hat.

"We're just about to go to a wedding," said Riggens. "We'll have to make this quick."

Riggens led Hoang and Westerby to a shed about thirty feet behind his house that was filled with drying animal pelts. Westerby pointed out three fox, two raccoons, and a dog. The animal Westerby called a "dog" was actually a coyote. Riggens opened a freezer door to reveal several boxes of wrapped venison. He reached in and pulled out a bear gallbladder. "Do you want this?" Riggens asked Westerby.

"Yeah," Westerby said and accepted the gall from Riggens. With Riggens still standing there, Westerby handed the gallbladder to Agent Hoang.

The men carried the boxes of venison back to Westerby's pickup, and Westerby loaded it into the utility box mounted behind the cab. He and Hoang said goodbye to Riggens and drove out to the highway where Jessup and Autrey were waiting by the front gate. On the way out to the gate, Hoang offered Westerby two hundred dollars for the bear gall. Westerby accepted.

"I'll have to pay you tomorrow," said Hoang.

"That's okay," said Westerby. "Just give the money to Henry. Me and Henry are partners. We've been in business together for over twenty years."

Agent Hoang rode with Henry Jessup back to Jessup's house. "Would you mind keeping the gall here until tomorrow?" asked Hoang. Jessup said he wasn't going to be home the next day and asked Hoang to make other arrangements. Jessup did not want to be caught with any gallbladders. Hoang said he would call Westerby and make arrangements to pay him the next day.

Agent Hoang made sure that he was not being followed as he made his way to an agreed-upon contact site. Warden Szody, Special Agent Packwood, Special Agent Anjola, and I were waiting there to debrief him. I gave Agent Hoang special funds for the next day's gallbladder purchase. We knew how tricky and possibly dangerous this assignment was for Agent Hoang and had been keeping undercover Fish and Game officers or U.S. Forest Service Special Agents close by whenever he was dealing with suspects.

Agent Hoang telephoned Jimmy Westerby at about 9:00 p.m. on the evening of January 24 and arranged to meet him the following morning at the Anderson Shell Station. Hoang would pay Westerby for the bear gallbladder at that time. The next morning at 8:45 a.m., Westerby drove up in a full-sized pickup. Hoang handed Westerby the two hundred dollars and thanked him for the previous day's hunt. Westerby was in a hurry, so the transaction began and ended in less than three minutes.

Henry Jessup and James Westerby were just two suspects in a large-scale, long-term investigation involving numerous suspects and over a hundred violations. The ultimate goal of the investigation was to find out the true extent of the bear poaching problem and step on its neck. It would have served little purpose to arrest Jessup and Westerby during 1996. We would only have alerted other suspects and essentially shut down the investigation. Because the gallbladder sales were all felonies, we did not have to worry about statute of limitations problems.

VI

It was August of 1997, and another bear season would be opening in a couple of months. Warden Szody and I were still very much involved in the undercover bear investigation. An elderly, longtime member of the local hound community contacted Szody and me on August 21, complaining about the rampant illegal killing of bears. We agreed to secretly meet with this man at his home.

"These guys are killing so damn many bears just for the galls," the broken-down, seventy-year-old houndsman said from the comfort of his easy chair. Recovering from recent surgery, he seemed frail and very thin. "It's going to ruin it for all of us. Buck Millsap's been braggin' about killing fifty-one bears last year. They're treein' the bears and sellin' them to the guides. The ones they don't sell they kill, take the gallbladders and leave 'em lyin' in the woods. Millsap hides the galls under the hood of his truck, passenger side."

All this was old news to Warden Szody and me, but it encouraged us to learn that not all the local houndsmen were outlaws. Some were upset about what was going on. We found it interesting that Buck Millsap's name always came up when bear-related violations were reported. He had been getting away with too much for too long and we hoped this would be the year we put an end to it.

Through our network of informants, Szody and I learned that Jason Lee planned to use the services of two new guides this year. They were none other than Ricky Nettles and Buck Millsap. Millsap was already a major player in our investigation and we were learning more about Nettles all the time. Even the other houndsmen didn't like or trust him—Henry Jessup made that clear to Agent Hoang during the 1996 bear season. According to Jessup, Nettles was going around buying up bear galls and could not be trusted.

Buck Millsap was sixty years old now and still up to no good. Like so many Northern California houndsmen, Millsap was believed to have come from the southern United States where running dogs was a way of life. It seemed to be in his blood and his only skill. Several of the local houndsmen, including Millsap and Nettles, were not licensed guides. These unlicensed houndsmen were treeing bears, advertising the fact over the CB radio, and essentially selling each bear for three hundred dollars or more to licensed guides with clients. They would often keep the bears treed for hours, waiting for the highest bidder to show up before they finished them off. This practice was highly illegal, under Fish and Game Code section 12012, which "prohibits the take or possession of mammals for commercial purposes."

During the summer of 1997, a young man named Ross Hamilton was working part-time in a Redding area taxidermy shop. Ross was in his twenties at the time. He was a tall, friendly, good-looking kid who had always wanted to learn the art of taxidermy. Clyde Shipley, the owner and operator of the shop, agreed to teach Hamilton if he would agree to work without compensation. Ross had a regular day job so he would come in on his days off and late in the afternoon on workdays. Most of the time Shipley kept Ross busy skinning out carcasses and cleaning up, but occasionally the enthusiastic young man got to do real taxidermy work.

Shipley had been a taxidermist for over thirty years and enjoyed a reputation as one of the best in the business. He specialized in big game and had mounted everything from deer and elk heads to full-bodied grizzly bears. Warden Szody and I had known Shipley for several years and made regular visits to the shop. We also became well acquainted with young Ross Hamilton. Ross hoped to work for Fish and Game someday, so he always had lots of questions and was anxious to help us in any way he could.

One afternoon, Szody and I were in the taxidermy shop talking to Shipley and Hamilton. Clyde mentioned a Korean guide, Jason Lee, who had brought several bear hides into the shop the previous season. According to Shipley, Lee was a tightwad who still owed him money for taxidermy work. Ross mentioned that for some reason Lee had taken a liking to him and was always asking him to go on hunts.

"Every time that guy comes in he treats me like I'm his long-lost friend," said Hamilton. "I gave him the impression that I had friends who hunt bears with hounds."

"Do you?" I asked.

"A couple guys at work are always talking about it," replied Ross. "I also know some of the bear hunters that are regulars here."

Szody and I were all too familiar with Jason Lee, as a result of our ongoing undercover investigation. I asked Ross if he would mind keeping his eyes and ears open and let us know any time Lee came in the shop. He and Shipley both agreed to keep us advised, although Shipley was not as forthcoming. He was concerned about hurting his business.

It was my experience that most taxidermists preferred to see as little as possible of Fish and Game wardens. Shipley was known to say, "It's bad for business to have game wardens hanging around." Shop freezers are generally filled with all forms of wildlife, most of it recorded correctly and taken legally. A good taxidermist, however, is sometimes tempted to mount something that was taken, possessed, or imported illegally. Most of the time it's a hawk or an owl that got hit by a car, but occasionally it's something more suspect, like an eagle, a bighorn sheep, or a mountain lion.

What I found over the years was that a taxidermist might turn an illegal customer away, but very rarely would he turn him in. As in Las Vegas, what happened in a taxidermy shop generally stayed in a taxidermy shop.

I asked Ross to drop by our office the following afternoon so we could talk further. He agreed. The next day, Szody and I coached the young man on how to handle himself, should Jason Lee come into the shop. We also provided him with a video camera and signed him up with the volunteer employee program.

On October 22, shortly after the 1997 bear season opened, Jason Lee walked in the front door of Shipley's Taxidermy Shop. Clyde continued working as Lee walked to the back of the shop and began talking to Ross.

"We're going hunting tomorrow. Why don't you come with us?"

"Where ya going?" asked Hamilton.

"We are going to use a bait pile up past Platina."

"A bait pile?"

"Yeah, we shoot a deer and rip it open. Then we throw it on the pile to attract the bears."

"I am off tomorrow. Would you mind if I videotape the hunt?"

"Do you have a bear tag?"

"I do."

"We have videotaped hunts before. I'm sorry but I'll have to charge you.

You know I have to pay my helpers, Buck Millsap and Farley Nettles."

Lee must have felt quite confident inside the shop because he was completely open about his illegal activities. Shipley was listening in on the conversation and held back a snicker at the mention of Millsap and Nettles.

"If you will promise to give me your gallbladder, I won't charge you," said Lee.

"I'd like to keep mine, but you're welcome to the bear's," replied Hamilton.

Lee, being all business and having no sense of humor, didn't laugh. Instead he stepped closer to Hamilton and leaned toward his ear. Shipley strained to hear but couldn't quite make it out.

"Do you have any friends you can trust who have bear galls to sell?" whispered Lee. "I pay from one hundred to two hundred dollars each, depending on the size."

Ross managed to hide his surprise at the question. He thought for a minute and agreed to ask around. "Don't worry," he replied. "I know who to trust."

Before leaving the shop, Jason Lee provided Ross with a phone number where he could be reached. He had rented a house in the nearby mountains for the duration of bear season. As soon as Jason Lee left the taxidermy shop, Ross Hamilton telephoned Dave Szody. Szody told him that he and I would no longer be coming into the shop, for fear of running into Lee. We would also have to stop meeting at the Fish and Game office, because bear hunters frequently came there to have their bear tags validated.

The following day, Szody and I met Ross Hamilton on a secluded road east of Redding. Ross recounted his recent conversation with Jason Lee. "Jason asked me if I knew anyone who had gallbladders to sell," reported Hamilton. "He even told me how much he usually pays for 'em."

Szody and I glanced at each other, our eyes wide with surprise. "Wow!" I said. "We've been trying to catch this guy in the act for the last two years. Now the kingpin is laying it on a silver platter for us."

Lee was openly soliciting new gallbladder business and he had definitely come to the right place. With opportunity knocking, I asked Ross Hamilton if he was willing to take the next step and actually sell gallbladders to Lee. Without hesitation, Ross said he was willing to do anything we needed.

Ross Hamilton telephoned Jason Lee on the evening of October 28, 1997. I had coached him on what to say. Lee began the conversation by telling Ross he had a client he was going to take hunting the following day.

"My client does not speak English. He just wants the gall," said Lee.

"Well, I have a friend with some gallbladders," replied Hamilton. "He said they were available."

"I do not want to meet your friend and I do not want him to know my name," replied Lee. "I will only deal with you."

"That's fine with him," said Ross. "He said he doesn't want to meet you either."

"How much does he want for the galls?" asked Lee.

Ross described the size of five gallbladders I had provided for the transaction. "My friend knows his stuff," he said. "He has a good idea what galls were going for and just wants to be treated fairly."

"All right, then," Lee said. "Bring the galls up to my rental house tomorrow evening."

Then he gave Ross directions, which was a huge boon for us: Szody and I knew Lee had rented a house in the mountains but, up until then, had been unable to locate it. We were recording the conversation—all recordings of conversations during the course of our investigation were pre-approved by the district attorney's office or the circuit environmental prosecutors.

Ross Hamilton met with Warden Szody and me, along with three other officers, at 1:30 p.m. on October 29. One of those officers was U.S. Forest Service Special Agent Don Hoang. At that point in our three-year investigation, we were engaged in several operations. Hoang was scheduled to make a gallbladder buy two days later, with Jimmy Westerby.

Five bear gallbladders had been packaged, photographed, and prepared for sale to Jason Lee. Hamilton was wired with a hidden microphone and instructed as to what to say. I had previously received approval from the Shasta County District Attorney's Office for the use of recording devices by civilian undercover operative Ross Hamilton. "We'll be just down the road, listening to every word," I reassured Ross. "If there is any problem we can be there in minutes." Ross appeared cool and collected. He would later explain that he had worked at boring, labor-intensive jobs since leaving school and this was the most exciting and worthwhile thing he had ever done.

It was 4:11 p.m. that afternoon when Ross Hamilton arrived at Jason Lee's mountain rental house, thirty miles east of Redding. He was carrying a grocery bag with five bear gallbladders inside. A quarter mile away, Szody and I listened intently. Jason Lee was busily skinning a bear in the garage as Hamilton approached. Several of Lee's clients were inside the house and Lee wanted to conduct business in private.

"Hi, Jason. What's that?" asked Ross.

Lee didn't understand him and responded, "Huh?"

"Is that a bear head?" Ross asked.

Lee didn't respond. True to form, he skipped the small talk and immediately got down to business. "Are you ready to go bear hunting with us?"

"Can you get Ricky and Buck to knock off the price as much as possible?" Ross countered.

Lee seemed distracted. "I'll try," he said as he opened the grocery bag to examine the bear galls that Hamilton had brought.

"Two of the galls look like they're spoiled and I don't want to pay for them," said Lee. "I will pay three hundred for the three good ones."

"Whatever you think," Hamilton replied.

A few minutes into the conversation, Jason Lee apparently had a change of heart.

"I want to help your friend so I will pay four hundred for all five galls," said Lee. "I will give you an extra hundred for making the deal." Lee counted out five one hundred dollar bills. "Are you sure you were not followed?" asked Lee.

"The only one who knows I was coming here is my friend with the gallbladders," Hamilton said. "Nobody followed me."

"Don't talk about this with *anyone*," Lee commanded. "I know lots of people who deal in galls, but I don't tell anyone."

Hamilton wisely changed the subject. "You should see this giant gallbladder that my friend has. It's huge!"

"Nice. Sure, I'd like to see it," Lee said. "I want to treat your friend fairly— you tell him that. I treat all my employees fairly. You know I pay Ricky and Buck five hundred dollars for every bear they tree for me."

"I have to get back," said Hamilton, "but I will tell my friend what you said." As Ross climbed into his pickup, Lee again reminded him to keep quiet about their business.

VII

On October 31, 1997, U.S. Forest Service Special Agent Don Hoang met with his old friend and hunting buddy, Jimmy Westerby. He had telephoned Westerby earlier that week to say he was coming through Redding and ask if Westerby had anything for him. Westerby said he did, so they arranged to meet in an Anderson parking lot. Agent Hoang was wearing a wire at the time and several of us were listening nearby. Westerby's reputation for being unpredictable and dangerous concerned us, so we took extra precautions.

"How you doing, buddy?" said Hoang, as he climbed out of his Mustang. Westerby was standing next to the cab of his pickup.

"What's goin' on?" replied Westerby, fidgeting. His eyes were darting everywhere.

"You got something for me?" asked Hoang.

"Three," said Westerby.

"Three?" Hoang asked.

"Yeah, right there in the SOS box," acknowledged Westerby.

Westerby pointed toward a yellow SOS scouring pad box sitting in the bed of his truck. Hoang walked over and picked it up. He was just about to look inside when a red sedan, with a woman driving, pulled up behind Westerby's pickup. Puzzled by the interruption, Hoang looked back at Westerby for an explanation.

"Don't worry," said Westerby, "that's my girlfriend."

Hoang examined the three gallbladders, hiding them with his hand and keeping his back toward the woman.

"So what's been going on?" Westerby asked. "I tried calling you a dozen times."

Hoang convinced Westerby that he had been out of the country.

"I figured you was," said Westerby.

"These aren't too bad," said Hoang.

Westerby began to act impatient. "What'll ya give me for 'em?"

"These aren't too fresh," Hoang said. "When did you take them?"

Westerby blinked a few times and looked around some more, as if stalling while he decided how to answer. "One was killed two days ago, one was four days ago and the other was five days ago. I'll be gettin' more, too," he added.

"Yeah?" said Hoang.

"I killed two cougars yesterday," said Westerby

"Wow!" said Hoang.

"Ya know, I just got home about two nights before you called," said Westerby.

"I'll give you four hundred," said Hoang.

Westerby puffed himself up and pursed his lips, unhappy with the offer. The diminutive undercover agent realized that the much larger man—a classic bully—was going to try to intimidate him, so he played along, milking his role as the timid, soft-spoken Asian. Agent Hoang had become quite proficient at his temporary job. The more he negotiated over price, the more convincing he appeared.

"I can get two apiece for 'em right up the road here," Westerby growled, gesturing wildly.

Having recently listened to a recorded conversation near Jason Lee's mountain rental house, Hoang immediately realized who Westerby was referring to.

"The guy right up the road gives me two for the small ones and three or three and a half for the bigger ones," Westerby boasted.

"Who are you dealing with?" asked Hoang.

The easily excitable Westerby launched into a tirade. "Every hound hunter in the world. Ya know what I mean? Hell, there's only a hundred hound hunters around here who have connections, ya know. And Jason does better than that."

Westerby's recorded statement validated what Szody and I had suspected for some time: many of the area houndsmen were selling gallbladders and most of them were selling to Jason Lee, either directly or indirectly. The cat was out of the bag.

"What's Jason offering?" asked Hoang.

A bit calmer, Westerby said, "Well, he pays me by the size. The guys normally say, 'Just give me the money for the small ones.' The small ones I get two hundred for right here."

"What about five-fifty?" countered Hoang.

"You just cost me money," Westerby shot back.

"I'll deal with just you, man," said Hoang, as he stepped back slightly. Agent Hoang was not intimidated by Westerby's bullying, but his law enforcement training had taught him to maintain a safe distance between himself and a possible recalcitrant.

No telling what this unstable character might do, thought Hoang.

Westerby paced back and forth beside his pickup, then turned to Hoang and said, "Yeah, we can do that. Just leave the galls in the box and take the whole thing."

Agent Hoang put the box in his car and began counting out the cash to pay Westerby. All along he had kept his back toward the woman in the red sedan. Westerby appeared relieved, as if he was under a lot of pressure to come up with money. As Hoang handed him the cash, Westerby said, "That guy up there gives me three and a half for the big ones, but to hell with him."

"So how many bears have you killed this season?" asked Hoang.

"Seven bears and three cougars," answered Westerby.

Hoang pretended to be impressed, all the time imagining how much Szody and I were going to enjoy lowering the boom on this guy. Cougars were totally protected and every tagged hunter was only allowed one bear per season.

"Ya know, them cougars is good eatin'," said Westerby, as he ambled toward his pickup.

Hoang had hoped that their transaction was over but Westerby suddenly did an about-face.

"Hey, what about that stuff we talked about before? I got some on the dryin' table right now."

"Really?" replied Hoang. "How much you got?"

"I ain't weighed it yet but it'll be two or three pounds. I know a guy over in Trinity County who's got a whole crop going. In the next thirty days there'll be a lot of it around. By the way, did ya happen ta bring any coke with ya?"

Agent Hoang thought about handing Westerby the bottle of Coca-Cola that was resting in the cup holder of his car. He knew exactly what Westerby was referring to, but wisely decided against joking around with a character as off-balance as this one. The agent dodged the question by saying that he was in a hurry and they could talk about that stuff on the next trip. Westerby seemed to accept Hoang's explanation.

"Drive safely," the man said, as Hoang was about to close his front door.

VIII

On November 1, 1997, Ross Hamilton was invited to join Jason Lee and his entourage on a bear hunt. The group consisted of Jason Lee, Buck Millsap, Millsap's tagalongs, Lee's tagalongs, and several Korean clients. Two of the Korean clients were young women. The hunt took place in the mountains west of Redding, a few miles east of the Trinity County line.

By 6:50 a.m., Millsap's dogs had already treed a bear. Ross found himself right in the middle of the activity and started his video camera rolling. *What a scene*, he thought. Dogs were baying and the entire group was milling around under the tree. Ross would later say that it looked more like a backyard barbecue than a bear hunt. Everyone seemed to be asking the same question—who is going to shoot the bear? Ross decided to find out. He walked over to Jason Lee.

"Jason, who's gonna shoot the bear?"

"I will," replied Lee, emphatically.

It was common knowledge that Jason Lee had a big ego but with two young, attractive women in the group, his ego took on new dimensions. Apparently everyone heard him except Buck Millsap.

"Hey, who's gonna kill that bear?" shouted Millsap, sounding impatient.

Lee scanned the crowd, looking for the two women. He found them standing off to one side in private conversation. One of them was cradling a lever action .30-.30 rifle that Lee had given her. Lee walked over and took the rifle from her hands. With everyone watching, he pointed the rifle at the bear and fired. The small, reddish-brown bear couldn't have weighed more than a hundred pounds, but it painfully endured a direct hit to the midsection without falling from the tree. Wanting to avoid further embarrassment, Lee took careful aim and hit the bear in the side of the head. It immediately fell limp, crashed through several branches and bounced on the hard ground.

If this had been a routine hunt, Lee might have ordered one of his flunkies to gut the bear. He was still trying to impress the ladies, however, so he gutted the bear and removed its gallbladder himself. Ross watched as Lee placed the gallbladder into a small plastic baggie, tied it off with a string, and secured it in his truck. Lee told Hamilton that he had intended to tag the bear with the woman's bear tag, but the bear was too small. Instead, Lee pulled an envelope from his pocket. Hamilton noticed that the envelope contained several bear tags with hunting licenses attached. One of the tags belonged to a man named Kim, who Ross later learned was still in Southern California at the time. Lee was killing bears and filling out bear tags for people who were hundreds of miles away. When Jason Lee wasn't looking, Ross tape recorded the information from the bear tag that Lee had fraudulently filled out.

Under California law, it is unlawful for anyone to have another person's license or tag in his possession while hunting. Lee had a whole handful of them. Every person who had given Lee his or her bear tag was also in violation. Legally, Lee was allowed to kill one bear per season, as long as he tagged it with the one tag that had been issued to him. Every time Lee shot an additional bear he was taking an over-limit.

The next day, November 2, Ross Hamilton was invited to go on another hunt with the same group of people. An average-sized bear was treed by Buck Millsap's dogs.

Jason Lee pointed to the bear and, looking Ross straight in the eye, said, "Shoot it."

Ross shot the bear and legally tagged it with his own bear tag. Lee gutted the bear, which had an unusually large gallbladder.

Ross didn't think anything more about the gallbladder that Lee had taken from his bear until Jason Lee walked into Shipley's Taxidermy Shop the following afternoon. Hamilton had been instructed to record his conversations with Jason Lee, which he did on that date. On tape, Lee told Ross that he routinely paid Millsap and Nettles five hundred dollars for each of the bears they treed for him and his clients. He also said that he had to pay Millsap five hundred dollars for Ross's bear because it had an extra large gallbladder.

Commercial transactions such as these are illegal—some being felonies— as per Fish and Game Code sections 2536, 12012, and 4758.

Ross Hamilton accompanied Jason Lee and his group on a November 9 bear hunt. This time the group members were Buck Millsap, Ricky Nettles, a Korean client named Hyun Park, and several of Millsap's tagalongs. They hunted the Trinity National Forest, near Clear Creek Campground. Ross was allowed to videotape much of the hunt.

Hamilton was riding with Lee and Park when Nettles came over the CB radio. "We got a bear cornered inside a culvert," said Nettles. Lee responded and advised Nettles that he and his client were on their way. At the time of the radio call, Lee's Bronco was a good half hour away from the culvert. By the time Lee, Park, and Hamilton arrived, the bear was already dead. Nettles had shot the bear with a pistol, then another man shot it, then Nettles shot it again.

Ross watched as two men dragged the bear out of the culvert. Although Hyun Park had not been in the area when the bear was killed, his tag was placed on the bear's ear. Several photographs were taken of Park with his ill-gotten trophy. Lee eventually gutted the bear and presented Park with the gallbladder.

Sport had nothing at all to do with it. Clients didn't seem to care who killed the bear as long as they got their package of magic bile.

Over and over again, flagrant violations were committed, with little or no attempt to abide by the law. These outlaws had gotten away with their crimes for so long, they had lost all fear of being caught.

Their most despicable act occurred on November 29. Fortunately, Ross Hamilton was there to witness and record the incident. Jason Lee was present, along with Buck Millsap, Stan Harder, Fred Belcher, some clients, and a few tagalongs.

At 10:05 a.m., a small, black-colored bear cub was treed on Behemotosh Mountain. Ross Hamilton immediately began videotaping Jason Lee and one of Lee's clients. Others could see that Lee was about to shoot the cub, so they attempted to stop Hamilton from filming the scene. Ross was so disgusted by the prospect of Lee shooting the tiny cub that he called out, "Jason, that bear's too small." Lee fired anyway and killed the bear.

When the cub fell to the ground, Jason Lee walked over and picked it up. With very little effort, he held it in his outstretched arms while a photograph was taken. Lee tried to appease Hamilton by saying that he had to kill the bear or the dogs wouldn't hunt. Since the cub bear was obviously unlawful to possess, it was left to rot at the bottom of the canyon.

On December 11, 1997, Ross Hamilton received a call from Jason Lee. Lee was going back to Los Angeles in a few days and needed gallbladders badly. Of particular interest to Lee was the very large gallbladder that Ross had told him about. Ross said he would call his friend and see if he could set something up. Arrangements were made and Ross called Lee back on December 13. Warden Szody and I were present when Hamilton recorded the phone conversation.

"My friend's dogs are better than Buck and Ricky's," said Ross. "He might be willing to work for you next season." Szody and I knew there was no love lost between Lee and those two mercenaries, Millsap and Nettles. We decided to sweeten the pot with a possible alternative, although we planned to have Lee in jail long before the next season.

"My friend wants to know how much you're willing to pay for each bear and how much you paid Buck and Ricky this season. He says if you make him a good offer, he'll get you more than they did," said Ross. That sounded pretty appealing to Lee. As he contemplated the possibility of hiring new help, Hamilton asked another question, "How many bears did Buck Millsap get you this year?"

"Well," replied Lee, "Buck got me twenty-eight or twenty-nine bears this year, but last year he got about fifty-eight. And Ricky probably got me eighteen or nineteen. I think I brought up about thirty clients from LA."

As Dave and I listened to the conversation, we were appalled by Lee's arrogance and total disregard for California's hunting regulations. Lee and his outlaw accomplices would kill the last bear in California if there was a dollar to be made.

"And you paid Buck and Ricky five hundred bucks for each bear they treed?"

"Yeah, but the deal for everyone else around here is three hundred."

"Buck Millsap must be rolling in money."

"Actually it was not a very good year. Very bad for everybody."

Ross tried to figure out, in his head, how much money Millsap had made from the bears he had treed for Lee. Then Lee volunteered the information: over ten thousand dollars.

"Ten thousand dollars?" blurted Ross.

"That not much money," Lee assured him.

Warden Szody and I felt that we had plenty of evidence to use against Jason Lee. We had already sold gallbladders to him on two separate occasions— all felonies—and there were numerous misdemeanor violations. Lee was persistent, however, about getting his hands on that extra large gallbladder Ross Hamilton had told him about. We advised Ross to agree to a final sale, which was arranged for December 14, 1997.

On the evening of December 14, 1997, Warden Szody and I were sitting in an unmarked vehicle at the south end of the Anderson Factory Outlet Stores parking lot. A hundred yards north of us, Ross Hamilton was meeting for the last time with Jason Lee.

"How many are there?" inquired Lee, as he climbed into Hamilton's pickup.

"I brought seven," replied Hamilton.

"These are all he has, right?" Lee asked.

"My friend does have more."

"What size?" continued Lee, licking his lips.

"I'm not sure," answered Ross. "I haven't seen them."

Jason Lee appeared desperate to get his hands on as many bear galls as he could before going back to Los Angeles. No matter how many Ross Hamilton came up with, Lee seemed to always want more. I wondered just how much money Lee was making off each gall. The thought occurred to me that Lee might have been transporting the gallbladders back to Korea.

"Can I get those when I come back?" Lee asked.

"I'll see what I can do," replied Ross.

"Two of the galls are spoiled so I will give you five hundred for the other five," said Lee.

Ross agreed, with Lee paying him five hundred dollars for the gallbladders and the usual one hundred dollars for making the deal. Lee started to walk away, but then he came back to admonish Ross not to talk to anyone about their transaction. He appeared especially concerned about being caught. Then he revealed why. Wiping the sweat from his brow with the back of his hand, Lee said in a low voice, "Stan Harder got busted by Fish and Game."

Warden Szody and I had recently secured a federal arrest warrant for Stanley Louis Harder. Harder was one of the outlaws who shot the mountain lion early in the investigation (December 1995), on National Forest land. This violation was witnessed by undercover Warden Al McDermott. Harder would be the first of many to be arrested, as we began to tighten the noose. Lee was actually trembling as he spoke to Hamilton about Harder's arrest. He alerted Ross to possible undercover officers. "And if they catch you they bust you," warned Lee. "Even if something go wrong, we not know each other."

Szody and I watched Ross Hamilton's pickup leave the parking lot. A few minutes later, Jason Lee drove away in the opposite direction. We waited five extra minutes before leaving and meeting Hamilton at a designated location.

Ross handed me the recording equipment, the ice chest that we had provided, and the six hundred dollars that Jason Lee paid him—all in one hundred dollar bills. Dave and I thanked Ross for the outstanding job he had done and told him that he had probably conducted his last transaction. After three years of evidence gathering, documentation, and remarkable undercover work, it was time to write search warrants, file criminal complaints, and begin making arrests.

IX

Conducting a three-year undercover investigation was a monumental task, with a long list of problems. As many as nine undercover agents and civilian operatives were involved. In an effort to maintain the integrity of the investigation, none of the agents or operatives knew the identities of all the others involved. There were statute of limitation challenges with the earlier misdemeanors: criminal complaints had to be filed within one year of the crimes being committed. An early arrest would have exposed operatives and eliminated any possibility of success, so affidavits were filed with the court, sealing complaints and arrest reports until the investigation was completed. All the bear gallbladder related charges were felonies and did not present that problem.

A year or two into the investigation, the California District Attorneys Association initiated a funded program providing environmental circuit prosecutors to rural counties. Two circuit prosecutors, Jennifer Scott and Larry Allen, worked out of an office in Redding. They collaborated with Szody and me throughout much of the investigation and all of the prosecution process. Much of our success can be attributed to Scott and Allen's extensive prosecutorial skills and total dedication to the project.

On January 23, 1998, I filed a criminal complaint in Shasta County Superior Court against Chung-Hee (Jason) Lee. The complaint charged Lee with sixteen felony counts of buying bear gallbladders (4758 California Fish and Game Code) and fourteen misdemeanor counts, including: taking an over-limit of bears, taking a cub bear, bartering for bears, possession of illegally taken bears (mother bear with cub) and numerous tag violations.

Immediately after filing the criminal complaint, I wrote three search warrant affidavits and secured search warrants for Lee's mountain home, his office in Los Angeles, and his residence in Los Angeles. On January 28, all three search warrants were served simultaneously. Most of the papers found at Lee's office and LA apartment were written or printed in Korean. He had several different business cards, alternately identifying him as a wildlife biologist, columnist producer, certified firearms instructor, personal protection instructor, and licensed guide. Lee even used the Department of Fish and Game logo on one of his business cards. Another card indicated that he was into "wildlife research." I wondered if Lee had gotten that idea from the Japanese whaling industry, which claims to kill whales in the name of research. Maybe Lee was trying to justify the killing of bears and other wildlife for the same purpose. A box of ziplock baggies was found at Lee's mountain house. That would not have been unusual, except for a length of green string inside each one—obviously in preparation for the many bear gallbladders that Lee planned to acquire.

As we learned more about Jason Lee, Szody and I started to wonder if he might have been living a double life—one as a bear guide in California and the other as a well-to-do entrepreneur in South Korea. We could only imagine how much money Lee might have received for bear gallbladders in Asian markets.

A felony arrest warrant was issued for Jason Lee, in the amount of $750,000. Szody and I arrested Lee as he walked out of an Anderson coffee shop on

January 28, 1998. He had a frightened, almost petrified look on his face when we applied the handcuffs, but didn't say a word. Lee was booked into Shasta County Jail. Szody and I later learned that Lee had been in Anderson to make yet another gallbladder transaction with Jimmy Westerby.

On April 7, 1998, I testified before the Shasta County Grand Jury, led by Environmental Prosecutor Jennifer Scott. A twenty-nine count indictment was issued. After several months of court proceedings, a negotiated plea was agreed to on September 28, 1998. Lee pled guilty to three felony counts of purchasing bear gallbladders. He was sentenced to three years in state prison, suspended; five years formal probation (with strict conditions), one year to be served in the Shasta County Jail, and ordered to pay a fine totaling twenty thousand dollars. As a convicted felon, he would never again be able to possess a firearm in California. Needless to say, his days as a guide and hunter education instructor were over.

Felony arrest warrants were issued for Elvin "Buck" Millsap and Henry Jessup in the amount of $100,000 each. Jessup was arrested and booked into Shasta County Jail on January 28, 1998. Millsap turned himself in shortly after that. On April 6, 1998, a meeting was held at the office of the Environmental Circuit Prosecutors in Redding. Jessup and his attorney were present, along with circuit prosecutor Larry Allen, Warden Dave Szody, and me. Jessup's attorney asked if I had any specific questions for Henry Jessup.

"Yes, I do," I replied. "On December 4, 2006, you sold thirteen bear gallbladders to Special Agent Don Hoang. You left for a time and returned with the gallbladders. We would like to know who you got those gallbladders from."

"Who I got 'em from?" repeated Jessup. "I got 'em from Buck Millsap."

"Out of the money that Agent Hoang paid you, how much of it went to Buck Millsap?" I asked.

"All of it," replied Jessup.

I reminded Jessup that Agent Hoang had paid him a total of $3,150. Jessup said he put the money in a bag or an envelope, then took it over to Millsap's house and gave it to him.

"How long after Agent Hoang paid you, did you go over and pay Millsap?" I asked.

"The same day," replied Jessup.

I asked Henry Jessup if he would be willing to testify to what he had just told us in court. He said he would. Jessup's attorney stated that she had already explained to Jessup that he would likely be asked to testify. I advised Jessup and his attorney that we could make no promises. Henry Jessup later testified in court against Buck Millsap.

Buck Millsap's day in court was a very long time coming. He was charged with fifty-four counts of serious Fish and Game violations. Twenty-five of those counts were felonies involving the sale or purchase of bear gallbladders. The court found him guilty, on July 20, 1998, and sentenced him to six months in Shasta County Jail. Millsap was ordered to pay a fine of $54,000 and was placed on formal probation for five years, with the following restrictive conditions: shall not hunt or be in the field with anyone who is hunting; shall not possess any wildlife or parts thereof; shall not run hound dogs; shall submit to warrantless search of his person, property, or vehicle at any time, by any peace officer and shall not possess a firearm or archery equipment.

Henry Jessup was charged with fourteen felony counts of selling bear gallbladders and one felony count of conspiracy. He pled guilty to selling bear gallbladders and was sentenced on September 8, 1998. Jessup's sentence included ninety days in the Shasta County Jail, a fine of $9,990 and restitution to the California Department of Fish and Game in the amount of $5,100. He was also placed on five years formal (felony) probation, with the same strict conditions that Millsap received.

James "Jimmy" Westerby was charged with four felony counts of selling bear gallbladders, unlawful take of a protected species (fisher), and one felony count of criminal conspiracy. Szody and I arrested Westerby on the streets of Anderson, minutes after what was believed to be his last gallbladder transaction with Jason Lee. Westerby pled guilty to selling bear gallbladders and taking a protected species. He was ordered to serve one hundred and twenty days in the Shasta County Jail and pay a fine and restitution totaling over $10,000. Westerby was also placed on five years formal (felony) probation, under the same strict conditions that Millsap and Jessup received. As a convicted felon, he could no longer legally possess a firearm in California.

Remember when Stan Harder and Larry Cogle shot and wounded that mountain lion back in 1995? They were each charged for that crime in federal court. Cogle was tried and convicted on June 30, 1998. Recommendations from federal probation included a five thousand dollar fine, forty-five days in jail, and three years supervised probation, including banishment from all federal lands. Harder received a similar sentence and was also charged in the case involving Bruce and Darrel Vanosek.

Without sufficient evidence that Ricky Nettles shot the bear in the culvert, Richard DeWayne Nettles was charged with license fraud and probation violations. Although his fine was minimal, Nettles was placed on probation for three years, during which time he could not hunt or be in the field with anyone else who was hunting. We served a search warrant at Nettles's residence, but found no gallbladders. Both Nettles and Millsap were suspected of keeping the gallbladders they had collected at locations other than their respective residences.

Bruce and Darrel Vanosek were found guilty and convicted of unlawful possession of an illegally taken bear on April 24, 1998. Although Warden McDermott believed the bear that Darrel Vanosek shot was a cub (less than fifty pounds) he could not have seized the bear and proved that charge without blowing his cover. Both Vanoseks were instead charged for unlawful possession of the same bear, as a result of tag (license) fraud. They were each fined a total of $640 and placed on three year's probation—they could not hunt or be in the field with anyone who was hunting.

Over fifty felonies and one hundred misdemeanor charges resulted from this three-year undercover investigation. Twenty defendants were brought to justice. Over $110,000 in fines and restitution were levied and over two years of jail time was ordered by the court. Buck Millsap's $54,000 fine was the largest game-related fine in California history. Four of the worst wildlife violators in California at the time were convicted of felonies and will never again be able to legally carry firearms in California.

For three decades, Dave Szody and I followed George Werden's advice. We played the "game" to the very best of our abilities. We studied our opponents and the rules they were required to play by—always trying to figure out their next moves before they made them. In the end, we left California's precious natural resources a little better off than they would have been had we never pinned on those badges. Nobody ever said working couldn't be fun.

We had a ball.

Steven T. Callan was born in San Diego, California, where he spent his early childhood. It was there that he first developed his love of nature, spending much of his spare time exploring the undeveloped canyons behind his house and learning to skin-dive in the nearby ocean. In 1960, Callan's family moved to the small Northern California farm town of Orland. Steve spent his high school years playing baseball, basketball, hunting, and fishing. With an insatiable interest in wildlife, particularly waterfowl, he never missed an opportunity to ride along on patrol with his father, a California Fish and Game warden.

Callan graduated from California State University, Chico, in 1970 and continued with graduate work at California State University, Sacramento. While studying at Sacramento State, he worked as a paid intern for the Sacramento County Board of Supervisors—using this golden opportunity to lobby for protected wildlife corridors in the county's general plan.

Hired by the California Department of Fish and Game in 1974, Warden Steve Callan's first assignment was the Earp Patrol District on the Colorado River. He was promoted to patrol lieutenant in January of 1978, leaving the desert and moving to the metropolitan area of Riverside/San Bernardino. While stationed in Riverside, Callan organized and led a successful effort to ban the sale of native reptiles in California. He also organized and led a successful campaign to stop a planned recreational development at Lake Mathews— establishing the lake and its surrounding wildlands as an ecological reserve for thousands of waterfowl and Southern California's largest population of wintering bald eagles.

Transferring north to Shasta County in 1981, Lieutenant Callan spent the remainder of his thirty-year enforcement career in Redding. While supervising the warden force in Shasta County, Callan created and coordinated the Streamside Corridor Protection Plan—working with city and county planners to establish development-free setbacks along the Sacramento River and its Redding area tributaries.

In 1995, Lieutenant Steve Callan and Warden Dave Szody conducted a three-year undercover investigation into the unlawful killing of California black bears for their gallbladders, possibly the most successful wildlife related criminal investigation in California history. Callan and Szody received the distinguished Frank James Memorial Award for their accomplishment.

Steve and his wife, Kathleen, a retired science teacher, are passionate about the environment. They are longtime members of no fewer than a dozen environmental organizations and actively promote environmental causes. They are avid bird watchers, kayakers, and scuba divers. Steve is a wildlife artist, using photographs he takes while scuba diving for inspiration. Callan has played competitive softball throughout the United States since his college days and, in 2004, was inducted into the National Senior Softball Hall of Fame.

You can find Steven online at callan.coffeetownpress.com.